PERSONAL AND PROFESSIONAL ASSESSMENT

Custom Edition for
Cardinal Stritch University

Taken from:

Transition Management: A Practical Approach to Personal and Professional Development, Fourth edition
by Sandra L. McKee and Brenda L. Walters

New Beginnings: A Reference Guide for Adult Learners
by Linda Simon

Learning Team Skills by Arthur H. Bell and Dayle M. Smith

Custom Publishing

New York   Boston   San Francisco
London   Toronto   Sydney   Tokyo   Singapore   Madrid
Mexico City   Munich   Paris   Cape Town   Hong Kong   Montreal

Cover Art: Courtesy of PhotoDisc/Getty Images

Taken from:

Transition Management: A Practical Approach to Personal and Professional Development, Fourth edition
by Sandra L. McKee and Brenda L. Walters
Copyright © 2002 by Pearson Education, Inc.
Published by Prentice Hall
Upper Saddle River, New Jersey 07458

New Beginnings: A Reference Guide for Adult Learners
by Linda Simon
Copyright © 2010 by Pearson Education, Inc.
Published by Prentice Hall

Learning Team Skills by Arthur H. Bell and Dayle M. Smith
Copyright © 2003 by Pearson Education, Inc.
Published by Prentice Hall

This special edition published in cooperation with Pearson Custom Publishing.

Printed in the United States of America

10 9 8 7 6 5 4 3 2

2009160505

LA

**Pearson
Custom Publishing**
is a division of

www.pearsonhighered.com

ISBN 10: 0-558-38207-X
ISBN 13: 978-0-558-38207-0

Contents

CHAPTER 3   Creating a Positive Attitude   35

CHAPTER 4 Developing Note-Taking, Studying, and Test-Taking Skills   55

CHAPTER 5 Strategies For Reading   69

CHAPTER 6 Strategies For Research   79

CHAPTER 7   Strategies For Writing   105

CHAPTER 8   Grammar Brushup   121

CHAPTER 13   Understanding and Resolving Team Problems   187

CHAPTER 14   Completing Collaborative Projects Through Teamwork   203

CHAPTER 15   Developing Intercultural Teams   217

CHAPTER 16   Moving Toward Your Goals   229

CHAPTER 17   Organizing Time and Tasks   247

CHAPTER 18   Confronting Conflict   267

CHAPTER 19 Assessing Learning Needs and Course Requirements   287

CHAPTER 20 Launching Your Career   303

CHAPTER 21   Lifelong Career Management   329

It's really simple, the reason I went back to school. I wanted to change my life.

Andy Sayles,
student

BECOMING A STUDENT

Y ou may want to make a career change, to learn skills that will help you gain a promotion at work, to enrich your leisure-time experiences, or to complete your education after an interruption. Whatever your goal in returning to school, that goal involves changing your perception of both yourself and the possibilities for your future. Through education, you hope to give a new direction to your life.

Adult learners return to school at different stages in their lives and careers. You may never have attended college, or you already may have experienced some form of higher education. You may decide to go to college after raising a family and working to finance your own children's education. You may log on at midnight to send a completed assignment to your instructor in an online class. You may come to class after a full day's work, after making dinner for your family, or before your night shift at the local hospital. You are mature, you are motivated, and you are busy.

There's one other trait that you are likely to share with other adult learners: You are feeling nervous about the journey ahead. Do you have the ability to do college-level work? Can your experiences outside of school help you succeed in class? Will returning to school be worth the considerable time and expense that you will devote to the effort?

This book will help you to answer "yes" to each of these questions. As an adult learner, you have considerable strengths that traditional undergraduates may not have.

Taken from: *New Beginnings: A Reference Guide for Adult Learners*, by Linda Simon

In this chapter, you will learn how to:

- assess your strengths
- begin to set long-term goals for yourself
- enlist cooperation and support from your friends and family
- build a good relationship with your instructors
- feel comfortable and productive in class
- see how this book will help you during your college career

LOOKING BACK AND MOVING FORWARD: APPLYING LIFE EXPERIENCES TO BEING A STUDENT

If you visualize the person you were at the age of 18, when many students begin their college careers, you'll see a different person from the one you are today. At 18:

- Your decision to be in school may have been influenced by peer pressure or demands from your family.
- You may have had a support system—such as your parents, school guidance counselors, or other trusted adults—to offer guidance and advice if you had problems.
- Your social life may have competed heavily with your academic work.
- You probably had not yet taken on such adult responsibilities as raising a family, supporting yourself, or paying taxes.
- You had less experience with the demands of the workplace.
- You may not have had a clear career goal.

In contrast, as an adult, you yourself are making the decision to return to school and take on the tasks associated with learning. Most likely, you have had experience in the workplace and/or with raising a family; this experience has helped you to see the *value* of education in daily life. Your life experiences have given you considerable strengths. For example:

- ability to juggle many activities at once
- experience in meeting deadlines
- experience in working collaboratively
- experience in recognizing the complexities of problems

Take a moment to think about how your life experiences can help you in your new role as a student.

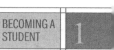

Juggling Responsibilities

Barbara is a young mother with two children under four years of age. Barbara completed only one year of college before she married, and years later, she has a goal for herself: When her youngest child enters first grade, Barbara wants to return to the workplace to supplement her family's income. But with one year of college, she feels that she will be at a disadvantage, competing against younger workers with college degrees. Therefore, she wants to earn an undergraduate degree. Although she has tentative plans of majoring in business administration, she is open to thinking about other possibilities. Her goal is simply to complete her undergraduate education.

For the past six years, Barbara has been working at home as a wife and mother, as well as participating in the cooperative nursery school that her older child attends. Juggling activities has been a necessary part of her life. From simple family-related deadlines, such as planning an anniversary dinner for her parents, to purchasing supplies for the nursery school, Barbara learned how to:

- break down big tasks into small, manageable tasks
- use lists, calendars, and planning books to set priorities
- be flexible when unavoidable problems (her son's ear infection or bad driving conditions) interfere with her plans
- take time for rest and relaxation so that she can approach tasks with a fresh mind and spirit

Assessing Your Strengths

1. What strategies have you used when faced with several tasks that compete for your time?

2. How have you found and evaluated outside opinions to help you solve problems?

3. With whom have you worked collaboratively on problem solving? What strategies have you used to make that collaboration successful? What problems arose?

4. How have you conducted research or found sources to help you solve a problem?

Evaluating Information

Rafael, who has just begun an online adult education program, is the oldest child in his family; his three younger siblings—a sister and two brothers—look to him for guidance in making family decisions. Recently, Rafael and his siblings had to make a difficult decision: whether or not to place their ailing mother in a nursing home.

Because the decision was so emotional for all of the family, Rafael took it upon himself to present information as objectively as possible. He met with his mother's doctor; visited local nursing homes and talked with staff members and

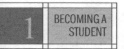

some patients; talked with a social worker about possible alternatives, such as a visiting nurse or home health care worker; and talked with a co-worker who had placed her father in a nursing home.

When the family gathered to talk about the decision, Rafael summarized what he had found out. Although the social worker presented a positive picture of home health care, his mother's doctor suggested that Rafael's mother was failing physically and would possibly need emergency care at times. Because the nursing home had its own medical facilities, she would be served better there. The doctor's opinion, then, carried more weight than the social worker's because he could predict his patient's future needs.

The staff at the nursing home wanted to sell the facility's services, so the information provided at the home did not weigh as heavily as testimony from the patients, who generally were happy with their care. In addition, Rafael's co-worker had had a positive experience after she placed her father in the same home. Weighing information allowed the family to come to an informed decision. From the process, Rafael learned how to:

- gather appropriate information from experts
- evaluate the information in light of the experts' special interests
- evaluate the information in light of his family's own needs

Working with Others

Ken works a four-to-midnight shift at his factory job as well as attending classes in an adult education program, so he is rarely home to see his children at dinner or in the evenings. When his wife told him that one of his sons—who just turned 13—seemed to be part of a street gang, he first became angry; then he decided to do something about it. If his son were able to participate in supervised after-school activities, Ken believed that he would not be as likely to get into trouble. His community, however, had no after-school programs.

For a month, Ken spent his days off looking for support for his idea. He spoke with the principal of the local middle school, where his son was in eighth grade, and he spoke with several local ministers. All offered to provide space if Ken could provide the personnel and find funding. Who would supervise the teenagers? Who would pay for supplies and salaries?

Concerned with his son's welfare, Ken developed a flyer describing the problem. The principal offered to distribute the flyer at the school and to call a meeting in the school's cafeteria. Although only a dozen parents showed up for the meeting, four of the parents were willing to work with Ken on the project.

Because Ken was accustomed to working independently on the job, committee work proved a challenge in itself. At first, Ken was afraid that the project

would fail just because the committee could not agree on its goals. Then he decided to use the "factory method" of solving the problem by giving each committee member a specific task: to find an appropriate space, to plan a reasonable budget, to investigate sources of funding, and to make a publicity plan for the program.

As the members worked on their tasks, they began to respect one another's efforts and opinions. When the most convenient space turned out to be the school's gymnasium, they agreed that a sports program would be a reasonable beginning for the after-school project. Once they made that initial decision, they managed to work together and started the program within six months. Ken's son was among the first participants.

From his experience in solving a community problem, Ken learned how to:

- articulate a problem to others
- enlist support
- listen and allow others to be heard
- generate support and respect within a group

Researching a Problem

Tony is returning to school with no college experience. After high school, he took a full-time job as assistant to the buyer of a local discount department store and, in five years, moved up to a more responsible position. But Tony wants the opportunity to move even further in business and marketing. He realizes that he needs an undergraduate degree to help him attain his career goals.

Tony's responses to the questions on page 3 focused on his purchase of his first car. Like many 18-year-olds, Tony was obsessed for months with the decision. He spoke to friends, visited used car lots, read magazines that tested and ranked cars, and even spent hours in the library reading some reference books that ranked used cars. By the end of those months, he knew the book value of every car in his price range; he could lecture on the relative merits of various cars. He finally felt that he had enough information to make a decision. When he purchased an eight-year-old Ford Taurus, he knew he had made the right decision.

From this project, Tony learned how to:

- find answers to specific questions from a number of different sources
- select the information that proved most helpful in the decision-making process

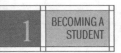

The situations that Barbara, Rafael, Ken, and Tony experienced have direct bearing on their work as students. As a student, you will need to:

- juggle class assignments, family life, and your job in order to meet deadlines
- evaluate and weigh information that comes from a variety of sources
- work collaboratively with others in finding information and solving problems
- do research and reading as you fulfill your course assignments

HOW BEING A STUDENT AFFECTS YOUR RELATIONSHIPS WITH OTHERS

Many adult students wonder how their becoming a college student will affect the relationships they have with others, particularly friends, family, and instructors. In the sections that follow, people who have been through the process themselves and who are eager to share their experiences with you discuss this important concern.

Friends and Family Members

Susan Bell discovered that some people she knew did not understand her motivation to return to school, and they made her question her commitment to take a new direction in her life. That questioning, however, only made her more certain that she was making the right decision. "Friends, family, and total strangers may make you uncomfortable about becoming a student," she comments; "they are used to you in a different role. Don't let the guilt trips knock you off course. Some people may be threatened, some envious, some just plain uncomprehending. It is up to you to believe in yourself and what you are trying to accomplish."

There are times when believing in yourself and your goals will not be easy. "As with any life change," Hollis Colby adds, "becoming an adult student requires personal sacrifices because it requires a commitment. In turn, you must become more protective of your time, and this, of course, can pose problems at home. First, you must accept your decision to return to school and make it a part of your life. Second, this helps others to accept the fact that there will be certain times when you need to do things that do not involve them, like study, for example. It is not always easy to make time decisions, but it gets easier as you go. And others tend to become more understanding and sometimes interested, too." You can generate that sense of understanding by sharing your experiences with friends and family.

Another adult student, Robert Vilardi, suggests that you set aside time for classes and studying, just as you set aside time to go to work or to do household chores. Make it a necessity, he advises, and others will begin to see it as an

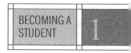

important part of your life. "Find a physically separate space and set a definite time for studying," Robert says. "Treat it like a *business* activity. When you return to your family and work from studying, you'll know that 'school' is taken care of, and you'll feel more relaxed."

Instructors

Instructors find that teaching adults is a refreshing change from teaching traditional undergraduates. As stated earlier: Adults have made the decision to come back to school; they are in class because they want to be there; they are highly motivated; their perspective has been enriched by their life experiences. These important qualities make teaching adults rewarding and revitalizing for instructors.

CLASSROOM PROTOCOL

As soon as you enter a classroom, you'll see that there is no prescribed uniform, no dress code, and no assumptions about what students wear. Some adult students will be dressed in jeans and a T-shirt; others may be wearing the suits and ties or the silk blouses and scarves they have worn all day at work. Even though you might come to class dressed casually, neatness, cleanliness, and appropriateness are important.

Even if there are no prescriptions about dress, however, there are shared assumptions about classroom manners. A classroom, after all, is a small community. Although the instructor is the leader in that community, each student is responsible for helping to make the classroom atmosphere conducive to learning.

Diversity

Academic communities value diversity among students and faculty. Diversity includes race, ethnicity, socioeconomic class, sexual orientation, religion, age, political beliefs, cultural experiences, work experiences, travel experiences, and values. The academic setting encourages respectful sharing of opinions and openness to other people's views. Many people hold stereo-

Dos and Don'ts in a Diverse Community

1. Do listen respectfully and allow others to express their views.
2. Don't ask one individual to represent the views of an entire group to which he or she may belong.
3. Do encourage others to participate in discussions.
4. Don't ask anyone to share personal information that he or she may not be ready to share.
5. Do ask questions respectfully.

types of others, but the academic community encourages its participants to examine and question those views.

Key Words in Academia

Throughout your academic career, you'll hear the words *argument* and *critical thinking* in many of your classes. In college, these words have a special meaning, different from their ordinary usage. Neither term has a negative connotation, and neither implies hostility or attack.

Argument refers to an assertion that results from analysis or research. If you argue a point, you make that point and defend it with evidence. If you present an argument in a history class, for example, you might be writing an essay about the causes of the Civil War, based on your readings and research. You will support your ideas with evidence from your sources. Another student may present a different argument, based on other evidence.

Critical thinking means analysis, not negative criticism. When you think critically, you ask questions, puzzle out problems logically, and bring your powers of reason to an issue. College gives you mental tools to hone your ability to think critically and analytically, rather than emotionally or impressionistically. When a professor asks you to write a critical paper on some question, he or she is asking for analysis and not a negative opinion.

PRESENTING YOUR WORK

Written Work

In most courses, written work should be presented in typed (or word-processed) form, double-spaced with one-inch margins, in 12-point (or equivalent) typeface. Papers should be fastened with a staple or a paper clip. Most instructors prefer that pages be numbered. All work should be identified with your name, class, and date. Some students, with access to countless font types and color printers, may be tempted to present work that is graphically inventive and colorful. Such presentations, however, usually are not appropriate at the college level. These are some general guidelines; you'll want to check the course syllabus for each instructor's requirements for presenting your work.

Oral Presentations

In many courses, you may present your work orally; sometimes you will hand in a written version of the oral presentation, as well. Rehearsing your presenta-

Guidelines for *Oral Presentations*

- **Stay within the time limit.** Generally, speakers allow two minutes to deliver each printed page of text. If you are not reading a prepared text, time your presentation by rehearsing it—even if you are the only listener.
- **Use a conversational tone.** Speak audibly, emphasize words that are important, and vary your pace, just as you would in conversation. Glance around the room from time to time so that all of your listeners feel included.
- **Practice.** You'll engage your audience more successfully if you make eye contact with them. Rehearsing will help you to feel comfortable with your presentation.
- **Outline.** Speaking from an outline or bullet points will help you to look at your audience rather than printed pages. You might project your outline or bullet points on a screen or chart so that your audience can see the shape of your presentation.
- **Be concrete.** Concrete information engages listeners better than abstractions. Examples and anecdotes usually are more interesting than statistics.
- **Define terms.** Think about what your listeners already know about your topic and what they might not know. Avoid using acronyms (WHO for World Health Organization, for example) unless you first tell the audience what the letters stand for.
- **Use visual aids.** Such materials include handouts, charts, slides, video recordings, and presentation software (such as PowerPoint).
- **Elicit questions.** Invite listeners to ask questions, and leave your audience with questions that your work has generated for you. By encouraging discussion, you actively involve your listeners.

tion in front of a friend or family member may help you avoid "stage fright" in front of the class. Your teacher usually will provide some guidelines for the presentation, such as length and availability of visual services (video player, computer).

Collaborative Projects

In some courses, students work on projects collaboratively. Collaboration means that each member in a group takes responsibility for part of the project.

Guidelines for Collaborative Projects

- **Know the assignment.** Make sure all the members of the group understand the assignment in the same way. If there are questions, check with your teacher.
- **Make a schedule.** Group members will have many obligations—other classes, work, family, or even a social life. Agree on a schedule that will work for everyone and lead to successful completion of the project. Keep a progress report or checklist to monitor accomplishments.
- **Share the workload.** Successful collaboration means that everyone contributes equally. If a member of your group cannot contribute, he or she should consult with the teacher for possible reassignment.
- **Check in regularly.** Meeting in person or by e-mail will help the group share accomplishments as well as problems.
- **"Play well" with others.** Even if one member is clearly more organized or prepared than the others, encourage all members to feel appreciated. Don't allow one group member to dominate discussions or decisions.

Collaboration depends on cooperation and dependability among all group members. Sometimes, each member will receive a separate grade based on his or her written work as part of the project; in some classes, the group as a whole receives a grade. Your teacher will explain how collaborative projects are graded in the class.

LEARNING ONLINE

Besides enrolling in courses on college campuses, many adult learners take online classes where they never actually see or meet their instructor or classmates. Some online classes take place in a virtual classroom, where all students log on at the same time, listen and respond to one another and their instructor, and work on assignments independently. This kind of instruction is called *synchronous communication*. Other online classes are self-paced, where students log on at any time and communicate to class discussions by posting comments on the course site. This kind of instruction is called *asynchronous communication*. Most courses incorporate ways for students to share ideas, such as chat rooms, bulletin boards, or e-mail connections.

Classroom Dos and Don'ts

- **Do participate.** When your instructor asks a question, she hopes that students will respond. All instructors want to create lively class discussions, and they welcome your contributions. Some students, especially at the beginning of their college career, hesitate to speak in class. But when you share your perspectives and ideas with others, you help to create a rich learning environment. When you do participate, remember that you are communicating with the whole class, not only with the instructor; the students in the back of the room want to hear your comments, too.

- **Don't monopolize class discussions.** Sometimes, in their enthusiasm for the course, a few students will try to answer every question the instructor asks, comment on everything any other student says, and interject questions or remarks throughout every class. Although instructors appreciate eager and engaged students, they want all of the class members, even those who may be shy and may lack confidence, to feel comfortable about speaking out in class. You can help the instructor by monitoring your own contributions.

- **Do come to class prepared.** Lectures and discussions build on what you have read and written outside of class. You will be a more valuable contributor, and you will learn more, if you do your homework.

- **Don't use class time to discuss personal concerns.** If you need an extension to complete a paper, for example, or if you want to inform your instructor that you will be missing a class, talk to the instructor privately before or after class. On the other hand, if you have a question related to the course material, the syllabus, or the course requirements—if you need a term defined or a concept clarified, for example—*do* ask. It is likely that if you do not understand something, others do not also.

- **Don't be distracting.** In the workplace, you know that staff meetings can be disrupted by a co-worker who spills coffee, whispers to a neighbor, or taps a pencil incessantly while others are trying to talk. A classroom is no different. Don't fidget, eat, rustle papers, whisper, pass notes, or otherwise distract your instructor and classmates. Turn off your watch alarm and cell phone, and make sure that your beeper or pager does not go off during class.

- **Do arrive on time.** You'll disrupt the class if you consistently come late. If you have a problem arriving on time, discuss it with your instructor. If coming late is unavoidable, remove your coat and take out your notebook and pen *before* you enter the classroom, take the first available seat, and make sure you catch up with any announcements that were made before you arrived. If you need to leave early, tell the instructor before class begins, take a seat as near to the door as possible, and put on your coat after you leave the room.

Becoming a student in an online course draws on many of the same skills and strengths as being a student in a physical classroom. In addition, however, here are some tips for success in the online environment.

TIPS FOR ONLINE LEARNERS

1. *Do participate.* Just as in a classroom, you have a chance to make your ideas known in a virtual classroom or through bulletin boards, chat rooms, or e-mail. All instructors want their students to participate by sharing ideas with them and with the rest of the class. You will get more out of the experience if you are a lively respondent.

2. *Don't dominate online discussions.* Sitting alone in front of a computer invites some students to digress or pontificate. Remember, your instructor, along with everyone else, is reading your message. Keep it relevant.

3. *Do write in a serious and respectful tone.* Messages to your professor and classmates are different from casual e-mails or text messages. Write in full sentences, avoid slang and colloquial terms, and be aware that your audience consists of a diverse community of learners.

4. *Do be prepared.* Unless you are attending a virtual class, you will need to exert self-discipline to complete assignments and keep up with class discussions. Before contributing to those discussions, make sure you have done the class work.

5. *Do set a realistic pace for a self-paced course—and then keep up with your planned schedule.* Make appointments with yourself to log on at specific times and do your homework regularly.

GETTING YOUR WORK DONE

Whether you work in an office or at home, you've evolved some strategies for getting your work done successfully. Those strategies can be applied to class work, as well.

Set priorities. You've learned how to organize your tasks according to deadlines, ease of completion, and importance. You've learned that if you have a large task to complete, it can be broken down into smaller components. The course syllabus will give you deadlines for work throughout the semester. Keeping a separate calendar for school can help you to break down your work responsibilities into manageable projects.

Communication and Goals

1. Write a letter to a friend or family member explaining why you want to return to school. As you read the letter, note which reasons seem stronger than others. Why are these stronger?
2. What reactions can you anticipate from the recipient of the letter?
3. How might you meet any objections that the recipient voices?

Organize. You probably have a filing system, a weekly planner, and a daily routine at work. You need a similar system for school. At work, your first task of the day may be to check e-mail and voice mail; at school, your first task may be to check your assignment book and syllabus. Establishing a study routine is as important as establishing a work routine.

Know your responsibilities. Your job description delineates your work responsibilities, and your syllabus tells you your course-related responsibilities. In a sense, the syllabus is like a contract between you and the instructor; it tells you what you need to do to complete the course successfully.

Make informed decisions. At work or at home, you know that the decision-making process involves gathering information and listening to others. Often, you need to seek that information and ask for help. Asking for information and help is not a sign of weakness, but rather it is evidence of your maturity as a student. Don't hesitate to use the many support services offered through your school. Chapter 3, "Identifying College Resources," discusses support services in more detail.

Identify helpful colleagues. Forming study groups, finding a peer reader for a paper, or just meeting a classmate for coffee to discuss the ideas of the course is a stimulating experience for most students. Some instructors distribute class lists with telephone numbers and e-mail addresses for all students enrolled. In other classes, you may have a chance to work collaboratively with your classmates on some projects. Even if these options are not built into your course, you'll be rewarded by taking the time to establish connections with your classmates.

SETTING GOALS

As discussed earlier in this chapter, adults have many reasons to return to school. Among those reasons:

- to complete an interrupted degree

- to begin a new degree program
- to prepare for a career change
- to learn new skills for career advancement
- for personal enrichment
- for intellectual challenge
- for a sense of community

Just as students differ in their goals, they differ in the time it will take to achieve their goals. Some students can attend school full-time; others can take no more than one course each semester. While some students may complete an undergraduate degree program in a few years, others envision themselves as students for a decade or more. Having a clear sense of your own goals is the first step toward realizing them.

ADDITIONAL RESOURCES

Carter, Carol, Joyce Bishop, and Sarah Kravits. *Keys to Success: Building Successful Intelligence for College, Career, and Life,* 5th ed. Upper Saddle River, NJ: Prentice Hall, 2006.

DiMarco, Cara. *Moving Through Life Transitions,* 2nd ed. Upper Saddle River, NJ: Prentice Hall, 2000.

Johnston, Susan. *The Career Adventure,* 4th ed. Upper Saddle River, NJ: Prentice Hall, 2006.

CHAPTER 2

Transitions and Life Changes

The average person today is expected to live approximately 80 years. During the 80 or so years of your life, you will experience many potentially life-changing events. These events will present you with many opportunities; each of which is a choice. A life event is an opportunity that brings you to the threshold of a new place, a new way of life. At each threshold you are faced with a choice. You can stay safely where you are or you can choose to pass through these doorways and establish yourself at a new level of maturity and satisfaction. This process, crossing the thresholds of life changes and settling into a new place in your progress toward a satisfying and fulfilling life, is a *transition*.

Once you learn a positive and constructive approach to life's challenges, you become the maker of the map that leads to the treasure of a full and happy life. Acquiring new skills to deal with life transitions allows you:

- To learn how to focus on solutions rather than problems.
- To feel in control of yourself and your life.
- To improve your self-esteem.
- To build future successes in managing your life transitions.
- To gain the respect of others.

Taken from: *Transition Management: A Practical Approach to Personal and Professional Development*, Fourth edition by Sandra L. McKee and Brenda L. Walters

We define the process of *transition* as **a shift in operating style that allows *successful adaptation* to a new set of life conditions.**

An example of a fairly difficult, but successful, transition process was Scott, a student at a small Georgia college. An athlete and a typical, active young male, he had a large circle of friends and a fiancée. In an instant, his whole life changed. A car accident caused injuries that resulted in brain damage, and suddenly, nothing in his life was familiar or doable. Family support and months of therapy to relearn simple things, like walking and talking, still did not return him to his former robust and active self. His fiancée broke off their engagement. Life had to start over for Scott on very different terms. His successful transition was predicated on his will to adapt. His new role has taken him all over the country as a motivational speaker. It has inspired him to make a valuable contribution to his community and has brought him a new life.

Scott's story, and others like his, might be summed up with the following: "We are not owed the right to an easy voyage through life, but instead are presented with opportunity to achieve some level of greatness. The real regrets in life only come from not doing our best. All else is out of our control" (Phillips, 2000, p. 10). What we can control, however, and improve on significantly, is our ability to manage transitions into more satisfying levels of fulfillment in our lives.

A transition is precipitated by a change—brought about either by you or by an external event. Learning to manage change and its effects ensures you continual forward movement with your life.

Face the Changes

"New stuff is a cause of confusion and a source of creativity" (Lowe, 2000). That quote sums up the effect and benefit of change in our lives. Anything that is different from what we have experienced before is a little confusing. Different conditions also give us the opportunity to be creative about the way we use or play out the change.

There is no escaping the fact that we will go through many transitions due to life changes. Some of these changes are unexpected, while some of the changes we create ourselves. Some allow us to merely add new elements to our lives, while others demand that we close a door on something (or someone) familiar. Choosing not to change in the face of changing conditions has implications of its own. Some changes we create because we see advantages in going through the change process, and others we choose in order to remove ourselves from circumstances that are unhealthy or unpleasant.

Any type of change has been described as an "upending of expectancies" (Shaw, 1957). This is what happens when what is expected does not occur at all; rather, something entirely different takes place, requiring us to be creative and enlarge our view, to stretch ourselves beyond our original boundaries to new and different horizons. Even good changes and changes we drive ourselves can leave us feeling "upended." But they allow us to make transitions that we might otherwise not have chosen.

To successfully navigate the transition process that change creates, you must:

- **become proactive**
- **overcome loss and fears**
- **engage reason and creativity**
- **take action**

Even if you are one of the lucky ones and have avoided major upheavals in your life, you should now begin to acknowledge that change is both continual in its occurrence and continuous in its effects. This means that:

- Change will occur over and over throughout life.
- Change forever alters conditions and people.

Because of these two facts, you must develop a repertoire of skills that you can use when change occurs in your life.

Ben was in special forces in the military for 10 years and saw some pretty heated action in foreign domains. When he chose to separate from the service to pursue a steadier, less dangerous life and have a family, he was faced with several challenges. Though he had acquired a degree in mechanical engineering during his years in the military, what he felt most confident of was his special forces skills. However, he wanted to make a clean break and move into a completely new life.

1. What might be Ben's first obstacle to overcome as he attempts the transition to a kinder, gentler life?

2. If you were to write a statement of redefinition, a new way for Ben to think of and describe himself, what would it say?

3. List three behaviors that Ben may have to learn to change in order to begin the transition to a new life.

Because change is likely to be common in your life, you must learn to develop strategies to manage change, rather than resist it. By developing these strategies, you prepare to take control and return to equilibrium quickly. These strategies give you a firm footing in the change journey and help you enjoy regular successes along the way.

Become Proactive

Cultivate Resilience

The first strategy, then, in managing change is to cultivate resilience. Resilience is the ability to bounce back, to get past the rough spots in life. When we become less agitated and more adaptable in the face of change, we reduce our stress level. Dealing with life events at a lower stress level gives us the opportunity to focus more readily on solutions and action. Therefore, we are better able to move through the crisis unencumbered by an excess of emotional baggage.

The most resilient people are those who:

- are in good health
- have solid support systems
- are on good terms with some sort of belief system

Good health creates a feeling of strength; this includes a good diet and enough sleep to maintain a stable emotional state. Connections at all levels—family, community, clubs, or social groups, even pets—provide additional emotional support. A belief system, whether you call it religion or a spiritual set of truths you live by, allows you to be a part of a larger world and gives you some assurances.

You can also cultivate resilience by "practicing" to be flexible. Taking different routes home, experimenting with new foods, associating with people from other cultures, or even changing your office around can all help to desensitize you to changing conditions. Something as simple as thinking of "what if" scenarios can be beneficial. In your day-to-day life you can become stuck in predictable patterns, consciously or not. By breaking the pattern regularly, you will find yourself adapting more quickly to new conditions—large and small.

TRANSITION TIP   *Jeff Tillilie, Buyer*

Travel takes you to see what other places have to offer and how other people look at things. You get a bigger picture of life if you live several months in another country. When you realize that there are lifestyles and values different from yours, then you become more relaxed about changes and differences. I would advise anyone to travel to another country, even live there for awhile, and you'll get a better understanding of what you like because you have some comparisons.

Increase Perception

Another part of responding positively to change is to increase perception. If you are aware of what is going on in your work or personal world, you are less likely to be taken by surprise. If you understand that business and industry are continually looking for ways to cut costs and downsize, you will be more likely to invest your time in careers that fit into the current trends, rather than follow more traditional careers.

From a personal perspective, if you understand what factors affect your relationships, you will be able to short-circuit crisis and beef up emotional connections to withstand stressful conditions. When you become more observant and begin to see patterns of cause and effect in relationships, you can plan changes in your life that will help you adapt to new conditions as they evolve.

Overcome Loss and Fears

Whether a change has an immediate positive or negative flavor to it, a first reaction might be a feeling of loss: the loss of the familiar that has gone before or has always been. Another could be fear: second-guessing the future, an inability to control how events will unfold. Even a potentially positive change requires you to leave the familiar behind and enter a new and unknown situation.

Loss

Strong feelings are especially acute in cases of unexpected catastrophic or traumatic events. When catastrophic changes occur, movement through a grieving process is required in order to separate from past events and move on. Those who refuse to acknowledge the feelings and, thus, squelch this process can become stuck emotionally, maybe even geographically, unable to transition to the next level or place of their lives. Comments from people who are stuck might include, "I'm just an unemployed assembler. There's no point in learning a new career now," or, "I can't leave here; it's just too painful."

By acknowledging the feelings of loss (you are having them at some level whether you admit it openly or not), you give yourself the chance to work through them and move on. The grieving process takes time because there is a myriad of emotions involved, such as:

- denial—"This isn't really happening."
- bargaining—"If I just had another chance . . ."
- anger—"I hate the person (or event) that caused this."
- depression—"I might as well just give up."

■ acceptance—"My life will be different, but I will go on." (Kübler-Ross, 1997)

1. What do you think Katie is going through?
2. What part do you think grief might play in the situation?
3. Predict some of the behaviors Kirsten might expect to see in Katie as she goes through the stages of this life change.

Kirsten and Katie, identical twins, had been inseparable while growing up. Both had chicken pox at the same time, lettered in basketball in high school, enjoyed the same concerts, and disliked the same foods. During college, Kirsten met Jake, and when graduated, they decided to marry. At first Katie was happy for her sister and thought Jake was a good choice for her. Eventually, though, Katie began making up excuses to avoid going with Kirsten to wedding preparation activities. She became ill-tempered and withdrawn.

Fear

Those who fare best under unexpected circumstances are those who accept that a certain number of these life upheavals just happen, and they refuse to live in fear of them. For example, refusing to drive a car because of the possibility of an accident is unrealistic. However, cultivating a heightened awareness of how to respond in emergency situations can help you to come successfully out of even the worst scenarios, personal or professional. The key is to avoid handing over control of your life to fear. You do not want to see yourself as a powerless victim of fate.

The fact that you feel some apprehension, even anxiety, about a prospective or occurring change is a good thing; a little fear heightens the thought processes. Too much fear, however, paralyzes. Understanding fear and how people deal with fear will help you as you face the unknown.

For example, it costs nearly $10,000 to fully train a police dog, so a rather elaborate process is used to assess pups for their potential for that kind of work. An important element in the dog's character is how the dog handles fear-invoking situations.

The following test is performed: The dog is brought out into an open area on a leash. At a specified distance, a gun is fired. Imagine the responses of three different dogs:

1. The first dog cowers and frantically tries to get away, even yanking the leash from the handler.
2. The second dog stands there in a blasé fashion, as if to say, "Gun? What gun?"

3. The third dog starts and even cowers for a second or two, then stands up and immediately starts looking around with interest.

Dog #1 is paralyzed with fear and would be of no use in a tight spot, no matter how much training was applied. Dog #2 does not feel fear at all—it is just not in his experience set. (Among humans, some mountain climbers, bungee jumpers, and other extreme sports or daredevil types fall into this category.) He would be worthless in police work because an awareness of danger is an important part of staying alive. Dog #3 is intelligent enough to recognize a dangerous stimulus. It felt the initial, instinctive fear, then rose above it to go to work to discover what the threat was. Dog #3 would likely be chosen.

Feeling fear is not an indicator of an inability to handle difficult or unknown situations. Recognizing that fear should not stop you from consciously assessing a situation and moving forward is the sign of a good transition manager.

Positive Expectation

An effective response to change is meeting it with a positive expectation. Sometimes our negative expectations are the result of past experiences with change that had disastrous or unpleasant outcomes: a parent dying, a best friend moving away, an appearance-altering injury.

ACTIVITY   2.1

List three change events that occurred in your life while you were growing up (until age 18 or so). Beside each event, describe whether it had a positive or negative outcome.

1. _____

2. _____

3. _____

Did any of the events that seemed to have an initial negative result turn out to be positive as you look back on them?

Many of the feelings you have about a present or anticipated change depend on your past experiences or attitudes. Some people view change as exciting. Others feel it is the worst thing that could happen to them. People who fear or dread change may react negatively regardless of the potential benefit of the outcome.

There can be endless argument as to whether positive expectations make positive outcomes, or whether accumulating positive outcomes shores you up and creates positive expectations. You might agree, though, that going through life with an anticipation of things turning out well is better than a day-to-day dread of negative events. If nothing else, a positive expectation makes you feel hopeful, and out of this hopefulness comes clear thinking that can lead the event to a positive outcome.

Engage Reason and Creativity

By definition, transition management, self-development, and effective living suggest a strategy of change, of dynamic movement, of adaptation, and of growth. By using reason and creativity to deal with the world, and the people and events in it, you embrace growth in the direction that will create the most happiness for you.

Reason

Change is the catalyst for who you will become in the future. Rationally, if you aspire to a full and satisfying life, you must respect the very nature of change and allow it to shape you into a strong and vibrant individual.

Rational people are able to see conditions in their lives that require change or can recognize changing situations that require adaptation. However, in many cases, change is likely to begin with the need to eliminate some discomfort in our lives. This discomfort can come from a general desire for more out of life or from crisis and pain that cause a quick and radical change. If you view discomfort as a motivator, as a reason to change to a new, more effective behavior, then it could become a welcome signal.

Though sometimes you might choose a change that can cause you to have temporary pain, you do it through reason, research, and conscious decision making, and you do it to make an improvement in your life.

1. What motivated Thomas to leave his home?

2. What obstacles might have existed to stop him from making the change he wanted?

3. What changes do you think he had to make in his life during the first year in the United States?

After a close friend was shot in a fight, Thomas decided that to make his life better, he had to leave Jamaica. When he was 18, he left the island his family had lived on for over 100 years and moved to a new culture in an American city. After attending a university, he completed a physician's assistant program and soon received a job offer in Dallas. Today, though he has little or no contact with his old life, he is quite happy.

Change requires movement. It is possible you will stay where you are right now in your life unless some sort of discomfort motivates you to make that move. Some of the most successful people owe their motivation to having grown up in poverty or fear. If you experience pain or unhappiness in your life, you might consider it as a signal for change.

ACTIVITY   2.2

Is there a situation or set of conditions in your life that you currently view as painful, disturbing, or unpleasant? If so, describe it briefly here.

_____

_____

Describe what changes this situation might motivate you to make in your life.

_____

_____

Some changes are complex, such as moving to a foreign country, securing an advanced degree, changing careers, or getting married to someone who has children. All of these changes require crossing a number of thresholds before a complete transition occurs and emotional balance is regained.

Creativity

Change can be a creative expression of your life and will. To stimulate creativity, you may want to begin with *visualization*. This is a technique that many successful individuals practice. In a quiet place or just before you fall asleep at night, begin by "painting" in your mind's eye the success scene you want to create for yourself. The more detail you can bring into this scene, the clearer your path to change will be. Each time you do this exercise, add more detail: people, places, specific circumstances.

If you are patient with the process and practice this simple technique over and over, both the scene and the activities required to reach your goal will become clearer. In addition, you will find that your sense of purpose and determination increase with each practice.

The only caution is that you focus on changes for yourself only. Attempts to create change in your life by wanting others to change or by wishing harm to others are ineffective and can be unhealthy. Your unconscious mind can be very powerful, so be certain that you are committed to a positive outcome. You may get everything you ask for. With your visualization, you become more aware of factors that can contribute to your goal—you recognize opportunities.

Reason leads you to see the need for a change or the need to adapt to an external change. Creativity helps you to frame the situation into an effective transition to a new level. Once you have used your reason and creativity to see your path, then you must embrace the change and take action.

Take Action

Remember, if your decision when faced with a need for change is to take no action, that is a choice also. Abdicating from the director's role does not relieve you of your part in the play—it only takes away a great deal of the control you have over what you do. Changes can have far-reaching effects and require that you go through many transitions in order to arrive at a sense of equilibrium. Sometimes these transitions are harder to make because you are not sure of the right steps to take. Sometimes you even procrastinate out of fear of failure and put off a potentially enriching experience.

The key to managing change is to live forward. What is past cannot be viewed as either a monument or a curse. It must, instead, be a springboard, a launch site.

Choose Change

Time and events go forward. People who do not also go forward run the risk of being weighed down by old events and bewildered by new circumstances. Your life will be different every day. You can choose positively: to grow, to learn, to move with change, to become more understanding about events, to develop new life and professional skills, to cultivate new relationships and improve old ones. Or you can stagnate—live a life devoid of growth, accomplishment, self-esteem, and pride in having overcome obstacles.

Albert, who had been with his company through three mergers and four management changes, explained his longevity to a coworker. "I go in the first day and ask the new management what they want me to do." He has chosen change over resistance. There might be many reasons to choose change:

- A change may be to your advantage.
- A change may promise to be interesting.
- A change may be a chance to learn something new and useful.
- A change may help you keep out the "cobwebs" of monotony.
- A change may take you a step closer to your goal.
- A change of your choice makes you feel powerful and in charge of your life.

Commit Effort

The next step is to make a commitment. In order to make your plans materialize, you have to commit to follow through on the work that will be involved in making the change. This commitment is the determination to be persistent, no matter how inconvenient or difficult the task may become. Without commitment, your effort will be halfhearted, leading only to partial success. Commitment is the driving force that steers you in the right direction. It assures you of the reward you seek.

Commitment and follow-through will take you further than any talent or particular advantage. Barry Mitchell, a professional football player for St. Louis, says, "Never quit. No matter if others say your dream is impossible, no matter if they laugh at you for even having such a dream, no matter if what it takes to get there is so hard you feel you can't go another step. Never quit and you'll win over all the others who do."

Operationalize Commitment

The next step is to put into practice the actions or thoughts that are required to get you to your desired outcome. Action brings you back to being in a balanced and stable state with a sense of confidence.

After you get a clear picture of the new conditions you are moving toward, decide what behaviors you must incorporate in your life to bring you to the success point. This part is crucial to your success. You may have to develop new skills; you may have to do some things differently. You may decide you need speech therapy or a new set of friends, maybe a new degree or professional certification. When you begin to practice these new behaviors, they may feel awkward at first. Don't worry about that. Remember your commitment to follow through and be persistent. Allow yourself several weeks to get used to the new way of doing things. Changes do not happen overnight, so be patient with yourself.

An important hint here is that practicing in your mind is often as beneficial as practicing an action. You can practice the skills related to managing changes by rehearsing scenes in your mind and applying your new knowledge to solving problems that may come up. Go back to your visualization technique and create a scene in which you successfully negotiate a raise or have a relaxed conversation with the object of your previously unvoiced affection. No one will see you do this, and you will be preparing yourself for the future.

Relax

The final stage of action is *relax*. Let yourself go through the change process in a calm way. Don't hassle yourself. Be prepared for unexpected occurrences. Above all, don't panic if the desired change does not occur immediately. These things happen in their own time—when you are ready—not when you think you are ready. Trust your subconscious to guide you in the direction you have set.

Wait

Sometimes we have to wait for our plans to unfold. Katie ran a bike and skateboard shop in a small community outside a large city. She was liked and respected by the sports and bike racing community. When a large, new indoor extreme sports park opened just 12 miles away, a competing skateboard and bike shop was invited to set up in the complex, guaranteeing a stream of customers and business success. Katie, disappointed, continued to offer service and support to area enthusiasts. Finally, in just a few months, the owner of the sports park and the management of the shop agreed to end their association after a disagreement. Katie moved in and her business is now thriving.

Observe

Another way you may have to relax is to observe something changing, rather than interfere with the natural evolutionary process. A change may come in a different form than you initially expected. You must be able to recognize that by relaxing and going with the change as it is occurring, you will be able to ride to the other side of the transition—to your new place of satisfaction. If you do not get the job with the advertising agency, you might instead find a contact in a Web page design company—similar environment, just a slightly different end product. Relax and let the process flow as it must without interruptions.

You can be a change agent for yourself. Remember, however, that you cannot change other people. You cannot make your parents suddenly become as you would like them. You cannot make a friend leave an abusive relationship or quit using alcohol or drugs excessively, and you cannot make your boss suddenly become even tempered. In some cases, relaxing means letting go of responsibility for someone else's choices. Focus on your own changes and enjoy the effects of those.

Life can be a creative process of directing your energy, anticipating changes in the world around you, and designing positive outcomes.

Change in the Professional World

Changes you go through as you make a transition to a new job will likely be compounded by changes that take place in your industry and your company. The job you have just secured may have been created due to a market shift or a change in technology. Many models and constructs have been used to describe change and its effects on business:

- systems theory, which looks at the organization as a system that interacts with and responds to forces in the environment
- terms such as *unfreezing* and *refreezing* describe the breakdown of old policies and long-standing procedures and the establishment of new ones
- paradigm shifts, which take place when people recognize that old assumptions and explanations no longer fit newly discovered discrepancies
- the idea that crazy times require crazy management

Today's information brokering has created an industry that has unlimited resources—there is no scarcity of information, and there is not likely to be. In fact, the opposite is to be expected. New distribution channels created by Internet commerce have opened up world markets in a way trade agreements never could. Companies are spawned by technology innovation and within a few years or even months create millionaires out of 25-year-olds, or they fold because they could not get to market before someone else did. Speculation and visions of riches from a technology home run may blind participants to the potentially harsh reality of risk in these industries and inspire new rounds of speculation, much like the lure of the lottery jackpot.

Increasingly sophisticated technical skills are needed to support all of these advancements. For this reason, companies are going outside national borders to find the talent and expertise they need. The influx of people from other cultures has changed the face of whole companies and even cities. Austin, Texas, for example, has recently gained a significant population from India that has come into the community to work in the growing high-tech industry. With these new residents comes their culture, including belief systems, customs, and foods. Larger numbers of foreign students are graduating from American Ivy League colleges and obtaining jobs outside their country of origin.

For these reasons trying to generate a model of organizational change processes in the twenty-first century becomes much like trying to capture fog in a jar or draw wind. But organizations are made up of people, and so they respond to change much as you or I would. Typically, organizations:

- resist change that is forced on them
- seek changes that eliminate pain
- implement changes that promise new vitality or profits

Resist Change

Resistance may come in the form of "digging in"—viewing change as an enemy to be overcome, or at least waited out. This way of thinking assumes that things staying the same is good. There is some logic to this because the company could be getting along quite well, for now, so changing conditions, competitors, or trends are seen as merely blips on the screen or temporary storms to be weathered. Many strong companies with adequate cash reserves can, indeed, get through some fluctuations in conditions. However, a failure to monitor and change with new circumstances can cause irretrievable losses.

Individual managers or employees can argue with upper-level decision makers or exercise power plays to try to circumvent plans that involve change. Ultimately, though, resistance takes considerably more energy and risk than skillfully managing change.

Seek Change to Relieve Discomfort

When competitive position begins to slip, delivery or manufacturing problems hamper the ease of doing business, personnel issues or information system problems cripple operations, or cash flow is in the wrong direction, companies actively seek to make changes to relieve the pain of these problems. There are a variety of ways this might be done, and all directly affect the first-year employee.

Bring in Consultants

Experts in the industry or professional consultants analyze the situation by doing a needs assessment. This involves interviews with employees at all levels of the organization, with customers, and possibly even with competitors. It also includes a detailed examination of the external and internal processes and conditions to find out what the problem really is and what is required to fix it. Then, the consultants make recommendations that could involve process or system revamping, reorganization of functional areas, elimination of certain departments, or even selling off whole units.

You will likely be interviewed in this process if you have been with the organization less than a year. Keep in mind the purpose of the interviews and monitor your assessment of the situation or your take on the best course of action. You may indeed have a beneficial, fresh approach, but it is also possible that you do not have a clear picture of the entire operation, so the scope of your responses should be in your own area.

As a result of the consultants' recommendations, it is possible that new people will be hired to support new strategic directions—while other staff may be laid off to reduce redundancy or costly areas in the existing structure.

Fresh into the workplace with a double major in business and engineering, Benyiata chose a large, stable company that she felt had a lot of opportunity for movement and challenge. After only eight months on the job, her manager asked her to share her "impressions" of the company with a consultant who had been brought in by management. After only 20 minutes, Benyiata had established a good rapport with the consultant, who began to hint to her some changes management was considering. One of the changes would benefit Benyiata directly, but would cause her manager to lose his job.

1. What do you think Benyiata is feeling?

2. Should she agree or disagree with the consultant's view of the situation?

3. Why would a company let go a manager who had been with them for some time and keep an entry-level person?

Reverse Engineering

Reverse engineering looks at processes and results that are central to the company's doing business. It is called reverse engineering because the approach is to go to the end or result, then figure out how to achieve that result. Often processes and procedures become unwieldy due to the repeated addition of short-term fixes as the demands of the business become more extensive and complex. Usually, people in the affected departments are put on a project team, possibly for the first time together, and occasionally an outsider is added for a totally fresh perspective.

Any department can be a part of a change team to improve the company's business, and any employee can be asked to join the team. You might be included on the team to represent your area. It is important that you know and can explain clearly what part your department or function plays in the total process. A change team can be a good way to meet and work with other employees and managers outside your immediate area. Sometimes, it is a way to let you in on the workings and strategies of the entire organization. You may be asked to make specific change recommendations. Ideally, you will be able to develop a well-thought-out formal document or presentation. Report writing and presentation skills are valuable in such situations.

Divest or Sell

As mentioned previously, to fix what a company sees as a drain on company resources, an irretrievable situation, or an irreversible trend, sometimes the board of directors or CEO decides that selling off part or all of the business is the best route. Cutting losses when investors are involved is sometimes chosen as a preferred strategy, even over the objections of management.

The companies with the most integrity tell all employees that this step is being taken and offer outplacement services or generous severance packages to those directly affected. However, in order to look good for a potential buyer or to prevent an untimely drop in stock prices, sometimes this kind of decision is held close by upper management until the very last minute. You cannot always see this kind of change coming, but diligent monitoring of your company's position in the market may alert you to anything drastic that might happen.

Seek Change to Ensure Growth and Ongoing Improvement

Some companies survive by being leaders in the continuous advancement of technology or service offerings. They constantly seek new markets, strive to respond rapidly to market changes, and work to develop new products or services ahead of competitors. Their structure is less rigid than companies that operate in more stable environments. Often, a single employee has duties in several different departments and reports to more than one project manager. In these companies, change is constant and change agents are valued.

Rapid Reactors

Rapid reactors are organizations that can retool or shift resources quickly in response to opportunities or threats in their operating environment, such as the removal of a competitor or the loss of a raw materials supplier. They are lean, without many layers of management; most employees do many different tasks, and everyone works long hours. If you are in one of these companies, be prepared to abandon a project and shift all of your energies and commitment to a new one on a day's notice. Taking too much ownership of a pet project can make you resent the organization's right to direct you wherever it wants. Keeping abreast of the competition and of market trends will help you to avoid being taken by surprise by one of these quick adaptations.

Proactive Leaders

Companies with large investments in research and development seek to maintain solvency by leading the market in some way: cost, time, or quality. Continuous improvement is a term often heard. Employees may be rewarded with cash or other bonuses for suggestions that advance the company's position or improve efficiency and productivity. Staying out in front gives them an advantage, as long as they can do that profitably. They are out on the edge of the technology in their industry and regularly unveil the newest advancements at trade shows and conferences.

To stay on that cutting edge, however, can sometimes be costly, and if your company does not have enough offerings that generate large, steady streams of income, capital reserves can be drained. You may be hired by one of these companies because they want fresh, up-to-the-minute skills and because they perceive you as an idea person. Do not let them down. Continue to develop what you have to offer the company, always meet deadlines, and focus study and thought on ways to constantly improve operations or market advantage.

ACTIVITY   2.3

Either in your current profession or in your intended field of work locate companies that fit these descriptions.

1. Large, stable

2. Small, lean, responsive

3. Cutting-edge technology leader or trendsetter

Monitor the companies you selected for 30 days to see how each plays out its approach. (Reading press releases or investor relations information on the company Web site or looking at industry publications will help provide this information.)

Some changes that may occur in your personal or professional life suggest pleasant or positive outcomes and evoke enthusiasm. Other changes can be extremely painful and require many weeks of adjustment. Both happy and painful change events can be stressful. In the midst of these change events, it is sometimes difficult to remember that those around us are likely undergoing the effects of these events also. Compassion and understanding of those who are close to you should be added to the skills for managing change that you have learned in this chapter.

Mapping Pathways for Change

As you move from the life of a college student to being a working professional, or from one career to another, you will make successful transitions if you internalize and practice the following:

- **Self-nurturing**—accepting responsibility for and taking care of your physical, emotional, and relational self.
- **Self-advocacy**—accepting responsibility for the development, direction, and ultimate satisfaction of your professional self.

Each time you finish a chapter in this book, you will have examined a new area of growth in your life. You will be asked to write down some goals in the areas of your life that relate to self-nurturing and self-advocacy. These goals help guide the transition process through the life changes you are experiencing and driving.

TRANSITION SKILLS SUMMARY

Face the changes

Become proactive

Overcome loss and fears

Engage reason and creativity

Take action

Observe change in the professional world

GOAL SETTING

My self-nurturing goals for managing change in my personal life are:

_____

_____

_____

My self-advocacy goals for managing change in my professional life are:

_____

_____

_____

C O A C H 'S   C O R N E R

"Improvisation is a natural event for all conscious beings."

Improv is the perfect response to the world we find ourselves in today. By definition, it summons up a picture of acting in adaptation to the moment, to whatever is presented to the performer. Thus, its methods certainly fit the world of industry, especially the quickening cycles of change we are seeing today: more changes in ever shorter periods of time. Improv, in spite of the way it may appear to an observer, does have specific guidelines for its application in unexpected and sometimes very surprising situations. Those same guidelines can help anyone, or any organization, that is hurling through the ever shape-shifting space and time.

First principle: Stay in the present moment.

At any given time, we are processing at many levels of complexity and awareness and in many places along the time line of our lives. A smell of bread baking reminds us of our youth in grandma's kitchen; a situation brings back fear of a similar situation that turned out horribly; a smile causes us to speculate about what could be possible with that person. Staying focused, like when an artist is concentrating on the detail of a person's face or when a martial arts or yoga practitioner works to perfect a position and then hold it, is difficult for most of us. In the present moment, change becomes nearly irrelevant because differences are in comparison to what went before and only intimidating in concern about what is coming after. Stress drops dramatically when we can concentrate on now and the events that are occurring, not replaying, comparing, or projecting to some other time.

Second principle: Strive to be completely honest with yourself.

Improvisation is a human occurrence, as is change. Change does not affect buildings or landscape, in that these being inanimate do not choose a reaction. Recognize in

(continued)

yourself what is going on at any given moment: fear, surprise, confusion, delight. The next level of honesty is recognizing the effects of outside influences on the moment. "I am really angry now, but looking at the situation, I can see that mostly I am disappointed that I was not chosen." Honesty with yourself is liberating, much like confession is for some.

Third principle: Be completely honest with at least one other person.

This does not consist of blurting out every thought you have about someone or some situation, but about being straightforward in what you do say. Honesty is related to happiness; if you are not hiding, you are sharing. Choose one person with whom you can be completely honest. This can be useful in the way you relate to others: I agree to tell you if your actions offend me, and you agree to do the same. We are playing the same game at the same time. If a change causes you to be fearful, have one person in whom you can confide this fear and with whom you can practice honesty and candor.

Fourth principle: You must put your work in public view.

This principle requires action, not contemplation or intellectualizing. You participate in the process; you practice your adaptations to the changing conditions. However, it is a step process, one at a time, where you practice being creative about your responses to different and evolving situations. Staying honest, you examine the results of your experimentation and evaluate whether that action achieved what you wanted. If it did not, then another creative approach should be tested.

ROBERT LOWE, coach, trainer, and author of *Improvisation, Inc: Harnessing Spontaneity to Engage People and Groups,* Jossey–Bass/Pfeiffer (2000)

CHAPTER 3

Creating a Positive Attitude

W e seek out positive attitudes in friendships, intimate relationships, employees, and sales people because people who are energetic, optimistic, open, and happy are just naturally attractive. We do this because they:

- radiate a sense of satisfaction about life
- seem centered, calm, and in control
- are pleasant to be around
- tend to have many friends
- have a spirited enthusiasm
- expect positive outcomes even in the most difficult times
- infect us with their upbeat spirit.

With all of the benefits of positive-attitude living, you might find it hard to imagine anyone who wants to view the world and life any other way. But, attitudes and behavior are learned over time. We are, after all, the sum total of our experiences and our attitudes about those experiences. Thus, a negative attitude can grow out of too many failures, hurts, and disappointments. Eventually, the negativity becomes a pattern; whining, despair, and helplessness win out over perseverance and expectancy.

Taken from: *Transition Management: A Practical Approach to Personal and Professional Development*, Fourth edition by Sandra L. McKee and Brenda L. Walters

In the same way, happy experiences lead to expectations of positive outcomes. But a pattern of happy life events is not the only reason a person develops an optimistic viewpoint. The world can be a hazardous, treacherous, and often frightening place, but it is also exciting and rich with gifts, heroism, and joy. Optimism is a choice—do you choose to see the poverty or the compassion, the hope or the depravity, the loss or the potential? Whatever you expect to see, you will.

The truth is, no one wants to be around a person who spews out negative thoughts and feelings. It makes others feel uncomfortable and it throws a damper on the general mood. If you find that you are in the group of people who use negativity excessively, you can, and should, disconnect its effect on you before you fall into the pattern or habit yourself. If you are one of those who view the world and the people in it with distrust and negative expectation, you can consciously change, creating a life of joy and satisfaction for yourself and those around you.

Understanding the Value of a Positive Attitude

The effects of a positive outlook are far reaching. It can make the difference between a life of dread and a life filled with peace. A positive attitude can have a dramatically beneficial effect on one's health also. Seeing the world as being full of opportunity and potentially good experiences prevents many of the physical effects of stress and the ensuing wear and tear on the body.

Characteristics of a Positive Attitude

Positive people are easier to be around and tend to uplift others around them, especially if they are in a leadership position. They are better to work with and for. Through their attitude, they generate confidence and help others stay calm in crisis situations. Because positive people are optimistic, they create opportunities for themselves by believing that solutions are just around the corner. They know that every problem has a point where a resolution lies. They see themselves as being able to get to that endpoint quickly. This attitude rubs off on others and fosters a constructive circle of friends, family, and coworkers.

A positive attitude is associated with high self-esteem. People with high self-esteem are desirable in the workplace for several reasons:

- They take responsibility for their work and future, including mistakes.
- They make good team players and are able to share success with others.
- They can commit because they are confident they will be successful.
- They are slow to anger because they do not carry grudges.

- They are candid, giving constructive criticism.
- They manage conflict well, valuing resolution over winning.
- They can take risks because they respect failure as a learning process, not a reflection on their essential value.

A positive attitude is powerful. It can help you realize your dreams because with an optimistic expectation, you feel free to dream.

Characteristics of a Negative Attitude

There are two kinds of negativity we deal with in our lives: our own negativity and that of others. We often are not aware that the troubled, uncomfortable feeling that nags at us is really negativity and its effects. Low expectations in our careers and relationships cause us to settle for something less than a satisfying life. The negative spiral downward is reinforced by the lack of real joy and inner fulfillment, further adding to the misery.

The characteristics of a negative person are as follows:

- They experience worry and fear almost daily.
- They often see themselves as victims of life.
- They feel powerless and overburdened by their circumstances.
- They are often described by their friends and coworkers as "naysayers" or "wet blankets."
- They approach tasks, aspirations, and relationships with low expectations.
- They project their negative view on others: "You'll never get that promotion; someone else has seniority."

The cumulative effects of negative thinking on us are dramatic. We become stressed out, self-esteem decreases, confidence fades, and we are unable to stay focused on our goals (see Figure 3.1).

Negative people "stomp" on ideas and possibilities.   **FIGURE 3.1**

No way.

This job stinks.

You don't have enough seniority.

That will never work.

Negative persons may experience an underlying hopelessness about life. Feeling powerless, they may struggle to gain some control. This struggle is emotionally draining and can actually cause situations to go badly. Adverse thoughts often become self-fulfilling prophecies, and the cycle of negativity continues.

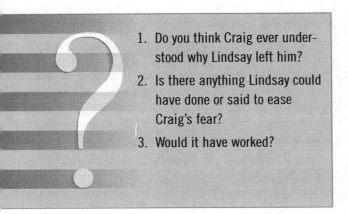

1. Do you think Craig ever understood why Lindsay left him?
2. Is there anything Lindsay could have done or said to ease Craig's fear?
3. Would it have worked?

Though Craig and Lindsay had been best friends since junior high school and dated all through college, Craig worried that Lindsay would leave him when she went to work. She had matured into a quite beautiful woman and drew admiring glances wherever they went. Though she was seriously committed to Craig, she began to be put off by his insistent jealousy and self-deprecating remarks. Eventually, his behavior led to several arguments, and Lindsay sadly broke off the relationship.

Negative communication with yourself and with others can become a habit that causes you to talk yourself into a dismal view of the world at large. It destroys expectations, and it alienates other people who don't want to hear pessimistic talk all of the time. The original cause for this doleful approach to life may have been a disappointment or even a tragedy. Though probably long forgotten, the initial life event left behind a pattern of negativism.

Alex, a computer specialist at a bank, was a worrier. He had come from a family who criticized him in an effort to make him improve and work up to his potential. He obsessed over his work and worried that he was not good enough for the job. He was very hard on himself if he made the slightest mistake and was openly critical of others' work as well.

Stephany was an executive secretary at a hospital that had just been bought by a managed health care organization. Stephany was still relatively new to her position and liked it very much. Her coworkers and the medical staff constantly expressed their fears and resentment over the changes that would be coming. Over the next several months, she felt more and more stressed and overwhelmed by her job even though her duties remained the same. When she got home in the evenings, she was exhausted. She had already been to her physician and he had found nothing wrong with her. She just could not figure out what was making her feel so bad.

Obviously, these examples are about negativity, but in Stephany's case the negativity was coming from her environment.

Negative thinkers usually have had much practice. Also, they probably are not even aware of the source of their own misery. They tend to blame their unhappiness on everything but their negative thinking. They use such statements as, "If only this would happen, I could be happy."

Those who communicate negatively also have negative expectations. They wait for life to change rather than beginning to change what they can. They usually wind up "waiting" most of their lives. Those few who have good fortune often cannot enjoy it because they don't know how.

ACTIVITY   3.1

Are you subjecting yourself to negative talk? Give some examples that you have used or heard others use.

1. Negative things I say to myself or others.

   a. _____

   b. _____

2. Negative things I have heard others say to me or around me.

   a. _____

   b. _____

Negativity in the office group dramatically inhibits productivity. The word *toxic* is often used to describe this effect. The stimulus can be a disgruntled, toxic worker who complains or criticizes constantly or it can be an organizational climate of fear or distrust. Even the rosiest personalities and the most highly motivated employees will eventually be adversely affected.

Improving Your Attitude

Although it is true that there is effort involved in changing old patterns, the effort is well worth it. You will find yourself feeling happier about life because you will feel a greater sense of control over your thinking. When difficult things come along, you can look for the silver lining, rather than lament about how you have been victimized.

Recognize Negativity as Learned Behavior

Both positive and negative thinking are most often a product of past experiences. We learn these patterns as children and continue to repeat them. These experiences usually occur when we are very young and do not have the intellectual capacity to question them. The critical judgments or the unflattering comments that we heard as children may have shaped us in directions we did not want to go. Young children's thought processes do not question or sift messages that come to them. Because of this, they do not have the ability to assess the accuracy of damaging statements, and, consequently, internalize them as truths. Because at some level in the child's mind the information is absolute fact, he proceeds to think about and operate on these ideas for many years.

The total effect of this is the development of a negative self-image. It is impossible to look constructively and positively on the world through eyes shaded by a negative self-image. These patterns become ingrained in our unconscious thinking and control our lives.

Conversely, those who have emerged from childhood with a generally positive self-image seem to be able to weather difficulties and experience less stress in adult interpersonal situations and life events. Contributors to this attitude might be anything from success as an athlete or with some hobby, excellence in schoolwork, or even the constant support of a doting grandparent or other "fan." This is why the way adults speak to children is so important. Regardless of the external reality of a child's life, positive and respectful treatment and communication can have lifelong beneficial effects.

3.2   ACTIVITY

Try to remember some negative comments made about you or to you when you were a child. See if you can come up with a positive statement that refutes the original comment.

1. Negative comment: _____

   Positive statement: _____

2. Negative comment: _____

   Positive statement: _____

Identify Worry Styles

Some of our negative learned behavior is worry. We spend far too much time feeling concerned about the potential for disturbing life events. Interestingly, the value we attach to something—whether it is interpreted as a good thing or a bad thing—is a learned identifier. For instance, eating less than the average person may be viewed by some as positive, a way to control weight and maintain good health. To someone else, not eating much suggests a loss of appetite and poor health—a cause for worry.

Our worry topics and style are often developed in very subtle ways during our youth. Your neighbor, for example, may have expressed concern about a drought and its effects, such as the local lake or river drying up. Or your brother worried about his appearance and whether people liked him. These examples are all filed away and emerge when some stimulus similar to the worry stimulus occurs. When you ask yourself why you are worried about your car breaking down even though you have an auto club, a cell phone, and a new car, you might remember a parent or relative worrying about such things.

The way people worry is learned as well. If your mother smoked when she was worried, you might have a strange desire to smoke when you are upset, even if you are not generally a smoker. Some people cannot sleep; some sleep a lot when worried. Some get quiet; others talk incessantly. Think about your behavior in the dentist's chair—a good indicator of one element of your worry style.

As soon as you understand why you identify an event or situation as a reason for worry and where you acquired your worry style, you can start disconnecting irrelevant and irrational responses. Constructive positive approaches to problems or dramatic life events is empowering and more effective than worrying.

When was the last time you remember your worry having any effect whatsoever on the outcome of a situation? Worry is taxing and interferes with clear thinking. Also, some worry behaviors can be extremely dangerous (e.g., a woman who drives when she worries could find herself in a very bad place at three in the morning, or a person who becomes cross or ill-tempered when worried may find himself alone or out of a job very soon).

Monitor Internal Dialog

We all talk to ourselves at some level, consciously or not. We play messages in our heads that we have received from others or we fill our thoughts with messages of our own choosing. Often, we are not immediately aware of this self-talk, and that is one reason why it controls our attitude and behavior so regularly—we never question what is coming into our heads. Once you begin to notice your internal dialog, you can act to change what is detrimental or pessimistic. No one has to live with negative thinking or its effects.

The more you talk to yourself in negative ways, the more you wind up frightening and agitating yourself. This kind of talk can:

- Create stress and panic attacks that can be debilitating.

- Make you feel that you are going crazy.
- Make you sweat profusely.
- Cause chest pains and make you feel you are about to die.

To maintain emotional and relational health and to progress in life, get a handle on your thinking patterns. Learn how to be kind to yourself and refute any unkind observations or comments that sneak into your thoughts. In addition, cultivate the habit of saying something positive or kind to someone each day.

When you take the step to notice what goes on in your head, you have begun the task of changing any negative internal programmed tapes to positive internal dialog. The change is not difficult if you maintain your awareness and short-circuit anything that you do not like. After all, you are the one in control of your thoughts. Even when negative thoughts float through your mind, you do not have to keep them there. You can learn to eliminate them and avoid the disturbing and taxing results. You might not be able to control what comes into your head, but you can certainly control what stays there.

Break Old Patterns

One of the most powerful weapons against negative thinking is its counterpart, positive thinking. Just as doleful or dismal thoughts become habits, upbeat and bright thoughts and communication can become a personal style. Following are the steps for breaking the negative thinking habit:

1. Note how you react to life events and become aware of the pattern. If your psyche is on auto-pilot, your mood or expectation is somewhat arbitrarily assigned. As soon as you begin looking for patterns, you start the process of disconnecting the unhealthy ones.

"I never noticed before, but every time my son suggests an alternative solution to a problem, I automatically dismiss it."

"At that meeting this morning I kept track and found I made eight comments to those around me, and all were critical or negative."

2. Decide the specific patterns you want to change.

"I notice I automatically assume there's going to be a problem when a customer calls. I would like to start answering the phone with a more helpful attitude."

"Whenever we start pushing toward a deadline at work, everyone, including me, seems to spend as much time complaining as working. I would like to keep my thoughts clear."

3. Catch yourself and others—don't allow your spirit to be bombarded with negativity from within or without.

If you think, "I forgot my wallet. What an idiotic thing to do," catch yourself: "Oops, there I go. How could I reframe that negative view?" Correct yourself and say, "Well, that's the first time in four years I've done that. Now, where might I have left it?"

4. Practice operating as a positive self-talker. Expect and verbalize positive outcomes: Not "I'll never get the boss to notice my good work," rather, "How can I get the boss to notice my good work?"; not "Alan won't call. He's always too busy for me," rather, "I haven't heard from Alan. Maybe I should call him."

When facing the challenges and frustrations of your daily life, you may find another approach to be helpful. By redesigning your responses to reflect a positive expectation, you build confidence in yourself. David Greenberg, motivational speaker and executive coach, says, "Of course, even positive, successful people have negatives sometimes—negative thoughts or events—but they don't allow the effects to stay with them long. If the computer breaks, don't consume your thoughts with the inconvenience, focus instead on the repair person who will come and make it work again and on how nice that will be." (See Coach's Corner at the end of this chapter.)

When you speak to yourself and others in positive ways, you make the statement that you believe in yourself and in your ability to cope with whatever challenge and frustration may arise.

Creating a Positive Environment

You might notice that there are others around you who have patterns of negative talk as well. Some people who would ordinarily have a positive life view and attitude find themselves in negative environments. These environments can affect the way we feel about our work and relationships.

Once you begin approaching communication in a more empowered and effectual way, you may notice how easy it still is to be infected or influenced by negative talk around you. If your friends constantly criticize each other or you, then that is creating a negative environment. Often when they say something unkind or sarcastic, they say, "I'm just telling it like it is." Perhaps they are, or maybe they are only telling the side they see from their own negative perspective.

Several approaches are possible to deal with negative environments created by friends or coworkers.

1. Defuse the effect the negativism has on you. This is easily accomplished when you recognize the dismal talk for what it is and laugh about it to yourself: "I can't believe how negative Angela sounds today!"

2. Stay away from the "gloom and doom" people and attach yourself to more positive and upbeat individuals. You will be amazed at how your energy level and your demeanor are affected positively by surrounding yourself with people who are positive and forward looking.

3. Confront the "wet blankets" and expose their negativism. Someone may say, "Gosh Nick, where on earth did you find that jacket?" Your reply might be, "That sounds like you don't like my jacket choice for the meeting today."

Sometimes people do not realize the habit they have let themselves develop. Your approach to this may be getting the work group to agree to improve conditions for everyone by choosing to have constructive conversations.

Renee is unhappy with her job. She loves the work as an accountant, but is becoming affected by the working environment. People complain a lot, and no one seems enthusiastic or motivated to do a good job. A coworker complains that the boss is too demanding. Another says that the workers are underpaid. Renee's officemate confides that she is looking for another job because she is not appreciated for the work she does. Renee decides to talk with the boss and recommend some changes to make the office more productive.

1. What are some "positive talk" ways Renee can make these recommendations?

2. How can Renee prevent becoming affected by the environment around her?

Positive thinking, demonstrated by using constructive internal and external communication patterns, is an effective tool to reverse negative directions in your life. It is your responsibility to use the tool to create the life you really want for yourself.

TRANSITION TIP

Jasyn Banks, Sales

One thing that keeps you motivated is being "hungry," wanting to go forward with making life the way you want it. As soon as you realize that choosing the easy route is not an option to get where you want to go, then you move forward with whatever it takes. Of course, there will be tasks along the way that you just don't want to do, even though you know you have to. Do those first when you're fresh, and then everything else that day is something you enjoy. Also, do something new all of the time: attend seminars, network to meet new people, learn to play golf; new stuff keeps your life interesting.

Changing old habits requires time. But, that time will be well spent and the payoff will be very rewarding. The key is to be persistent: that will bring you ever closer to the destiny you choose. Sometimes you have to engineer positive experiences to help that process along.

Activating Joy in Life

If you want to receive the most from life, you had better not wait passively for happy circumstances to come your way. You can take some positive steps that will lead you to greater satisfaction with the life you have today. Following are a few simple observations and suggestions from people who have made excellent and rewarding lives for themselves and have taught others how to do the same:

- separate fantasy from reality
- acknowledge gifts
- recognize contributions
- clean house periodically
- revel in your own experience

Separate Fantasy from Reality

Identify fantasy events and people for what they are: isolated, serendipitous events. These fantasy situations should not be the standards by which you rate the rest of your experience. The man (or woman) who is too perfect to be true, really is. Mr. or Ms. Wonderful is generally a carefully created, temporary persona designed to be appealing for a specific purpose. No one can be "perfect" over time and relationships with real people are messy and complicated.

The same holds true for events as well. The perfect dinner, weekend, gift, vacation, or even job is generally a single occurrence—a fantasy that should be enjoyed and savored. These events should be viewed as pleasant memories that accumulate over time and help nourish your spirit. Trying to plan and re-create such situations, though, nearly always fails because the synergistic element, the unexpected coming together of several exciting or pleasurable conditions, is part of the wonder of the experience.

Acknowledge Gifts

Recognize and take time to be grateful for talents, unexpected kindnesses, and interventions that come your way.

Your Own Gifts

Uncovering your own natural talents and gifts is sometimes a function of your environment. If you grew up in an athletic family, but your innate talent is music, you may not know how really gifted you are. However, trying to label talents often limits our view of what those are. Jennifer may not see her ability to organize almost any activity or space as a talent. Sunil, at age 40, took a computer basics class and discovered a natural ease with programming he never knew he had.

Your talents may be in an area to which you have not yet been exposed. Many writers published their first book after age 50. Some people who have never had children find they are good teachers of young people. Other people have the gift of making people around them feel calm and at ease (highly valued in an emergency room nurse or trauma doctor). Everyone has something important to contribute and feel good about (Gardner, 1993). Taking time to note your unique gifts helps you affirm yourself in specific ways.

3.3   ACTIVITY

Look at your life in the larger picture (not just grades or job skills) and list three categories of things that you do well and feel good about when you do them. For example, "I can get people who don't know each other to talk together in a short time." Or, "I am quick at sizing up a situation and figuring out what needs to be done, whether I would be the person to do it or not."

This might take some thought on your part because we often do not look at ourselves in this way—in terms of our gifts.

Gift 1. _____

Gift 2. _____

Gift 3. _____

Life Events

You may have heard of children being called gifts, but there are also many other delightful things that happen in life that add to our joy and satisfaction. Making a difference in someone's life in a positive way, arriving in Honolulu and discovering the full moon over Waikiki beach, or even happening on a close parking space on a rainy day can all contribute to our happiness. When

Virgaletha became bored with her job and could not figure out what to do about it, she received an unexpected phone call from her college roommate who offered her an interesting new position at her company. These events come to us, often through no particular planning or specific work on our part, yet they add significantly to our enjoyment of life.

Caution must be observed here, however. Expecting such "breaks," as many call these gift events, creates a climate for constant disappointment. You do not place an order for a gift; you accept it graciously for the addition it makes to your life. So many people live, as one retired "hustler" put it, "on the verge of a cinch." Welcome the unexpected events that bring you those moments of joy and allow them to enrich you; do not live your life waiting for the next one to occur.

Other People

People will come into and out of your life, each leaving something behind that becomes a part of your experience. Never forget to acknowledge to yourself, and to them, the important contribution they make to your happiness. Just knowing certain people, even for a brief time, can alter your life completely. A single conversation at an airport may give you an insight that opens up a whole new world of experience for you. Someone may appear just when you need help or comfort, then go out of your life just as quickly when you are no longer in need. There is no point trying to find that person to thank him. That conversation or help was a gift; be grateful for it and hope you have the chance to contribute to someone else's life in the same way you were enriched.

Recognize Contributions

Growth in understanding a task or life adds considerably to happiness. Education in the classroom is only the beginning. To profit from the instructional value of events and people, you have to pay attention. If you believe that people come into your life so you can learn something from them, then everyone you meet takes on a new importance.

Life events are the same way. You can look at an experience and say, "Glad that's over." Or, you can view the same experience for the new insight you gained from having gone through it. The more you understand, the more sense you can make of your life, and the better you can shape it. Remember, though, the person or event that has the greatest contribution to make to your growth and insight will not come with a label that says, "I am here to teach you." Life's wisdom does not come by way of ghosts in the night, as occurred in Dickens' *A Christmas Carol.*

You have to involve yourself enough in the ideas and experiences of the people who seem to purposefully cross your path to figure out what each has to contribute. This viewpoint makes you begin to treat everyone in your acquaintance with a new respect and a positive attitude. You appreciate people and events for the richness they bring to your life.

Clean House Periodically

Regularly look around you at your physical space, your responsibilities, your activities, and your beliefs. The longer you live, the more you tend to accumulate things because they had value to you at one time. You take on more and more responsibilities over time because you want other people in your life. Also, you engage in numerous activities so you have a reason to get up in the morning.

Physical Space

Have you ever moved into a new house or apartment? If you have, you remember the cleanness and simplicity of the bare walls and floors. Your field of vision was uncluttered everywhere you looked. Though there is a starkness to that visual experience, there is also a calm. Then, you acquire items through gifts, yard sales, or other purchases and clutter begins to take up the free space. Many of these items have, or had at one time, sentimental value from how or when you acquired them. Turning the acquisition clock back and clearing your physical space can be refreshing.

There are several methods for doing this:

1. Move—this forces you to move everything out and make decisions about keeping different items. Surprisingly, the value you place on some items changes when you have to pay to keep them in your life.

2. Store—choose some of the items in your house (e.g., pictures, furniture, silk plants, certainly clothing) and rent a storage place for three months. At the end of that time, if you have not really missed the items in storage, or cannot even remember what is there, a garage sale or large-scale donation is in order.

3. Donate—the sofa you are going to sell, the screens you took off when you installed the storm windows, the leftover paint, and the lumber and tools you no longer use are all valuable to charity organizations. Shelters and organizations that help homeless or abused families to start over can use most anything. If it is not usable, throw it away—you are probably never going to get around to fixing it and it just makes you feel bad that you mean to but do not. The few dollars you could get for many of these things do not compare to the tremendous good a donation will do and the great benefit you will receive.

4. Sell—take the plunge; sell everything and start over. This tactic sounds somewhat drastic, possibly, but is amazingly liberating, especially if you are making a life or career change. Purging yourself of most of your possessions this way allows you to reinvent your environment to accommodate a new lifestyle or attitude.

Responsibilities

Adults have many responsibilities in life, so many more than young people do that adults sometimes want to retreat to a younger, simpler time. They may do this by buying frivolous things on a whim, drinking too much, skipping work, and many other ways of "acting out" the need to get away from over-whelming responsibilities.

Laying down responsibilities is an excellent road to happiness, but it must be done selectively or the repercussions could be serious. Responsibilities seem to accumulate over time: housecleaning, then yard maintenance, car maintenance, financial obligations, clubs, work, maintaining friendships, looking after aging parents or grandparents, children, and something as sim-ple as food—it does not appear unless you prepare it or go get it. Of course, you cannot avoid all of these responsibilities, but reducing the number helps.

A condo or an apartment, for example, allows you to avoid yard work; mass transit allows you to avoid having to maintain a car; paying a maid frees you from cleaning; meal services replace cooking; electronic fund drafting makes bill paying less time consuming. Choosing not to have a pet, spouse, children, or involvement with others will simplify your life dramatically. But, at some point, you must examine the value of the trade-off. A dog may be a hassle, but the unconditional love, good humor, and forgiveness may be worth the trouble.

Three tactics are useful to address the responsibility issues. First, examine the number of responsibilities to determine which you can abandon. For example, the club that you are president of will be unhappy if you step down, but you may find a new freedom in giving up that responsibility. Second, retain only those responsibilities that enrich your life. Teaching Sunday school is a responsibility, but you may gain a feeling of renewal when you do it. Third, take regular "holidays" *before* you need them. Set aside a day for relief on which you take off from work, board the dog, or arrange for the kids to stay with a friend. Treat the day as a mandatory day of no responsibilities. Do not clean, go to bed at 8:30 if you want, take pictures of flowers—do those things that you believe your responsibilities prevent you from doing.

Holidays are often most therapeutic if taken in small increments at close intervals, such as a long weekend every month instead of two weeks together. Maybe just going in late one day a week would help. Right now, the focus is on stepping off the train occasionally and reveling in the freedom of knowing that you have chosen responsibilities that enrich your life. Abandon the ones that do not contribute in some way to your joy.

Activity

Excessive activity often comes from people defining themselves by what they do, not who or what they are. Parents, particularly, fall into this. Children, even teenagers, often confess that they just want their parents to spend time with them—not plan elaborate activities or fuss over clothes or food—just be in their lives. Munira has her children, ages six and nine, fix supper one night a week while she sits in the kitchen and talks with them. The meal is often cereal or peanut butter on crackers, but everyone enjoys the time together.

Shane, a single man, gets caught up in meeting friends for tennis, basketball, drinks at the sports bar, networking lunches, and washing the car every Saturday. The fact that he has fewer responsibilities than a parent, does not mean he has fewer activities that he has to squeeze into every day or week. He has now begun relaxing alone in a bookstore coffee shop one evening a week and has noticed a great improvement in how he feels about everything.

Today's society attaches little prestige to the nonpurposive expenditure of time. We have become a population of frantic activity-mongers: "Yeah, I shot nine holes of golf after work." Or, "I spent three hours on the Internet researching investments." Rarely do you hear, "I took a walk in the woods today and watched a squirrel bury nuts," or "You know, I'm going to just stay home tonight and think for a few hours." Sometimes each of us just needs to stop. It might be uncomfortable at first because frenzy has become a way of life. But for those who need help stepping back from that way of life, fishing is excellent training. And, if you are lucky, the fish will not bother you too much.

Ideas and Beliefs

Over time, what we know and have come to understand and accept may not be valid anymore, and hanging on to those old ideas and beliefs becomes more than just burdensome. They get in the way of our ability to experience joy. The woman who was taught to clean the refrigerator every Saturday morning at 6 A.M. can probably abandon that practice with no ill effects.

Couples with both spouses working often struggle with the feeling that their life should be like their parents', but the world has changed dramatically, as has the view of family. Different does not have to be worse and clinging to an impossible-to-attain image of what *should be* is better replaced with energy used creatively to shape what *is*. Values are important; they give us a moral compass, and rituals connect us to a reassuring predictability in our lives (Fulghum, 1996). However, there are many old habits, beliefs, and practices that should be examined for their current relevance.

ACTIVITY

3.4

Look objectively at all you have around you and all of your activities with the goal of setting some aside.

1. What can you do to reduce clutter in your physical space?

2. What activity feels stressful to continue to do even though you enjoyed it at one time?

Revel in Your Own Experience

"I cried because I had no shoes, until I met a man who had no feet. . . ." This old adage speaks a simple truth of our existence. We tend to forget how well off we are because we compare our present situation to how well off we want to be instead of to how inadequate our life could be.

Your definition of life happiness is only relevant to you—you do not have to be as prestigiously employed or as educated or as smartly dressed as everyone thinks you should be. You only have to be in a good place physically, financially, spiritually, and intellectually. The term *good* means emotionally and physically *healthy*.

Sometimes an examination of your values is required to put your good fortune into proper perspective. If you do not have the life you think you want, you might do well to look at your situation differently, look at its potential for happiness. Wanting more is part of the human experience, but ambition can be as paralyzing as apathy. If being consumed with developing a better body or portfolio or power position is keeping you from finding joy where you are, then perhaps it is time to reflect on how you define joy. When each day is a celebration, upending your entire existence to get to someone else's idea of a party becomes unnecessary.

This does not mean to dismiss growth and change; they enrich everyone's life. It does mean, however, that framing your own experience is purely under your control. A list for just such an exercise was found hanging on the wall of an auto repair shop.

Today I can grumble about my health or rejoice that I am alive.

Today I can mourn my lack of friends or I can embark upon a quest to discover new relationships.

Today I can whine because I have to go to work, or I can shout for joy because I have a job to do.

Today I can complain because I have to clean the house or I can feel honored because I have shelter for my mind and body.

Any time you have difficulty finding something to love about your life, go volunteer at a homeless shelter or help build or refurbish a house for someone. When you are lost in not having enough, you can reclaim your spirit by giving of your time and energy to others. Cultivating happiness in others has the wonderful side effect of multiplying your own.

Positive thinking is not the result of a happy life, it is the method for building one. An expectation of beneficial and constructive outcomes creates a more positive and effectual you. A positive and effectual operating style attracts opportunity and upbeat, positive people: the recipe for a happy life.

TRANSITION SKILLS SUMMARY

Choose optimism

Recognize and eliminate negative patterns

Adopt a positive style

Create a positive environment

Activate joy

GOAL SETTING

Self-nurturing: I will make my emotional and relational life more positive by

_____

_____

_____

Self-advocacy: I will make my professional life more positive by

_____

_____

_____

COACH'S CORNER

The most positive and successful people all have GAS.

Goal

Attraction

System™

GAS occurs when two elements come together: the brain's filtering system and the law of attraction.

The brain's filtering system allows you to see what you want to see. Your lover, for instance, appears wonderful to you while you think he or she is wonderful. When you begin looking for faults, however, you see negatives. You can change what you choose to see—focus on the good and tell the brain what is important to you. When you program your goal, best stated in writing as a contract with your subconscious, you will begin to see opportunities all around you to achieve that goal.

The law of attraction is simple: what you think, comes to you. You think of someone you haven't seen in years, and that person calls or contacts you in some way. You think of an old song, and suddenly it comes on the radio. This isn't something we can explain, really; it just is.

So, your subconscious draws to you whatever you have stated you want. You cannot have a negative goal, though; the subconscious draws whatever you focus on. For example, if you say to yourself in a restaurant, "I don't want this spaghetti to fall on my crisp white shirt," all your brain records is "spaghetti on crisp white shirt."

Commit your thoughts and fine tune your attention on what you want. Don't cloud the focus by worrying about how you will get there. If the *what* is clear in your mind, then the *how* will come to you, literally. The same is true of opportunity. As long as your focus is on the job you have, you cannot focus on another, more satisfying job. If you focus on the fear of not knowing exactly how you might move to another position, then you will not see an opportunity that will get you to that new place.

DAVID GREENBERG, motivational speaker, executive speaking coach.
E-mail: GreenbergSpeaks@aol.com.

Part of what I've learned is *how* to learn.

Patricia Adams,
student

DEVELOPING NOTE-TAKING, STUDYING, AND TEST-TAKING SKILLS

N o matter which classes you take, you'll be asked to learn and to think about new information and ideas. During class, you'll be listening and taking notes that can help you to recall what you have learned. Your learning may be evaluated in several ways: by your participation in class discussions, by your written work and projects, and by your performance on tests. At the end of the course, you'll be assigned a grade that reflects your performance. Like many adult students, you may feel out of practice in such academic skills as taking notes, studying, and taking tests.

In this chapter, you'll learn how to:

- take useful notes from class lectures
- study effectively
- take tests with less anxiety
- understand your grades

TAKING NOTES FROM DIFFERENT KINDS OF INSTRUCTORS

In Chapter 6, you'll learn some useful strategies for taking notes from texts and source material. In this chapter, you'll learn some strategies for taking notes

Taken from: *New Beginnings: A Reference Guide for Adult Learners*, by Linda Simon

from class lectures. The key to taking useful class notes lies in listening: You need to listen for and identify the main ideas that your instructor presents.

As you become a more effective listener, you'll discover that you can identify different kinds of information and ideas from any lecture:

- main ideas, generalizations, laws, or theories
- definitions of key words or phrases
- examples or illustrations of main ideas
- important questions about the topic being presented
- important names, dates, events, places, or other factual information
- bibliography references for further research

Instructors have different styles of conducting a class. Even in a lecture class, teachers differ in the amount of time they relegate to answering students' questions, the amount of material they note on the board, the number and types of handouts they provide for students, and the way they organize their lectures. In the following paragraphs, you'll read about three different kinds of instructors and learn some helpful strategies for taking notes in their classes.

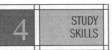

No matter what kind of teaching style your instructor has, however, it is important that you come to class prepared by completing all assigned readings. If you are familiar with main ideas, key terms, and important questions about the topic of the class, you will be able to listen more productively and take more effective notes.

The Organized Lecturer

The organized lecturer announces the day's topic at the beginning of the class and, during the lecture, writes main ideas on a chalkboard or an overhead projector. At the end of the class, the board contains a complete outline of the main points of the lecture. This kind of lecturer often will emphasize material by offering **pointing phrases**, which are helpful verbal cues (such as "the two main problems," "the four causes of the war," "the most significant source of opposition"). This kind of lecturer often supplies handouts to reinforce class lectures.

TIPS FOR TAKING NOTES

1. Copy all material from the board.

2. Make sure you understand the definition of all key words and phrases that the instructor uses. If you do not understand these terms from the lecture, look for clarification in class readings or ask the instructor.

3. Always be prepared for class by doing reading assignments. The organized lecturer expects students to be organized, too.

4. When studying from class notes, elaborate on the instructor's outline by filling in your own examples and putting ideas in your own words. Your instructor wants you to understand the material presented, not merely reproduce that material on a test.

The Storyteller

The storyteller may be an entertaining lecturer, offering vivid illustrations and examples to help students understand and connect with the ideas of the course. Sometimes, however, students become distracted by the stories told in class and cannot identify the main ideas, key terms, and significant questions of the course.

TIPS FOR TAKING NOTES

1. At the beginning of each class, create your own outline in your notebook. The outline may look something like Exhibit 4.1.

EXHIBIT 4.1 SAMPLE NOTES IN OUTLINE FORMAT.

Topic for this class:

1. First example or illustration: What is the idea behind it?
   a. key word and definition
   b. key word and definition
   c. key word and definition

2. Second example or illustration: What is the idea behind it?
   a. key word and definition
   b. key word and definition
   c. key word and definition

3. Third example or illustration: What is the idea behind it?
   a. key word and definition
   b. key word and definition
   c. key word and definition

2. As you listen to the lecture, remind yourself to ask "What is the point?" or "What am I learning?" as your instructor gives illustrations and examples. What is this story an illustration *of?* What is this example demonstrating? The outline will direct you to answer this question.

3. Ask questions. During the question period or, if necessary, after class, make sure you have filled in your outline to your satisfaction. If not, ask your instructor to underscore the main idea. In an Economics class, for example, you might say, "You told us a dramatic story about a software entrepreneur, but would you just go over the economic principle you were trying to get us to understand?"

4. When you study, make sure you can relate the ideas and definitions given in your textbook or class readings to the examples and illustrations given in class. Make sure, also, that you are clear about the material you are expected to know for a test. Often, the storyteller assumes that you can learn main ideas from the readings and, therefore, prefers to use class time to relate those ideas to real-life situations or to expand upon the examples given in the textbook.

The Discusser

Your instructor may use the **Socratic method** of teaching: asking open-ended questions and eliciting responses from the students. This kind of instructor assumes that students will come prepared by doing class readings and will participate seriously and thoughtfully in the dialogue of the class. If you are used to taking notes only from what an instructor says, you may leave class with only a few sentences. In a class led by a discusser, you need to identify important points made by students, as well. The discusser often will highlight such important ideas by:

- affirming the idea ("Yes, that's right" or "Good, that's a key idea")
- summarizing the idea ("As Carlos said . . .")
- paraphrasing the idea ("Yes, in other words," or "Put another way")
- showing how the idea leads to another idea ("Once we've established this," or "What question does this bring up now?")

TIPS FOR TAKING NOTES

1. Always be prepared by doing class readings, and come to class with your own summary of the important points.

2. Listen for the instructor's cues about the value of ideas discussed. If the instructor highlights an idea, write that idea in your notebook.

3. In your notes, distinguish between a main idea and an example or illustration.

4. Use your notes for recording your own responses to the instructor's questions, even if you don't voice each of your responses in class.

5. When you study, compare the ideas in your class notes with the main ideas and key words from your class readings. How did class discussions expand upon or modify those ideas or definitions?

Exhibits 4.2 and 4.3 show two samples of notes from students in American Literature.

EXHIBIT 4.2 NOTES SAMPLE ONE.

Portrait of a Lady.

Isabel Archer is American girl, age 23 when story begins.
She gets taken to London by her aunt who is very eccentric
and pretty funny. The aunt is married, but lives apart from
her husband. Name: Lydia Touchett. She soon inherits a lot
of money. Problem: How is she to live? She thinks she is
special. Other people think so, too. She wants freedom.
Characters discussed today. Cousin Ralph Touchett, dying of
tuberculosis. Suitors: Lord Warburton, very rich. Henrietta
Stackpole, new woman, journalist. Caspar Goodwood, American
businessman. She refuses them. Besides freedom wants to
travel and experience life. Gilbert Osmond, daughter Pansy.
Madame Merle, mysterious relationship to Osmond. Goodwood
lack of cultural refinement.

As you can see from the first note sample, the student has written down ideas without order and without high-lighting what is important.

Another student used an outline. In the second set of notes, you can see that the student is organizing information in a way that will make it easy to study, to find main ideas, and to distinguish minor points of information (such as Mrs. Touchett's humor) from important information (such as Madame Merle's mysterious qualities).

EXHIBIT 4.3   NOTES SAMPLE TWO.

Portrait of a Lady

I. Characters:
   1. Isabel Archer, American, 23, inherits fortune from uncle
   2. Daniel Touchett, uncle
   3. Lydia Touchett, aunt, who lives apart from uncle
   4. Ralph Touchett, cousin, dying of tuberculosis
   5. Henrietta Stackpole, journalist, friend of Isabel's
   6. Madame Serena Merle, friend of Mrs. Touchett and Osmond
   7. Pansy Osmond, daughter of Gilbert Osmond

II. Suitors:
   1. Lord Warburton, rich British nobleman
   2. Caspar Goodwood, American businessman
   3. Gilbert Osmond, American expatriate, loves art

III. Plot
   1. Isabel inherits money
   2. thinks about the course of her future
   3. has to choose between three suitors

IV. Questions
   1. Why is Serena Merle so mysterious?
   2. Why does Isabel choose to marry Osmond?
   3. What is the function of money as she makes her decision?

eneral Pointers for Taking Class Notes

1. Be prepared with a notebook and at least two pens or writing implements. If you are an auditory learner, ask your instructor if you may tape-record lectures. Even if you record lectures, also take notes.
2. Keep a folder for each class in which you can collect and organize handouts.
3. Choose a seat where you can hear easily and can see the lecturer, the chalkboard, or any visual aids such as an overhead projector or map.
4. Avoid sitting near distractions such as a friend, a window, or a source of noise (such as an air conditioner or heater).
5. Listen for cues from the lecturer. Some lecturers:
   - pause before an important point
   - write an important point on the board
   - repeat an important point
   - make a point, give examples, and then repeat the point
   - change volume or inflection before an important point
6. Summarize rather than attempt to copy every word.
7. Write in outline form rather than in paragraph form.
8. Underline main ideas.
9. Fill in points right after the lecture. While the class is still fresh in your mind, jot down some words or phrases to remind you about the most important ideas of the lecture or discussion and make a note of material to reread or study. If you have a tape recorder, make verbal notes of ideas to study or to follow up in your reading.
10. If your instructor tells you that certain material will be tested, make sure to identify this material by starring, underlining, or highlighting it.

STUDY SKILLS 4

As soon as possible after class, take a look at your notes and answer the following three questions:

1. What is the most important idea I learned from class today?

2. What are three important terms I learned to define or understand?

3. What question do I want to answer (either from class readings or the next class discussion) to help me understand the material?

Responding to notes soon after class helps to reinforce what you have learned, provides an orientation for the next class, and helps you when you study from your notes to prepare for a test.

HOW TO PREPARE FOR TESTS

Besides writing papers, tests are the source of greatest anxiety for all students, adults included. Preparing for tests is a two-part process: assessment and study time.

Assessment

There are basically three kinds of tests:

1. Multiple-choice
2. Short-answer
3. Essay question

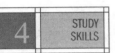

Sometimes, instructors will combine these forms of testing, asking you to complete 50 multiple-choice questions and answer two out of three essay questions, for example. Because the form of test will affect your study plan, be sure to ask your instructor to explain the test in as much detail as possible. Many instructors set aside time to discuss a test a few weeks before it will be given. Be sure you know the answers to these questions:

- What kind of test will be given: multiple-choice, short-answer, essay question, or a combination of these?
- How long will you have to complete the test? Is the test given during class time, or is there a longer period of time allotted for the test?
- Is the test an open-book test? An open-book test allows you to bring texts, readings, and lecture notes for reference during the test. Although you can bring such materials, you still need to know the course material thoroughly.
- Can you bring a dictionary to class? Especially if English is not your native language, a dictionary may help you to express yourself clearly and correctly.
- What material will the test cover: the entire semester, the last few weeks, or a particular unit of study?
- What sources will the test cover: textbook, lectures, outside reading?
- What sources does the instructor think are most important?
- Are old tests available for use as practice?
- What might a typical multiple-choice question look like? A typical short-answer question? A typical essay question?
- What is the purpose of the test? Is it to see how well you have memorized key terms? To see how well you synthesize ideas presented throughout the semester? To see how well you can develop your own analysis or argu-

ment about the issues of the course? Knowing the purpose of the test can help you to anticipate the kinds of questions that will be asked.

Study Time

Test preparation begins when you take notes in class and from assigned readings. When you take notes, make sure that you define key terms as you go along. If your notes are clear and well organized, they will be useful for test review. If you have missed any class lectures, it's a good idea to get notes from a classmate whose work you respect.

Some students find that if they prepare for a test too far in advance, they forget what they have memorized; a week's intensive review is more helpful. Other students find that several weeks of studying and review plant ideas and concepts firmly in their memory. Whatever study schedule you choose, remember that cramming the night before the test is a poor strategy. You'll arrive at the test exhausted, anxious, and unfocused. Reviewing the night before, however, can refresh your memory and leave you feeling more confident.

STUDY
SKILLS
4

Some students find it helpful to study with a partner or in a group. Study groups can be useful if they are focused on reviewing material rather than on open-ended discussions, complaining, or worries. If you form or join a study group, make sure the other members are people whose work you respect and who have kept up with assignments and attended lectures. Study groups should meet several times before a test and set a clear agenda for each meeting.

Preparing for a Multiple-Choice or Short-Answer Test

Multiple-choice and short-answer tests draw upon your ability to define terms and distill concepts into a few words or phrases. The key to studying for these tests is memorization. One way to memorize is to *write down key words with a short definition.* Using 3 × 5 index cards is a timeworn strategy to help you memorize key terms. On one side of the card, write the term; on the other, write a brief and precise definition. A multiple-choice test will try to trip you up by offering a definition of a term that is similar to the correct definition but is worded in a way that makes it incorrect.

If your textbook lists key words as part of a chapter review, make sure that you transfer all of these words, with their correct definitions, to your index cards. If your instructor has used key terms in class lectures, make sure these terms also are among those you learn. As you are studying, if you find that you need clarification of certain terms, be sure to ask your instructor.

If you are an auditory learner, you may want to work with a study buddy so that you can repeat key words and definitions aloud; then listen as your partner does the same. Using a tape recorder may also be an effective study tool for an auditory learner.

If you are a kinesthetic learner, you may want to write and rewrite key words and their definitions. You also may want to associate words with images or action as much as possible. Visualizing terms as part of a picture, image, map, or structure may help you to remember them.

Preparing for an Essay Test

If your textbook has questions as part of a chapter review, one option for study is to *write answers to the questions and keep track of the length of time it takes you to answer them.* Part of the skill of taking an essay examination is being able to answer questions adequately within the time limit of the test. The more practice you do before the test, the more quickly you can respond to questions and the more successful you will be.

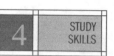

If your textbook does not have a chapter summary, ask your instructor for a few examples of essay questions. These examples should give you an idea of what your instructor is looking for: summary of specific readings, synthesis of several readings and class discussions, analysis of a text, or your own argument based on readings and class material. Once you have these questions, write answers to them.

If getting sample essay questions is not possible, you can formulate your own by turning topic sentences from chapters or sections of chapters into questions.

For auditory or kinesthetic learners, it may help to first discuss your responses with a partner or study buddy. As you talk, take notes to help you write an outline for an essay response; then write the response, being sure to keep track of your time.

TEST-TAKING

Get a good night's sleep, eat something before the test (but not so much that you'll feel sleepy), and arrive a few minutes early. Bring to the test everything that you need: pens or pencils, calculator, and books (if the test is an open-book test). Wear a watch or sit in a place where you can see the clock. Take a deep breath; then follow these eight steps:

1. Look over the test before you begin.

2. Make an estimate of the amount of time you will need to complete each section of the test.

3. Begin with multiple-choice or short-answer questions, answering those you're sure of and placing a dash or dot next to those you are not sure of.

ypes of Essay Questions

Your instructor asks you to respond to essay questions in order to see how deeply and thoroughly you have thought about the course material. Rather than test your ability to memorize facts and information, the essay question tests your ability to analyze source material or synthesize what you have read. In general, essay questions fall into five categories. Understanding the purpose of each kind of question may help you be more successful in responding:

1. **Agree or disagree.** This question gives you a statement by an expert. Using readings and class notes, you formulate an argument agreeing or disagreeing with the expert. Don't be afraid to disagree. If no disagreement were acceptable, your instructor would not give you the question.

2. **Support a generalization (or a theory) with examples.** This question gives you a statement by an expert. Using class readings and notes, you are to provide examples to show that the statement applies to specific events or ideas you have learned about in the course.

3. **Analyze a text.** Usually, this question will ask you to focus on what meaning is conveyed by a text (poem, essay, story, work of art or music, etc.) or how the text achieves its effect. You will be expected to apply the strategies of analysis that you have learned during the course.

4. **Make a comparison.** This question asks you to look at two or more texts, events, thinkers, or ideas and show some important similarities or differences among them. As in all essay questions, you want to focus on specific points to make the comparison. When you answer this question, you may discuss first one text and then another, or you can set up an outline point by point, returning to discuss each text as you move through the points of comparison.

5. **Put a text, event, or idea in context.** This question asks you to show how a text you have read for the course fits into a larger social, historical, cultural, or artistic context. In answering this question, you want to define the context in as much detail as you can; then you specifically show how the text, event, or idea responded to or grew out of that context.

STUDY SKILLS 4

Sometimes, answering the questions that are easier for you acts as an on-the-spot review, helping you to recall more information.

4. Go back to the troublesome questions. In a multiple-choice test, eliminate the obviously incorrect choices and then make the best choice from whatever remains.

5. Assess the essay questions. How much time do you have for each one? Again, begin with the easiest question, making it clear in your response booklet exactly which question you are answering.

6. Write an outline. Begin by responding directly to the question in a sentence or two. Then, make a list of at least three concrete points that will support your answer. Students often lose credit on essay questions because they repeat generalizations rather than refer to specific material from readings or class lectures.

7. Organize the outline. Make sure that the three points you make are logically connected.

8. Write or print legibly.

UNDERSTANDING YOUR GRADE

The grade you receive for a course reflects the quality of your work, not the quality of you as a person. It is not a reflection of how much the instructor likes you. Getting a low grade in one course does not mean that you have no ability to continue as a student; getting an A in a course does not mean that you can expect to get an A in every other course you take. These statements may seem commonsensical, but it's likely that you'll reread them several times during your college career. Getting a grade means being judged, and being judged is not easy for anyone.

Instructors often include criteria for grading in their syllabus or set aside a few minutes of class time to discuss grading policies. In general, teachers consider the following five criteria in grading:

1. Test scores
2. Grades on papers
3. Class attendance
4. Quality of class participation
5. Extra projects

Different instructors weigh these criteria differently, placing more or less emphasis on test scores or participation, for example. You should understand your professor's criteria for grading in each course you are taking.

At the end of the semester, if you receive a grade that is a surprise to you—usually because it is lower than what you expected—you may want to contact your instructor so you can understand how the grade was computed and learn what you can do in another course to improve the quality of your work. You may find that you have evidence to dispute the grade, and sometimes an instructor will agree to change a grade.

The following, however, are *not* reasons to dispute a grade:

1. *You worked very hard.* Remember that the grade reflects the work you produced, not the effort that you put into that work. In a difficult course where material is unfamiliar, you may have to work much harder than in a course in your field. Still, you are not being graded on effort, but on the products that result from that effort.

2. *You need the grade to keep up your grade point average (GPA).* Sometimes, your admission to a degree program or your standing in a program depends on your maintaining a certain GPA. Sometimes, your employer will reimburse you for tuition if you earn a high enough grade. Your instructor, however, is not responsible for that GPA or your employer's tuition policy—you are. Take the opportunity to find out how you can improve rather than dispute a grade that you earned.

STUDY SKILLS **4**

3. *The person who sits next to you got an A, and she's no smarter than you.* Remember, the grade reflects your work, not your general intelligence or aptitude. Many factors can influence the quality of your work, some course-related (you missed a few lectures), some personal (you had unusual family responsibilities during the semester). Your classmate may have been better prepared for the course than you because she took a few other courses in the department.

If grading causes unusual anxiety for you, you may want to seek help from your academic advisor or personal counselor. Everyone would like to earn an A in every course; not everyone does.

The next several chapters, like this one, focus on the skills you need to do your best in all of your classes.

ADDITIONAL RESOURCES

Carter, Carol, Joyce Bishop, and Sarah Lyman Kravits. *Keys to Effective Learning,* 4th ed. Upper Saddle River, NJ: Prentice Hall, 2005.

Carter, Carol, Joyce Bishop, and Sarah Lyman Kravits. *Keys to Success*, 5th ed. Upper Saddle River, NJ: Prentice Hall, 2006.

Hancock, Ophelia. *Reading Skills for College Students*, 6th ed. Upper Saddle River, NJ: Prentice Hall, 2004.

Holschuh, Jodi, and Sherrie L Orist. *Active Learning: Strategies for College Success*.

LearningExpress. *Math Skills for College Students*. Upper Saddle River, NJ: Prentice Hall, 1998.

LearningExpress. *Vocabulary & Spelling Skills for College Students*. Upper Saddle River, NJ: Prentice Hall, 1998.

Majors, Randall E., and Joan Marie Yamasaki. *Is This Going to Be on the Test? And Ten Other Questions That Can Save Your College Career*, 3rd ed. Upper Saddle River, NJ: Prentice Hall, 1997.

Ooten, Cheryl and Emily Meek. *Managing the Mean Math Blues*. Upper Saddle River, NJ: Prentice Hall, 2003.

Pauk, Walter. *How to Study in College*, 8th ed. Boston: Houghton Mifflin, 2004.

Wong, Linda. *Essential Study Skills*, 3rd ed. Boston: Houghton Mifflin, 2000.

> The main part of intellectual education is not the acquisition of facts
> but learning how to make facts live.
>
> *Oliver Wendell Holmes, Jr.,*
> *Supreme Court Justice*

STRATEGIES FOR READING

I n most of your college courses, you are likely to be assigned many different kinds of reading material: textbooks, theoretical books and articles, critical books and articles, fiction, plays, and poetry. In college, all of these various kinds of reading materials are called texts. Based on these texts, you may be asked to:

- memorize information
- respond to an author's arguments or analysis
- develop your own questions about the material presented
- use the readings as a basis for writing assignments
- show your understanding of the readings on examinations

Reading course material is different from reading the morning newspaper, an office memo, or John Grisham's latest thriller. College texts may be more difficult to understand; you have to *learn* as you read, not just come away with vague ideas. You have a responsibility to process and think about what you read; in the end, your course grade may depend on your skills as a reader.

This chapter offers you some strategies for honing those skills, for becoming an active reader. You'll learn strategies for:

- reading actively
- reading a textbook
- reading a theoretical or critical book or article

- reading fiction
- reading poetry

TAKING AN ACTIVE APPROACH TO READING

Simply put, an **active reader** responds to texts. This means an active reader:

- takes notes
- asks questions
- discovers patterns
- looks for main arguments
- thinks about how evidence supports an argument

Active reading, then, is different from the kind of reading you may be accustomed to doing. It takes more time, more concentration, and more skill. Here are six general guidelines for becoming an active reader:

1. Read in a quiet place.
2. Be comfortable—but not so comfortable that you'll fall asleep.
3. Keep note-taking materials at your side.
4. Keep a dictionary handy.
5. Remember that reading an hour every day is more productive than reading for several hours at once.
6. Set aside a few minutes of every reading period for review.

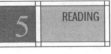

 ## READING A TEXTBOOK

Introduction to Economics, American History, Principles of Literary Theory: The titles of textbooks announce that they convey essential course information. Textbooks, which are the main reading material for many courses, offer a special challenge for any student. There seems to be so much information that it's hard to know what is important and what is not. What will appear on a test? What is necessary to remember? Here are some strategies for making textbook reading more successful.

Get oriented. Like other books, textbooks are organized into chapters that present information on various topics. Unlike other works of nonfiction, though, textbook chapters themselves are organized into sections that focus on specific areas of information. This structure is designed with learners in mind: Textbook authors want to present material in manageable amounts to help you assimilate it as easily as possible. Looking at the structure of a chapter is the first step toward learning the material.

Here, for example, is the organization of a chapter from *Fundamentals of Investing*, an introductory textbook used in a business course:

Chapter title: Investment Markets and Transactions

    Section 1: Securities Markets
        Subdivisions: Types of Markets
                        Organized Securities Exchanges
                        The Over-the-Counter Market
                        NASDAQ
                        Regulation of Securities Markets
                        General Market Conditions: Bull or Bear
    Section 2: Making Security Transactions
        Subdivisions: Stockbrokers
                        Basic Types of Orders
                        Basic Types of Transactions
                        Transaction Costs
    Section 3: Summary
    Section 4: Key Terms
    Section 5: Review Questions

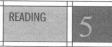

READING 5

The structure of a chapter gives you a useful outline of the information presented and provides a map to guide you through the material you need to learn. In *Fundamentals of Investing*, as in many other textbooks, the authors provide a summary of main points, a list of key terms, and questions to help you test your knowledge of the material.

Read and write. Some students read with a highlighter, turning their black-on-white textbook into a rainbow of yellow and pink. In fact, for kinesthetic learners, highlighting in different colors is a useful strategy for identifying key terms or ideas. But highlighting alone leaves out an important processing step: your own summary, in your own words, of what is important.

Reading with a pen and index cards (or a notebook) may be a bit slower, but it will be more efficient in the long run. As you read, summarize, and write, you are processing information and producing a useful study tool for examinations and paper writing.

Skim as you go. You don't have to read every word of every chapter. You do, however, need to read and understand key definitions and main points. Here, for example, is a section from *Fundamentals of Investing*. As you read this paragraph, think about what is important to note:

The risk of not being able to liquidate an investment conveniently and at a reasonable price is called *liquidity risk*. The liquidity of a given investment vehicle is an important consideration for an investor who wishes to maintain flexibility in an investment portfolio. In general, investment vehicles traded in *thin markets*, where demand and supply are small, tend to be less liquid than those traded in *broad markets*. However, to be liquid an investment must be easily sold at a reasonable price. One can generally enhance the liquidity of an investment merely by cutting its price. For example, a security recently purchased for $1,000 would not be viewed as highly liquid if it can be sold only at a significantly reduced price such as $500. Vehicles such as bonds and stocks of major companies listed on the New York Stock Exchange are generally highly liquid, whereas others, such as an isolated parcel of raw land in rural Georgia, are not.

This paragraph defines *liquidity*. In your notes, you would include that definition, but you would not necessarily include the information given after the words "for example". If you understand the definition of liquidity, then this part of the paragraph can be skimmed.

Look for definitions and blocks. Graphics are an important textbook feature. Key words and definitions often are italicized or printed in boldface; important concepts often are separated from the rest of the text in shaded or framed blocks. Memorizing definitions is an easier task when you have created your own flash cards from the textbook or, if you are an auditory learner, when you have recorded key words and definitions into a tape recorder.

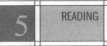

Ask questions. Textbooks convey information in the form of statements or assertions. When you frame those statements as a question, you take a useful step in the process of reviewing. Here are three questions you might ask after reading the paragraph on liquidity:

1. What is liquidity?
2. Why are some investments less liquid than others?
3. How can an investment be made more liquid?

Your instructor might ask questions like this in class or on an examination. When you formulate questions as you read, you will feel better prepared for both experiences.

Review. Build in a review period—10 or 15 minutes—every time you read. You can review by skimming a chapter and looking at the topic headings for each section, or you can review by looking at your notecards. Reviewing each time you read will make preparing for examinations much more efficient.

READING A THEORETICAL OR CRITICAL BOOK OR ARTICLE

A theoretical or critical book or article gives you an author's interpretation or argument about some topic. A literary critic may show you a new way of looking at a novel or short story; an economist may offer a way of interpreting recent market trends; a historian may offer a perspective on interpreting events of the past.

Criticism, as academics use the term, does not mean a negative assessment of something. In ordinary conversation, if I criticize your cooking, I may be pointing out its shortcomings. But when scholars *criticize a text,* they analyze it and interpret it. If you are studying *Hamlet* in a literature course, for example, your instructor may ask you to read a critical article or book interpreting the meaning of the play or the behavior of the characters.

The steps of active reading apply to a theoretical or critical book or article, as well as to a textbook.

Get oriented. An active reader of a theoretical book or article looks first for the author's main idea. In a book, this idea will be presented in the preface, fore-word, or introduction. In an article, the main idea appears in the first few paragraphs. The preface to a book or the beginning paragraphs of an article offer a useful guide to the rest of the text, helping you to understand:

- the author's motivation in writing the text
- the sources to which the author will refer and the evidence the author will use
- the problem the author wants to solve

READING   5

Read and write. As you read, respond to the author's assertions in marginal notes, in a note-book, or in a reading journal. Keep in mind that the author is a real person writing to you, a real reader. Your comments and marginal notes, then, become part of a conversation that the author began by writing the text.

Some students find it helpful to write a "letter" to the author, after reading a text, summarizing the main ideas, responding to points with which they agree or disagree, and asking questions. This "letter"—not sent, but used as a study tool—is one strategy of an active reader.

Skim as you go. Thinking about the author's aims and intentions will help you to connect with important ideas in the text. Once you identify the author's main argument, you can construct your own outline of the supporting assertions or main points. These assertions usually are developed in clusters of paragraphs—similar to the subsections of a textbook—that support the assertions with evidence and examples. As you gain experience reading a theoretical or critical text, you will be able to identify more easily the beginning of each cluster of paragraphs.

Look for definitions. The author's argument depends on *key words* defined and explained within the text. You know that you have found a key word when it recurs throughout an argument and when the author defines or discusses its meaning.

As you read a theoretical or critical book or article, you may encounter either unfamiliar terms or words you know used in an unfamiliar way. Here, for example, is a passage from *"Dracula's* Backlash," a critical article about Bram Stoker's famous novel, *Dracula*:

> It is certainly true that Dracula, the narrator's pivotal vampire, is a male, but the world in which he operates is a world of women, the world of Eve, a world in which reversion and acculturation are at war.*

Among the difficult terms in this passage are: *pivotal, reversion, acculturation.*

What do these words mean? Sometimes, it is possible to deduce the meaning from the text. *Pivotal*, you might guess, means crucial or important; calling Dracula the *pivotal vampire* implies that there are other vampires in the novel, but he is the most important. Even if you did not guess the meaning quite accurately, since *pivotal* serves only as an adjective, its importance in the sentence is minor compared with nouns and verbs. But *reversion* and *acculturation* are more difficult terms and, as nouns, apparently more important. If you have a dictionary beside you as you read, you would want to stop here and make sure you understand the meaning of these words.

Ask questions. Here are ten questions that will help you to connect with the author's aim:

1. What is the author's main point?
2. What problem or question does the author consider?
3. Whom is the author addressing? Who is the audience for this text?
4. What assumptions does the author make about the reader?
5. To what extent does the author want to change the reader's way of thinking or acting?
6. What is the author's tone in this text: Informal? Conversational? Friendly? Distant?
7. What words, phrases, or images recur throughout the text? How do these words, phrases, or images help to fulfill the author's purpose?
8. How has the author's analysis changed or enlarged your understanding of the topic?
9. What point(s) do you agree with? Why?
10. Where do you disagree? Why?

Review. Build in time to take one last look at your notes. Have you given yourself a sense of the structure of the argument and the author's main points? When you look at your notes, do you discover a place where you explain the author's main point?

*Bram Dikstra, *"Dracula's Backlash,"* In *Dracula: A Norton Critical Edition*, eds. Auerbach and Skal. New York: Norton, 1997: 460.

READING FICTION

In such courses as literature, women's studies, and even history, works of fiction—novels and short stories—often are assigned as texts. Fiction offers a different kind of reading experience from textbooks or theoretical and critical texts. When you read a story, it may seem that there is nothing more to say about it than to describe what happened to which characters. Your instructors, though, will be asking you to analyze these texts, not merely to summarize them.

A summary, however, is a useful first step after reading a fictional text. In a summary, you condense the plot and give brief descriptions of the characters. While writing a summary, you may think of questions that you want to ask about the author's choices in creating a text: Why is one character angry? Why is the story set in the Australian outback? Why does the main character seem so self-destructive?

After you have written a summary of the text, you are ready to move on to analyzing the text. The following 12 questions will help you think about fiction in a deeper way than you may have approached such texts in the past.

1. What events in the story are most significant? Why?
2. Who are the main characters? How would you describe the personality traits of each?

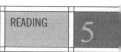

3. How do these characters change?
4. What do the characters learn?
5. How does the author make you care about the characters?
6. Where does the action take place? What is the setting?
7. How does the setting relate to the plot? To the characters?
8. Who is narrating the story? What is the relationship between this narrator and the other characters?
9. What is the relationship between the narrator and the author?
10. What problem does the author present in the text? What main idea does the author explore?
11. What images recur throughout the text? How are they important?
12. How does the author's style help you to understand the problem or main idea of the text?

Questions such as these—and you will invent some of your own—help you move from merely telling what the story says to exploring how the author communicates with you, the reader.

READING POETRY

Poetry is a particular form of creative writing that some students find difficult to read. Certainly, one of the main features of poetry is that it is elliptical: Words are deliberately omitted so that a poem does not read like a sentence. Poems, however, can be exciting puzzles to figure out; they can provide rich reading experiences.

Here are eight questions to help you discover the meaning of a poem:

1. Who is the speaker in the poem, the poet or someone else?

2. Who is the intended audience for the poem?

3. What problem or issue is the poet exploring?

4. What images, words, or phrases recur throughout the poem? Why does the poet emphasize these images, words, or phrases? How do they relate to the meaning of the poem?

5. What sounds are repeated or emphasized in the poem? Why?

6. What is the form of the poem? Does it have stanzas? Does it have a regular rhyme scheme? Does it have a regular rhythm? How does the form relate to the meaning?

7. What feeling or emotion does the poem evoke in you? Why?

8. What images or words in the poem stand for other ideas? Why did the poet choose these particular images or words? How are they effective?

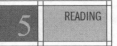

Practice applying these questions to the following short poem by American poet Emily Dickinson:

My life closed twice before its close

My life closed twice before its close—
It yet remains to see
If Immortality unveil
A third event to me

So huge, so hopeless to conceive
As these that twice befell.
Parting is all we know of heaven,
And all we need of hell.

Source: Emily Dickinson's poem "My Life Closed Twice Before Its Close."

It's easy to see that Dickinson is writing about death, but what is her point? Here are some questions that one student asked as he read the poem:

■ How do we experience death before we actually die ourselves? What possible experiences might Dickinson have had that were huge and hopeless?

Analyzing Your Reading Assignments

After completing a reading assignment, use this list to analyze what you've read.

1. What is the main idea of this text?
2. What words cause difficulty in comprehension? List those words, look up their meanings, and record the definitions.
3. What are the author's key words? List them and write a brief definition for each.
4. Identify the most important passages. Why do you think these are important? Write a brief explanation.
5. Write several questions in response to the text.

- Dickinson mentions heaven and hell: How does she understand these two "places" that figure in Christian religion?
- Why does she emphasize the word *parting* by placing it at the end of the poem and relating it to heaven and hell?

In response to these questions, the student wrote the following paragraph interpreting the poem:

> Physical death is the most final experience of separating one human being from another, but it is not the only experience. Emily Dickinson sees any kind of parting—one person leaving another—as a death experience. She tells us in this poem that she has had two such experiences. Separation, maybe abandonment, makes her feel that her life has closed. We do not know what she believes about the possibility of heaven as a reward or hell as a punishment. For her, both "places" are evidence only that the departed person is no longer with her, and so in a sense both places are equal in not being able to soothe her pain.

Although Dickinson's poem is short and fairly self-explanatory, the student who wrote this interpretation read the poem several times before really understanding it.

Reading is the most basic academic skill that you will need to master. In this chapter, you've learned six strategies for becoming an active reader:

1. Get oriented.
2. Read and write.
3. Skim as you go.
4. Look for definitions.
5. Ask questions.
6. Review.

As you apply these strategies to different courses and different texts, you are likely to discover an improvement in your ability to read productively.

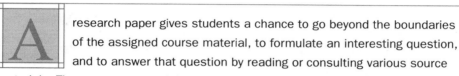
To learn is a natural pleasure, not confined to philosophers, but common to all men.

Aristotle

STRATEGIES FOR **RESEARCH**

A research paper gives students a chance to go beyond the boundaries of the assigned course material, to formulate an interesting question, and to answer that question by reading or consulting various source materials. Those source materials might include books or articles found in a library; information found on the Internet; interviews; films; television programs; and works of art, music, dance, or theater.

A research paper, however, is not merely the kind of report that you may have written in high school. In college, a research paper (just as any other college essay) involves interpretation, analysis, and argumentation.

In this chapter, you'll learn how to:

- choose a topic for research
- formulate a question
- define your terms for online searches
- practice Internet search strategies
- evaluate Web sites
- take notes
- document sources
- organize notes
- avoid plagiarism and overdocumentation

Taken from: *New Beginnings: A Reference Guide for Adult Learners*, by Linda Simon

CHOOSING A RESEARCH TOPIC

A **topic** names the area of interest that you want to pursue in your paper. In a philosophy class, a topic may be an abstract term, such as morality or ethics. In an accounting class, a topic could be the impact of tax law on financial planning. In an art history class, a topic might be as broad as American Impressionism or as narrow as Winslow Homer's early works.

Finding a topic sometimes seems daunting: If you are very much interested in a course, you may have trouble narrowing down your interests; if you are cool toward a course, you may have trouble coming up with a topic that excites you. In either case, however—and in all cases in between—finding a topic results from active thinking. When you take notes in class and as you read, use the opportunity to jot down questions as they occur to you. When you think about the implications of what you are learning, you'll find that questions are bound to occur to you. What issues or problems puzzle you? What are you curious about?

Topics often arise from personal interests. In a course called *The City in America,* one lecture focused on the ways that immigration changed the housing needs in some major urban centers. A student whose grandparents had been immigrants was curious about his own family's experience. He decided to investigate the topic of immigration and city planning for his research paper. Another student in the class, who happened to be a single mother, decided to research the topic of women workers in cities.

Choosing a topic, however, is only the first step in the research process. A topic does not provide enough focus for a college essay. Writing about women workers in cities, for example, could be the focus of an entire book. Once you have a topic—a subject area that you want to research—you need a focused question that will narrow down the topic to make your research and writing manageable.

FORMULATING A RESEARCH QUESTION

To write a good research paper, you will need more than general ideas on a broad topic. Your paper should be grounded in concrete information that will bring your topic to life and convey its flavor and immediacy. A specific focus in your research will lead you to such concrete information.

If you are having trouble achieving a specific focus, ask yourself questions about your topic. What do you want to know about your topic? The student interested in immigration and city planning, for example, needed to write a ten-page research paper. The topic, of course, was much too broad for such a small paper. To narrow down the topic, the student asked six key questions:

1. Who? (Who are these immigrants?)
2. What? (What kind of community did they create in their new place of residence?)

3. Where? (In what city did they settle? Where in that city did they go?)

4. When? (When did they come?)

5. Why? (Why did they choose that particular city?)

6. How? (How did the city adapt to their presence, and vice versa?)

These questions helped the student to limit the topic to a workable focus for a research paper: How did city planners in Portland, Maine, respond to the arrival of Irish immigrants in the middle of the nineteenth century?

Posing a similar series of questions, the student who decided on the topic of women workers also formulated a focused question: How did the city of Toledo, Ohio, respond to the needs of women workers in the 1950s?

You can see that the focused questions of these two students are of the right breadth for their papers: The students will be able to provide well-researched and precise answers to their questions. But there is more to a good question than its size. A good question also generates your interest as you do research, and your readers' interest as you translate your research into an argument. Good questions have *significant* answers—reasons why your readers should care about your topic.

A good way to ensure that your question is significant is to ask yourself why you are interested in answering it. Will you provide a new way of looking at a particular historical event? For instance, the student writing on nineteenth-century Irish immigration in Portland can provide a unique perspective by discussing his own grandparents' experience. Will you convince your readers that they are involved in your topic in some way? A student writing on a new lunch program in the Boston public schools can suggest the implications of new nutrition research for us and our health. Doing research will help you to appreciate and articulate the significance of your topic.

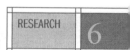
RESEARCH 6

DISTINGUISHING PRIMARY AND SECONDARY SOURCES

Research papers are based on two kinds of sources: primary and secondary. A **primary source** does not contain someone else's interpretation of the material; rather, it may be a novel, a work of art, economic statistics, laws, maps, letters, or a film, depending on the research topic.

Suppose, for example, that you are writing a research paper about the economic conditions of farmers in Connecticut at the end of the nineteenth century. A diary kept by a farmer would be a primary source. Billing records from a local supply store would also be a primary source, as would photographs, letters from farmers to their relatives, and nineteenth-century newspaper articles relevant to farm issues. All of these sources would provide evidence that you, as the researcher and writer, have to interpret and analyze.

Secondary sources are materials that offer interpretation or analysis of primary sources. Biographies, histories, literary criticism, art criticism, and economic analyses are all secondary sources. For the paper on economic conditions of nineteenth-century Connecticut farmers, for example, a history of Connecticut would be a secondary source. A scholarly article about farm life in the *New England Quarterly* also would be a secondary source.

Secondary sources can help you discover background material, find references to relevant books and articles, and learn how scholars use evidence. In your own paper, however, you must make sure that your argument is supported by evidence from primary sources—that you don't just repeat the arguments you find in secondary sources.

Both primary and secondary sources are important in a research paper, and they are easy to locate once you understand how to look for information in libraries or online.

USING THE INTERNET FOR RESEARCH

The Internet has been described as a "network of networks"—a universe of information sources connected in cyberspace. You can access vast amounts of information on the Net; much of it is organized in ways you will find helpful. For instance, if you have a defined research interest, you can consult sites at which in-depth specialized knowledge is available by subject. If, on the other hand, you are still trying to settle on a topic, the Internet offers plenty of opportunities for following links from one subject to other related subjects until you find something that really interests you. You can find just about any information you want on the Internet, and the sources of information are not limited to American or English ones, as your library's reference books often are. The Internet is global, which means you can obtain news and publications in foreign languages and from any region on earth where the Internet exists.

The World Wide Web is not the same as the Internet; it is a facet of the Internet, the one you will use the most in research. The Web is a system of sites or home pages that provide links to other pages. These links are in the form of "hyperlinked" (often underlined or highlighted) text, images, or icons. By clicking on one of these links, you can move from site to site as you do research.

One caution about Internet research: Be wary of unreliable information. Anyone with Internet access can post something—anything—on the Net. If no source is listed for a piece of information you find on the Net, try to find out where it came from by querying the Web site by e-mail. If you can't find the source, don't trust the information.

Another drawback of the Internet is that even documented Web sites often contain abbreviated information. For instance, there is a company that publishes reference books on American doctors and hospitals; it has a database on the Internet that contains all of the information appearing in the reference books. However, there is *also* a site on the Web for this company—but it does not contain all of the information that appears in the reference books, so the unsuspecting researcher may consequently miss crucial information. Likewise, older materials are often not available on the Internet: You can get this week's issue of *The New Yorker*, but for an article written in that magazine in 1967, you'll have to go to a library.

Nevertheless, the Internet and the World Wide Web can be important sources. If you are not familiar with using these sources, it may be useful for you to take one of the many orientation courses offered. Your college is likely to offer such courses through the library, the technology center, the computer laboratory, or other such support services.

Evaluating Internet Sites

Because anyone can mount a Web site, users need to evaluate the reliability of sources. The most reliable sources are hosted by a reputable institution such as a college, museum, or professional organization rather than a single person. The most reliable sources are designed for educational, rather than entertainment, purposes.

Here are some questions to help you evaluate an Internet site:

- What does the domain tell you? The domain name is the group of letters after the dot. Common domain names are
    com—a commercial site hosted by a profit-making business
    edu—an educational institution, such as a college or university
    gov—a government organization
    org—a nonprofit organization or business
    net—a network
    mil—military
    uk—a site originating in the United Kingdom
- Who is the author of the Web site? Is the site hosted and managed by an individual? If so, what affiliation does this individual have? If the site is hosted by a group, what authority does the group have to offer information?
- Who is the intended audience? Does the site address children? High school students? Advanced professionals?
- How reliable is the information? What evidence does the site offer to support assertions and claims?
- How current is the information? Often, a site will let you know when it was last updated. Sometimes, currency of information (about political issues, for example, or scientific research) will be relevant to your research.

nternet Lingo

Here are a few terms you should understand in order to do research on the Internet.

- **Telnet.** This is a program that lets you log in to a remote host computer on the Internet and run programs resident on that host computer. Telnet, therefore, is a service that can connect your computer with hundreds of host computers. Your library may provide Telnet to connect with other libraries around the world.

- **Browser.** A browser allows you to view World Wide Web documents. Browsers provide a way to navigate the Internet by pointing and clicking on text or icons. Netscape Navigator and Microsoft Internet Explorer are common examples of browsers.

- **Search engine, search directory.** These are tools to help you find information on the Internet. Examples of search engines are Librarian's Index, Alta Vista, Infoseek, Excite, and Lycos. Examples of search directories are Google, Yahoo!, Magellan, Galaxy, Excite, and Infoseek. Besides these information-finding tools, there are also Internet collections, which are subject directories of Internet resources compiled by individuals. Such directories may focus on archaeology, art, mathematics, government, history, literature, and so forth.

Here are three useful Web sites with links to most online libraries:

http://sunsite.Berkeley.edu/LibWeb

www.metronet.lib.mn.us/lc/lc1.html

http://library.usask.ca/hywebcat

- **Discussion group, newsgroup (Usenet), chat group.** Discussion or chat groups should not serve as your principal sources, but they are useful for finding leads to other sources. Different groups emphasize different issues or topics; if you subscribe to a particular group, you can receive e-mail—relevant articles, transcripts, etc.—on its topics.

Two Web sites can help you find Usenet newsgroups:

www.deja.com

www.tile.net

Some organizations and publications have their own groups. If you go to the address of any group and log in, you can "talk" to other people who are also connected, and thus issue a question to the world at large. You may need to leave your e-mail address and just wait for responses, or you may be able to read all the messages directly on the group's site. For example, National Public Radio's afternoon talk show "Talk of the Nation" has a chat group where you can "converse" with other listeners about the topic being discussed on the air.

Two Web sites can help you find mailing lists:

www.tile.net/lists

www.liszt.com

ONLINE SEARCHES

To find information on the Web, you'll use a search engine, such as Google. Most likely, Google is familiar to you if you've shopped online, looked for helpful tips about anything from symptoms of illnesses to gardening, or planned a trip. Google is not the only search engine—other popular search engines are yahoo.com and ask.com; whichever search engine you choose, the process is the same.

Let's follow a search for research about women's roles on farms in nineteenth century America. To begin, you would enter a few **key words**: *women, farm,* and *nineteenth century.* Key words are terms that a search engine will use to find sources. You might have entered other related terms: *agriculture, female,* and *1800s* for example. You'll see, as soon as you press *search,* that you come up with hundreds of thousands of results. It would be a daunting task to sort through all of them; usually in a search, the first dozen or so are sufficient to provide some useful sources.

With so many apparently relevant references, how can you decide which ones might be helpful to your research? First, spend a few minutes examining where the reference comes from by looking at the *domain name.* The domain name is the identification that comes after "www." In one reference that emerges from this search on Google or Yahoo!, you'll see the domain name *connerprairie.org.* "Org" signifies a nonprofit organization, such as a museum.

Generally, sources hosted by an educational or nonprofit organization are more reliable than sources from a commercial site. If you click on the link for the *connerprairie.org* reference, you'll find an essay about farm women's roles in the late nineteenth century. But from the essay, you still won't know what *connerprairie* is. For that information, you need to click on "Home," to discover that Conner Prairie is a history museum in Indiana. Knowing where your source originates is the first step to deciding on its usefulness.

Some references you may find come from a source identified as JSTOR.org. This source contains references to articles in the humanities and social sciences from many scholarly journals and books. The difference between scholarly publications and popular magazines is a process of selection called *peer review.* This means that other scholars read the essay before it is accepted for publication and decide that it is sufficiently important and well written to deserve being published. Books published by academic publishing houses (Oxford University Press, Harvard University Press) go through the same peer review process.

Using the key words mentioned earlier, you are likely to find a reference to the book *Bonds of Community: The Lives of Farm Women in Nineteenth Century New York* by Nancy Grey Osterud. This book may be in your college library, or it may be available on loan from other libraries through a service called *interlibrary loan*. Your college reference librarian can help you make a request. Since this book is directly relevant to your research, you'll want to look at its bibliography to see what sources the author used. One way to build your own bibliography is to check sources in useful books and articles.

A library online catalogue entry for *Bonds of Community* looks like this:

Author:	Osterud, Nancy Grey, 1948-
Title:	Bonds of Community: The Lives of Farm Women in Nineteenth-Century New York/Nancy Grey Osterud.
Publication Information:	Ithaca: Cornell University Press, 1991.
Description:	ix, 303 p. : ill., map ; 25 cm.
Notes:	Includes bibliographical references (p. 289-295) and index.
LC Subject(s):	Rural women —New York (State) —History — 19th century. New York (State)—Rural conditions.
Record number:	ocm22004130
Call Number:	HQ1438.N57 O88 1991

It's useful to look at the Library of Congress (LC) Subject terms for this source. Using *rural women* or *New York (State)—Rural conditions* as key words can help you as you proceed in your research. If this book proves helpful to you, other books and articles that emerge from a keyword search of these subjects also may be helpful. Also, online catalogues allow you to search for other books at the same Call Number. Clicking on HQ1438.N57 O88 will show you other titles that are adjacent to this one on your library's shelf.

Others references from an internet search might lead you to the following kinds of sources:

- *com* in the domain name refers to a commercial site. Although designed to publicize a business or sell merchandise, a commercial site still may offer interesting material or links to educational sites. You need to be careful, though, because material on commercial sites generally does not undergo a peer review process.

- *edu* in the domain name refers to an educational site. These sites may lead you to libraries, collections, or archives, which may contain manuscripts, letters, unpublished material, or, in the case of nineteenth-century women, newspapers and magazines from the period. Sometimes, archives can provide photocopies of some of their holdings for students who are engaged in research. Clicking on the link can tell you about the collection, whether it is accessible, and how to find out more information.

- *Amazon.com* frequently appears in searches, leading you to references for books published on your topic that can be purchased through the online bookstore. These titles, though, may be in your library, or you may request the title through interlibrary loan.

ARTICLE DATABASES

Databases in your library may provide indexes and full texts for journal articles, abstracts, reports, and other material in various fields of study. Libraries can subscribe to hundreds of online databases. Some databases are devoted to a single discipline, like PsychLIT for materials written in the field of psychology. Others are multidisciplinary, like Lexis (or LexisNexis), which assembles news pieces from hundreds of papers and journals.

Examples of databases that are available at most large libraries are ERIC (Educational Resources Information Center, for material in the field of education), MLA Bibliography (Modern Languages Association Bibliography, for material on linguistics, literature, and languages), and PAIS (Public Affairs information Service, for government documents and policy periodicals).

Databases also offer you access to abstracts, full-text articles, and images in journals, archives, and other collections. An *abstract* is a brief summary of a longer work, such as a scholarly article or research report. The abstract will contain a full citation for the longer work so that you can locate it in a library or, if the service is available to you, request the longer work from your library's Interlibrary Loan Office. Some databases contain links to full-text articles, so that you can download the article from your own computer and print it out. Databases also may contain links to sources of current or historical images. Hundreds of databases cover a wide range of topics. Your instructor often can recommend databases that are best for your research. As in an Internet search, you can use key words to find references and sources.

Some Useful Databases

Ebscohost.com

Access to a collection of databases for the humanities, social sciences, behavioral sciences, business, educational literature, environmental sciences, and other fields.

ARTstor.org

Access to images of paintings, photographs, and other art forms.

Search.eb.com

Encyclopedia Britannica. Although Wikipedia is a popular source for succinct entries identifying people, places, ideas, and things, the Encyclopedia Britannica continues to be a professional, reliable source of information.

LexisNexis.com

Access to a number of specialized databases focused on education, business, law, and news.

WorldCat

A library catalogue that can tell you where in the world you can find a book you are looking for.

LIBRARY RESOURCES

Once you have a topic and a focused question, you are likely to head to a library to begin your research. Depending on your topic and question, use the following good research sources.

Dictionaries

The range of dictionaries goes far beyond the familiar *Webster's* or *American Heritage*. The *Oxford English Dictionary (OED)* is a multivolume resource that offers historical information on word usage. When is the first time that the word *multicultural* appeared in print? What is the origin of the word *thing?* You can find the answers to those questions in the *OED*. The OED also has an online site at www.oed.com.

In addition, there are specialized dictionaries for science, business, biography, and many other fields. Dictionaries are useful as a first step: They help you to define terms and find basic information about your topic.

Encyclopedias

Just like dictionaries, encyclopedias may be all-inclusive *(Britannica, Americana)* or specialized. The *Encyclopedia of Philosophy,* for example, contains entries, written by experts, on major philosophers and philosophies. The *Encyclopedia of American Industries* contains summaries of hundreds of important industries, offering basic factual information for each. Wikipedia is an online encyclopedia that has generated controversy about its reliability. If you find information on Wikipedia, it's best to compare it with a generally accepted source such as the *Encyclopedia Britannica* or scholarly encyclopedia.

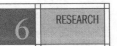

Popular Magazines

Magazines can be important sources of information. But how do you find an article pertaining to your topic? One of the many online or print guides to periodical literature can help you. The *Reader's Guide to Periodical Literature* is widely used and available in many public libraries, as well as in college libraries. When you look up key words for your topic or question, you'll find an entry that gives you the author, title, magazine name, publication dates, and page numbers for an article that may be useful to you. This reference source will help you find information published in such popular magazines as *The Nation, Ladies Home Journal,* and *Reader's Digest.*

Professional and Scholarly Journals

Specialized guides to articles in professional and scholarly journals include the following:

- *Education Index*
- *Art Index*
- *Business Periodicals*
- *Humanities Index*
- *Index to Legal Periodicals*
- *Social Sciences Index*
- *Applied Science and Technology Index*
- *Public Affairs Information Service Bulletin*
- *Essay and General Literature Index*

Most scholarly journals are now referenced in online databases.

Dissertations

Doctoral dissertations that are not yet published as books can be valuable resources for research. To locate a dissertation pertinent to your topic and question, there are several sources you can consult. Among them are the *Comprehensive Dissertation Index, Dissertations in English and American Literature,* and *Dissertation Abstracts International.*

RESEARCH   6

Book Review Digest and *Book Review Index*

This source contains excerpts from reviews of many popular books published in the United States. If you want to quote from a book review, you need to find the review in its original source. Do not quote directly from the *Book Review Digest* because entries offer only summaries of longer reviews; these summaries are not considered a scholarly resource. The *Book Review Index* can be found online for reviews published after 1965.

Biographical Indexes

Biographical indexes offer information on well-known or influential people, past and present. Some indexes, like the *Biography Index,* refer you to other sources of information about prominent people. Others, such as *Contemporary Authors* and *Modern Scientists and Engineers,* offer biographical accounts, which vary in length according to the index. *Current Biography* includes both references to other sources and biographical information. Biographical indexes are generally multivolume series of books, arranged alphabetically by name or profession, which are updated regularly. Usually, an index series has a separate cumulative index volume.

Newspaper Indexes

Newspaper indexes offer complete citations, by subject and author, to news articles. Many major newspapers, including *The Los Angeles Times* and *The Christian Science Monitor,* have their own indexes of articles. *The New York Times Index* is one of the largest and most consulted of these newspaper indexes. *The National Newspaper Index* is a larger index, available on CD-ROM and online, which compiles citations to many newspapers. *LexisNexis* is also a usual database for news articles.

Online Catalogues

In many libraries, an online catalogue contains information on a library's own holdings. This sort of database—generally called an online catalogue— is an updated version of the old-fashioned card catalogue. In card catalogues, the library's holdings are arranged by author, subject, and title. Online, you can do all three searches in one place; in addition, you can conduct searches by publisher, key word, and other features. The online catalogue will produce a list of all the works in the library that match the search word you enter. You can view the long display for each work or choose only those you really want to see. At some computer terminals, you can print the information that appears on screen and take it with you when you search the library shelves.

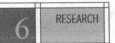

Both card catalogues and online catalogues provide complete bibliographic information on the library's holdings (one minor difference is that a work's title is sometimes abbreviated in online catalogues). A listing from either sort of catalogue will include the title, author(s), edition, publisher, city of publication, date of publication, total number of pages, number of illustrations (if any), the size of the book (in cm), subject headings, Library of Congress catalogue number or other identification number, and the work's call number and location.

Online catalogues have several advantages. They are continually updated, so you can find out immediately whether and when the work has been checked out and when it is due back. They also include key words and suggest related subjects, which you can search using particular search commands. Some online catalogues allow you to check the book out by computer, using your student ID number. In most online systems, the screen will display a list of possible commands that are fairly self-explanatory, which you type or select. The list should include a "help" command, which will give you specific information on how to operate the search system.

CD-ROM

Most university libraries and larger public libraries have computers on which you can conduct research by CD-ROM. CD-ROM is a way of storing vast amounts of information in very limited space: Information, organized into databases, is stored on CDs, which you "play" in a computer disk drive the way you'd play a music CD. Some disks contain bibliographic information—indexes of titles, authors, and so forth—which directs you to other resources in the library. Some disks have summaries of articles and other written material. Still other disks contain the written material itself that you are looking for—the full text of an article, for instance. Most of the reference publications listed above are available on CD-ROM.

Doing research by CD-ROM is quite easy. Once you have selected a CD, you can type in search words (key words), or you can select words from a menu or list offered by the database. The computer searches the database for information on the subjects you have selected and reports the number of entries on those subjects that it has found in the database. You can then look at a list of entries and choose to view the long display on any of them. On some databases, the display will show bibliographic information only; on other databases, the display will include the full text of an article.

CD-ROMs are produced by several database companies, and the search process may differ slightly depending on the company whose CD-ROMs you are using. Different databases also emphasize different sorts of information. In general, on any database, you should be able to access both indexes and the full text of magazines, journals, newspapers, and other publications, which are often arranged by professional sphere (e.g., academic publications) or by general subject matter (e.g., the *Biological and Agricultural Index,* available from H. W. Wilson).

TAKING NOTES BASED ON YOUR RESEARCH

Once you are equipped with a focused question and know how to find the information that will help you answer that question, you are ready to take notes.

Taking good notes will urge you to read more carefully; conversely, reading carefully will help you to take good notes. You have already learned some reading strategies for doing efficient and thorough research. Taking notes involves selecting and synthesizing the most important information from your sources. Note-taking will help you to develop ideas and arguments and to gain a thorough knowledge of your topic.

You can respond to the sources you consult in many ways; in this section, you will learn ways to:

- copy factual information
- copy quotations
- paraphrase
- summarize
- ask questions
- follow up ideas with research

Observations, ideas, and questions will occur to you while you read and consider sources. These responses represent your own perspective and creativity; they will help you to write an interesting and coherent paper. Some students jot down key words and generalities that later will suggest directions to pursue and connections to make. Others take a break from note-taking to follow through fully on a thought.

One student, for example, was doing research for her paper on architectural restoration in historic but low-rent neighborhoods in Chicago. She came across a newspaper article on rent-districting policies, which reminded her of a book she had read on residential overcrowding in urban areas. She stopped reading the article to list the possible ways in which architectural restoration in some neighborhoods might produce overcrowding in others by influencing rents. She later used this list to develop the thesis of her paper. Another student may have made a brief note of the relationship between restoration and overcrowding and waited until he got home to think more about it. If you are reading carefully, you may find it useful to analyze and interpret the source at that moment; if you are skimming, you may want simply to note digressive responses briefly and reserve more thoughtful work for later.

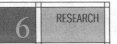

In the beginning stages of your research, it may be difficult to tell which information is worth noting. It is better, in this case, to take more notes than fewer: Even seemingly irrelevant information may become quite useful to you at a later stage in your thinking. It is not a waste of time to write down more information than you will use in your paper; thorough note-taking will give you the flexibility to choose the best evidence for your paper.

Using Quotations

Direct quotations are the easiest notes to take and document. Although you may write down many quotations in the course of research, remember that quotations are *evidence* for your own assertions or analysis. Quotations cannot substitute for your own analysis; rather, they can be used to support your analysis. When you read and take notes, try to limit the number of direct quotations you list. Look for particularly pertinent passages: those that speak most strongly and directly to your point and those that are well phrased (clear, specific, descriptive). These passages are the best candidates for quotations. Quotations are also valuable when they derive from people who are well known or who are strong, respected authorities—in other words, from authors whose opinions are important.

You can test the quotability of a text by trying to paraphrase or summarize it. If you can't do either—if it simply doesn't make sense to put the passage into other words—but the content of the text is still important, then you should quote it. For example, Alex, a student who is writing a 20-page research paper on modern travel writing, is in the process of reading some travel narratives. One of these, Paul Theroux's *The Pillars of Hercules: A Grand Tour of the Mediterranean,* opens with a line that really appeals to Alex:

> People here in Western Civilization say that tourists are no different from apes, but on the Rock of Gibraltar, one of the Pillars of Hercules, I saw both tourists and apes together, and I learned to tell them apart (1).

Alex can use this sentence in his paper to demonstrate Theroux's style, perspective, and intentions, but to do this, he must use Theroux's exact words. The sentence will not be valuable if it is rephrased.

If you wish to quote a passage of a text but don't need each and every word in that passage, you can use ellipses to show your interruption of the original text. In the following passage from Theroux's book, Alex notices something he thinks is characteristic of modern travel writing:

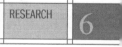

RESEARCH 6

> We soon came to a checkpoint, with Bosnian soldiers, and some policemen who entered the bus and bullied civilians, denouncing them for carrying doubtful-looking identity papers. There were Croatian checkpoints, too, at Omis, Makarska, and Podgorje: the same routine. Usually the victim of the policeman's wrath was a squirming, cowering woman. In this sort of situation the cop had absolute power: he could arrest the poor woman or boot her off the bus, or send her back where she came from (241).

Alex decides that he doesn't need to quote the entire passage. Instead, he transcribes only the most relevant part of the passage and inserts ellipses (three dots) to signal the part of the text he has left out:

> We soon came to the checkpoint, with Bosnian soldiers, and some policemen who entered the bus and bullied civilians. . . . Usually the victim of the policeman's wrath was a squirming, cowering woman. In this sort of situation the cop had absolute power . . . (241).

The part that Alex quoted is the part he needed to make his point.

Once Alex identified the passage he wanted to include in his own paper, he knew he needed to introduce the passage so the reader would know who contributed it. Here's how Alex accomplished integrating the quotation into his own paper:

> As Theroux described his trip to Bosnia, readers can feel the daily tension. "We soon came to a checkpoint, with Bosnian soldiers, and some policemen who entered the bus and bullied civilians," Theroux reported. "Usually the victim of the policeman's wrath was a squirming, cowering woman" (241).

Paraphrasing

Paraphrasing is tricky because it is the form of note-taking that lends itself most easily to plagiarism. It is useful to think of paraphrases as reports: For instance, when you "report" an opinion you heard on the radio about the new Congressional tax policy, you are uninvolved in the opinion—your interpretation is not required—but when you report the opinion, you do so in your own way, in your own language. You should paraphrase when you don't want to quote directly, either because it is not called for (for the reasons listed above) or because the language is difficult (overly scientific, full of jargon, etc.), yet most of the content of the paraphrased material is needed.

The important thing to remember in paraphrasing is that you want your paraphrase to resemble the original passage only in its main points—not in length, style, or structure. The first step in paraphrasing a passage of a text is to read it through. Once you understand the content of the passage, you can select its important points—those key to the author's argument (*not* necessarily key to yours). You may rearrange these points in the order that makes the most sense to you: You have the opportunity here to edit and clarify the author's writing. Finally, you are ready to restate the author's points in your own words. Here, you should not simply "translate" an author's sentences into very similar sentences of your own, which differ only in vocabulary. Rather, you should try to write the paraphrase in your own style. It will be easier to know your own style once you start writing your paper; at that stage, you may wish to change the paraphrasing you have done in your notes.

Paraphrased sources need to be documented by a footnote, endnote, or parenthetical citation, just as you would do with a quotation. It also helps the reader if you introduce a paraphrased source by referring to the author or the source in your own sentence. You want the reader to know that this passage of your writing really has a basis in someone else's work.

Alex has read several primary sources for his paper, and he is now consulting secondary sources as well. One of his secondary sources is an article by Adrian Furnham called "Tourism and Culture Shock," in which Furnham offers his own interpretation of travel. Alex finds one of Furnham's observations particularly striking:

6 RESEARCH

Anyone who lives in a popular tourist city or town soon becomes aware of the fact that it is not only the tourists who experience culture shock at the behavior and beliefs of natives, but also the natives who experience culture shock at the unusual habits of tourists (53).

Although this sentence contains an important insight, it is somewhat unwieldy, and the writing style is not appealing to Alex. He decides to paraphrase the sentence. When he discusses Furnham in his paper, Alex writes:

Adrian Furnham shows us the flip side of the conventional travel perspective in his article "Tourism and Culture Shock." After reviewing the psychological literature on the effects of travel on tourists, he considers the experience of people who are subjected to tourism (Furnham 1984: 53). Furnham argues that people who live in tourist areas experience the same kind of "culture shock" that tourists do: Tourists and "natives" are equally strange to one another.

Here, Alex effectively combines a paraphrase with direct quotations of key words—"culture shock" and "natives"—from Furnham's article. He selects what is most important from Furnham's text and restates it in his own writing style, which is easily distinguished from Furnham's.

Summarizing

In comparison with using quotations and paraphrasing, summarizing involves more reading and less writing. Summarizing requires that you understand the main points of a passage and not be distracted by details that the author includes to support those points. A summary consists mainly of generalizations.

You can usually judge whether to summarize a passage rather than paraphrase it on the basis of its length. You wouldn't want to paraphrase a 30-page chapter of a book, but you can easily summarize it.

In summarizing, as in paraphrasing, you should read a text thoroughly and to the end. While you read, look in paragraphs or groups of paragraphs for topic sentences. These are sentences that state a section's main point, for which the rest of the information is supporting argument or detail; they are the sentences you might underline or highlight if you were reading your own copy of the work. In some sources you consult, you will not find clear topic sentences. In this case, you will need to gather parts of the author's main points from a number of sentences.

When you have finished reading, use the main ideas you have identified in topic or other sentences to write your summary. You should write these main points in your own language and in the order that makes the most sense to you. Because you will be omitting many of the author's finer points, your summary should represent a different arrangement of ideas from the original.

DOCUMENTING SOURCES

When you take notes, you will need to record complete information about every source you consult. However, you may not want to rewrite all of this information for each piece of information you jot down. It may be easiest to transcribe full bibliographic information from your sources onto a master list of sources, to which you can add in the course of your research. You can then refer to these sources in abbreviated form in your notes.

In your master list, you should record the following information:

- author(s) and/or editor(s)
- complete title
- city of publication
- publisher
- edition
- year of publication (if the source is a reprint or numbered edition, you'll need the original and the most recent copyright dates)
- volume (with scholarly journal articles, you may need to note volume and number, e.g., vol. 3, no. 1)
- page numbers (for a section of a book, a journal, or a newspaper article)

When you are ready to compile a bibliography of works you have consulted in your research or cited in your paper, this master list will be invaluable.

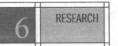

There are several acceptable ways to document your sources; you should ask your instructor which style is appropriate for your paper. To start, you should know the difference between bibliographic entries and footnotes or endnotes. Your bibliography is a list, arranged alphabetically by author's last name, of all the works you cited or consulted. The bibliography typically does not provide page numbers for material taken from books. For instance, Clara wrote a paper on the dramatic uses of heat in a novel by Doris Lessing. Her bibliographic entry for the novel looked like this:

Lessing, Doris. *The Grass Is Singing.* New York: Plume, [1950] 1978.

Note that the entry is not indented. If an entry requires more than one line, all lines after the first line should be indented five spaces. You should double-space bibliographic entries and skip two double-spaced lines between entries.

Footnotes and endnotes are the actual citations of sources: You use them to provide information about the sources you quote, paraphrase, summarize, or otherwise reference in your paper. Footnotes and endnotes are numbered consecutively to match the superscript number in the text of your paper. Footnotes appear at the bottom of the page of your paper where the cited material appears; endnotes appear in a list at the end of your paper. In addition to source information, you can also provide additional facts or commentary in a footnote or endnote. Clara quoted Lessing's novel in the following section in her paper:

> Mary's increasing anxiety both flows from and exacerbates the intense South African heat: "And it really seemed to her that she could not stand another morning with the hot sun on her neck, with the dazzle of heat in her eyes, although she felt sick with the heat when she stayed in the house. . . . As time passed, the heat became an obsession."[3]

Clara's corresponding note at the foot of the page (or in a list at the end of the paper) looked like this:

> [3]Doris Lessing, *The Grass Is Singing* (New York: Plume, [1950] 1978) 75. Such descriptions of the heat recur throughout Lessing's book—one reason it is known for its vivid realism.

Notice that, among other differences between the note citation and the bibliographic entry, the note's first line is indented and the subsequent lines are not.

If you use full footnotes or endnotes such as Clara's, you may not need to attach a separate bibliography at the end of your paper because all the information that would appear in a bibliographic entry will appear in your notes instead. You should provide all of this information for a source only the first time you cite that source. Thereafter, you can use the short form: Simply include the author's last name, the year of publication if you use more than one source from that author, and the page number where the cited material appears.

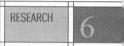

Another option is to use only the short form for all of your footnotes or endnotes. In this case, you will need to attach a bibliography or list of works cited.

Another way to document sources is to use parenthetical citations, which are internal or textual notes. These notes include abbreviated source information and appear in parentheses in the text of your paper. If you use internal notes, you must provide a full bibliography or list of works cited. You can then refer to the bibliography in your notes.

If Clara had used parenthetical citation, she would have written:

> Mary's increasing anxiety both flows from and exacerbates the intense South African heat: "And it really seemed to her that she could not stand another morning with the hot sun on her neck, with the dazzle of heat in her eyes, although she felt sick with the heat when she stayed in the house. . . . As time passed, the heat became an obsession" (Lessing 1978: 75).

This parenthetical note includes the author's name, the year of the work's publication, and the page number where the quoted material appears. This information leads the reader to the source in the bibliography.

Styles of Documentation

Well-known manuals for documentation style include the *MLA Handbook for Writers of Research Papers,* which is the standard style for humanities papers, and the American Psychological Association's *Publication Manual,* which is the standard for social science papers.

MLA style of documentation. Although your professor may ask you to use footnotes or endnotes, preferred MLA style cites sources within parentheses. After quotations or paraphrased material, indicate the author and page number of the cited work, the way Clara did when citing Lessing, in the example above. The citation is then expanded fully in a list of works cited. Here are examples of bibliographic entries in MLA style:

> Furnham, Adrian. "Tourism and Culture Shock." *Annals of Tourism Research,* Vol. 11. 1984: 41–57.
> Theroux, Paul. *The Pillars of Hercules: A Grand Tour of the Mediterranean.* New York: G.P. Putnam's Sons, 1995.
> Wonter, Janine. "Tourism Totters in the Mediterranean." *The Granham Flier.* 31 Aug. 1994: 67–68.

APA style of documentation. In the social sciences, the date of publication often is crucial in evaluating a source's significance. Therefore, you'll notice that the date of publication comes earlier in the citation in the APA style than in the MLA style. If you use the APA style, you will cite sources not with footnotes or endnotes, but with internal (parenthetical) notes. You will attach a list of works cited in the bibliographic form that you see in the examples below:

> Furnham, A. (1984). Tourism and culture shock. *Annals of Tourism Research, 11,* 41–57.
> Theroux, P. (1995). *The pillars of Hercules: A grand tour of the Mediterranean.* New York: G.P. Putnam's Sons.
> Wonter, J. (1994, Aug. 31). Tourism totters in the Mediterranean. *The Granham Flier,* pp. 67–68.

Online sources may offer standard bibliographic information. For instance, if you read an article from *The New York Times* on the Internet—either at the newspaper's official Web site or posted by an individual at a different site— you should document it as if you were reading it in hard copy. Other online sources may not include such information. In this case, record the date on which you read the information, the electronic source (Internet address, database), and the author or sender of the information.

ORGANIZING YOUR NOTES

The method you use to organize your notes may depend on your experience, library facilities, and advice of classmates and instructors. Whether you use note cards, a notebook, or a computer, you should make sure to identify the source of each note on the note itself. Head each set of notes with a source reference, a subject or key word, and the page numbers concerned. For direct quotes, the page numbers you list should be only those pages on which quoted words appear; for paraphrases and summaries, list the numbers of all the pages from which you draw information.

When you take notes, make sure to keep your personal responses separate from quotations, paraphrases, and summaries. If you write responses and notes in the same place—on the same note card, sheet of paper, or computer file—you can distinguish your responses by bracketing them or putting headings on them. However, it may be safer to write responses and notes on separate note cards, on the front and back of the same cards, on different pages or sections in a notebook, or in different files on a computer (you can keep both windows open at once).

Index Cards

Index cards impose great discipline. This form of note-taking is sometimes arduous and cumbersome, but it will improve your organizational skills.

RESEARCH 6

Index cards make it easy for you to keep brief notes—whose content can fit on a card or two—and to keep notes on different topics in different places. Often, using different-colored cards for different subject areas helps you to keep the cards organized. They also allow you to cross-index your notes. For instance, if you have copied down part of a senator's speech that covers crime rates and employment statistics, you can keep two different note cards in two separate files: one on crime and one on employment. Cross-indexing will let you remember what notes you have and therefore help you make the most efficient use of them.

If you take notes on index cards, keep separate cards for different sources, different quotes, distinct points, and so forth. To organize these cards, try writing a subject heading on each one. Later, when you are ready to start writing your outline and your paper, you can spread all of your cards out (on a table or the floor) and see them all at once. You can then try different ways of arranging the information you have collected. In addition, the extra step of filing your note cards will permit you to estimate how much information you have on each point for your paper; it will also remind you of what notes you've already taken so that you don't duplicate your efforts.

Index cards have some disadvantages. For one thing, they are easy to lose. For another, they are quite small and will not allow you to take long, substantive notes easily. You can, of course, take one set of notes on multiple index cards. If you do this, you will need to attach cards with a continuing note together or make sure to rewrite the same heading on each one. Otherwise, you risk losing the source for a set of notes, which means you will have to go back to the library to find it.

Notebooks

Notebooks offer more room and flexibility than index cards. Notebooks are preferable if you like to read hard copy rather than computer screens and if you think best while writing as opposed to typing. If you do use a notebook, make sure that you invent an indexing system: You can organize notes into sections by subject, source, or some other meaningful feature.

One disadvantage of using a notebook is the inability to spread out your notes and look at many at once: You can see only what is on one page.

Tape Recorders

Especially if you are an auditory learner, the tape recorder may be a useful tool for recording notes. Some students find that they can work more quickly if they read into a tape recorder rather than copy material from sources. At the same time, reading aloud helps them to process the material.

Computer Files

Computers have a much larger—nearly infinite—capacity for storing information; if you are planning a massive amount of research, they are your best bet. Computers also permit continual reorganization: If you take notes on a computer, you will be able to make corrections and additions easily, without disrupting the order of your notes. Another advantage of note-taking by computer is that when you get to writing your paper, you can transfer notes directly from a note file into your paper's file: You won't have to rewrite everything (as you do if you take notes on paper). If you prefer to read and work from hard copy rather than from a computer screen, you can always print your notes before starting to write your paper.

With most word processing software, you can keep several note files open at once and simply shift between windows. This capability will be quite helpful if you find that a source is useful on several subjects, or if you are keeping separate files for your personal responses and your notes. You can organize these note files into folders by subject, source, or whatever organizational scheme you prefer. This way, as you take more notes and add files for them, you will have to choose a research category for each new note. This will help you to stay on target and avoid distractions in your research.

PLAGIARISM AND OVERDOCUMENTATION

Although it should now be clear to you *how* to document a source, you may still have questions about *when* you should do it. This section will help you make good decisions about citing the information you use, directly or indirectly, in your paper. You must document a source if you use quoted, paraphrased, or summarized material. You should cite other people's original insights, observations, and arguments, as well as their data, figures, and research results. Take particular care to document information your readers may want to look at for themselves in the original source, either because it is surprising or because the source contains additional useful information.

On the other hand, you do not have to document everything you learn from your research. You do not have to document information that most readers may know and statements they would generally accept, for example, general facts about major historical events (the French Revolution started in 1789); the names and roles of public and mythic figures (the British Prime Minister Tony Blair was elected in 1997); or even more specific information that is both indisputable and widely available. Likewise, elementary scientific facts and explanations (heat rises, meat is a source of protein), general observations (commuters read newspapers), and other sorts of common "truths" are the property of everyone, including you. Of course, your own ideas, arguments, and analyses do not need to be documented.

What Is Plagiarism?

Students sometimes encounter cases in which the basic, commonsense documentation guidelines do not seem to apply. When you do the sorts of research we've discussed in this chapter, it will often be clear which evidence you should cite in your paper. For instance, Joe was writing a paper on lung cancer rates in American cities. He knew that he had to cite the useful figures he found in an article by Dr. Lamm, an urban oncologist. He also knew that he should cite Dr. Lamm's analysis of the figures because it supported Joe's own argument. However, it was less clear to Joe *how* he ought to cite this evidence, especially since he was having trouble distinguishing his thoughts from Dr. Lamm's.

This is the kind of situation in which plagiarism can occur. Plagiarism is a term most people recognize but don't clearly understand. Because plagiarism is a serious legal and moral issue with significant consequences for your career as a student, it is important for you to have an adequate grasp of what it means.

Broadly speaking, **plagiarism** means that you take credit—either deliberately or by accident—for observations, ideas, arguments, phrases, and figures that you gather in the course of your research. There are obvious and subtle forms of plagiarism: A direct quotation that appears in a student's paper without quotation marks is a fairly clear case; an idea that is partly the student's but partly a well-known essayist's is less apparent—but still plagiarism. Recall the passage from Adrian Furnham's article that Alex used in his paper on travel writing:

> Anyone who lives in a popular tourist city or town soon becomes aware of the fact that it is not only the tourists who experience culture shock at the behavior and beliefs of natives, but also the natives who experience culture shock at the unusual habits of tourists (Furnham 1984: 53).

Earlier, in the section on taking notes, you saw how Alex used an acceptable paraphrase of this sentence. A different student poorly paraphrased the same sentence and did not cite Furnham at all:

> Tourists are not the only ones who get culture shock. People who live in places that tourists visit are "shocked" by the "culture" of the tourists, too.

Here, Furnham's idea is merely rephrased; even the order in which his ideas are arranged is conserved. Without a citation, this paraphrase is plagiarism.

Equally bad is the following version, in which another student copied portions from the original text directly:

> It is a fact that the natives of popular tourist cities experience culture shock. The behavior and beliefs of tourists are as disturbing to natives as natives are to tourists.

Another student, who was interested in finding support for his own disapproval of tourists, engaged in a more complex form of plagiarism in this paragraph:

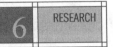

> Tourists are not at all sensitive to the natives of the regions they visit. Tourists experience "culture shock" when they meet these people, who are very different from them in their customs, appearance, and perspective. Natives, although they also may experience culture shock when faced with the rude behavior of tourists, are less blameworthy: They did not ask for their shocking experience, whereas the tourists are the sole cause of their own discomfort (Furnham 1984: 53).

This version is an interpretation, not a representation, of Furnham. Furnham is cited, but it is not at all clear which of the ideas expressed belong to Furnham, and it looks as if Furnham is credited with ideas and opinions that we know do not appear in the original article. As this example shows, documentation must be specific.

When Does Plagiarism Occur?

Plagiarism does not have to be intentional. In fact, most often, it is a consequence of hurried work. If you do not have adequate time to take notes—which means not only writing complete bibliographic information for each source you consult, but also reading each source carefully and thinking about how it may be useful to you—you may find yourself either short of ideas or full of ideas that aren't yours. Also, people make poor decisions when they are tired or under stress—feelings familiar to many students. To avoid plagiarism, it is best to be prepared with good notes and a firm grasp of your own ideas *before* you start to write, so you don't have to rely solely on your state of mind.

Sometimes, students plagiarize because they don't quite know how to use their sources properly. Particularly with a research paper, you may feel unequipped to judge the evidence you are required to use as support for your argument. You may feel overwhelmed by the volume of expert opinions published by professional critics, essayists, and scientists. You might think you have nothing additional to say, or perhaps you don't feel qualified to dispute anyone else. These experiences are common for students who rely too heavily on others' opinions—that is, on secondary sources—rather than concentrating on the primary sources about which they need to develop their own opinions.

Useful Guides to Research

The following guides may help you with general and specific research concerns:

Berkman, Robert I. *Find It Fast: How to Uncover Expert Information on Any Subject, In Print or Online.* New York: Harper Perennial, 1997 (including a particularly detailed section on the Internet, in addition to full information on library resources).

Booth, Wayne C., Gregory G. Colomb, and Joseph Williams. *The Craft of Research.* Chicago: University of Chicago Press, 1995 (helpful for devising topics and questions, and for weighing and using evidence).

Johnson, Jean. *The Bedford Guide to the Research Process.* Boston: Bedford Books, 1992 (especially strong on advice for note-taking).

RESEARCH   6

How Can You Avoid Plagiarism?

The best strategy for avoiding plagiarism is to use the note-taking methods of quotation, paraphrasing, and summary, as described above, as a model in your writing. The rules you follow in taking notes are the same rules you should follow in writing; if you do not plagiarize in your notes, you are unlikely to do so in your writing. You should attribute every quote, every paraphrase, and every summary to a source. You also should write good paraphrases and summaries—ones that capture the essential points in an author's argument but that are written in your own style.

Note-taking will help you avoid plagiarism in another way. In taking good notes, you are taking the time to read your sources carefully, to think about them, and to identify which parts of which sources you will use for which purposes. Your notes are your written records of these processes; they will make it much easier for you to remember where the line is between your ideas and those of other people. If you are not careful taking notes (simply copying sentences without thinking about how they fit into your own ideas and plans for your paper), you may not even realize, later on, that an idea that has "just occurred" to you actually came from someone else.

When you incorporate sources into your paper, signal the origins of those sources: "Dr. Ann Kaliphos, in her new book *The Vegetarian Life,* suggests that the principal health benefit of abstaining from meat is an increased vitamin intake." You may flag your own ideas with the first-person voice: "I, on the other hand, will argue that the true vegetarian success is a moralistic one." You should be careful to take credit for your own ideas, not bury them in a summary or paraphrase of someone else's point of view.

Are You Overdocumenting?

People who are anxious about plagiarism sometimes overcompensate by citing each and every idea expressed in their papers. If you are in doubt about whether to cite a piece of evidence, you should err on the side of caution. But if you find that you are documenting almost every sentence, you may be writing nothing more than a report of other people's ideas. You need to do the work of interpreting, analyzing, and responding to the evidence you find.

Research is an essential part of academic work, and it can be fulfilling and productive once you learn the strategies discussed in this chapter. Once you have done your research, read your sources, and taken notes, you will be ready to begin the next step: writing a college paper. Chapter 7 offers help on the writing process.

ADDITIONAL RESOURCES

Buckley, Peter and Duncan Clark. *The Rough Guide to the Internet.* London: Rough Guides, 2007.

Gibaldi, Joseph. *MLA Handbook for Writers of Research Papers,* 6th ed. New York: Modern Language Association, 2003.

Leshin, Cynthia B. *Student Resource Guide to the Internet: Student Success Online.* Upper Saddle River, NJ: Prentice Hall, 1998.

Publication Manual of the American Psychological Association, 5th ed. Washington, D.C.: American Psychological Association, 2001.

Sometimes I sit at the computer and nothing happens. Nothing. The blank screen just stares back at me, and the longer I sit the worse it gets. It's like a face-off at the OK Corral, and eventually the computer wins.

Jon Everett,
student

STRATEGIES FOR WRITING

Every writer—at one time or another—has sat in front of a computer screen or typewriter keyboard with nothing to say and a deadline to meet. Contrary to popular myth, however, writer's block is not an incurable disease. It usually is caused by a problem at one stage of the writing process—a process that begins much earlier than the moment you sit down in front of the ominous blank screen. Writing a successful paper starts when you get your assignment and ends when you complete the final revision of your work.

In this chapter, you'll learn how to:

- understand your assignment
- generate and develop ideas
- draft an essay
- revise globally and locally.

WRITER'S BLOCK: WHAT IS IT AND WHAT CAUSES IT?

The chilling experience that some writers call **writer's block** is an inability to generate ideas. Usually, that feeling of powerlessness and despair has one of five causes.

1. *You don't understand the assignment.* Suppose someone led you into a workshop where you found planks of wood, a can of nails, a saw, and a hammer, and that person told you you'd be paid when the job was done. Certainly you'd want to know exactly what you were expected to build, for example, a

Taken from: *New Beginnings: A Reference Guide for Adult Learners*, by Linda Simon

Writing Assignment Checklist

Here are some questions to ask yourself about any writing assignment:

1. Is this assignment testing my knowledge of class lectures and readings, or is it asking me to go beyond that material?
2. Am I required to use outside sources? If so, what sources are appropriate?
3. Is the thesis or argument given to me by the assignment, or do I have to invent my own?
4. Am I focusing on one text or comparing one text with another?
5. Do I need to define key terms?
6. If I am analyzing a text, does the assignment ask me to consider any of the following?

   - the author's background or life
   - the author's motivation for writing the text
   - the historical or cultural context of the text
   - the original audience for the text
   - the writing strategies used by the author
   - the main themes of the text
   - the form or structure of the text
   - the emotional or intellectual effect the text has on me

7   WRITING

desk or a dog house. The more information you had, the more likely it would be that you'd build something pleasing to your employer. Without that information, you'd probably develop a case of builder's block.

Any writing assignment should clearly explain your task as a writer, tell you what sources you should use, indicate how long the paper should be, and give you a due date. When you get a writing assignment from your instructor, make sure you understand what you are asked to do. If you feel confused or unsure, *ask your instructor* as soon as possible. Don't wait until the day before the assignment is due.

2. *You haven't done the required reading for the class.* If you haven't kept up with reading assignments, you'll have trouble with writing assignments. Even when you tackle assignments that require additional research beyond class readings, your instructor will expect that you have listened to lectures, participated in class discussions, and done all the required work. Sometimes, falling

behind in your class work—and therefore developing writer's block—is a result of poor time management.

3. *You haven't done preliminary writing.* Any athlete will tell you that if you try to run, swim, ski, lift weights, or do anything physically demanding without warming up, you won't perform well. It's the same with writing. Before you sit down to begin your paper, there are some strategies that can help you to "warm up" and generate ideas. In the next section of this chapter, you'll learn some of those strategies.

4. *You're afraid of being judged.* "I have quite a bit of difficulty separating the product from the person," Patricia Adams admits. "When I write, I feel as though I am taking a piece of myself, a very private and intimate piece, and putting it on paper to be judged by anyone who can read." Your instructor, who will give you a grade on your work, does take on the role of judge. But more important, she is interested in helping you develop your ideas. Writing serves as an important way of communicating those ideas.

If fear of being judged is getting in the way of your writing, make an appointment to see your instructor to discuss the problem. You'll find that your instructor's understanding and sympathy will go a long way toward easing your fears. Many instructors will look at early drafts or passages from your paper and offer suggestions for revision or simply let you know that you're on the right track. Communicating with your instructor as early as possible in the writing process may give you the support you need to overcome writer's block.

5. *You didn't leave enough time.* Writing takes time. Even if you have done all your reading, research, preliminary writing, and outlining, you can count on producing about four or five pages of writing in a few hours of work. If you have to produce a ten-page paper, you may need two four-hour sessions of writing to complete a first draft and, a day or two later, another few hours for revision. If you sit down in front of your computer or typewriter the night before a paper is due, your anxiety about time may well result in writer's block.

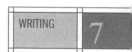

GENERATING IDEAS

No one can write a good paper without good ideas. How do you come up with those ideas? By thinking, recording your ideas, reflecting on those ideas, and thinking some more.

Good ideas come from good questions. Sometimes your instructor will provide you with a question to address in your paper. Often, though, it is your responsibility to come up with a question of your own. A good question for a college essay:

- asks you to make an argument or analysis
- cannot be answered by a simple yes or no
- is focused enough so that it can be answered in a college-length essay
- genuinely interests you and therefore is likely to interest your readers

Here are a few examples of questions that could result in good college papers:

Course:	*Nineteenth-Century American History*
Topic:	Theodore Roosevelt
Question:	How did Theodore Roosevelt's relationship with his sons reflect his ideas about manhood?
Sources:	Roosevelt's letters to his children

Course:	*Health Services and the Law*
Topic:	Nursing home regulation
Question:	What can Florida's regulatory measures teach legislators about state intervention in nursing homes?
Sources:	*Miami Herald* articles, Florida statutes on nursing home care, interviews with nursing home administrators

Course:	*Economics of International Business*
Topic:	Marketing American products in Asia
Question:	Coca-Cola has shaped its marketing strategy to respond to national tastes in Thailand, Cambodia, and Viet Nam. Where has the company's strategy proved most successful? Why?
Sources:	*Wall Street Journal* articles, *Business Week* articles, Internet sources, Coca-Cola annual reports

In the examples above, these questions are specific enough to discuss in a college essay. The sources that will help a student to answer the questions are all primary sources.

So how do you get started? Most students find that ideas will flow if they sit down and write in a journal or notebook, on index cards, or on their computer. Without worrying about the final product, without the pressure of organizing their thoughts, they find that freewriting exercises, in whatever form, help them to think creatively.

Journal Writing

A journal can take many forms: a computer file in which you make a daily entry, a notebook in which you jot down ideas as they occur to you, or even a tape recorder, into which you can talk as you commute to or from work. Busy students find that making a record of ideas helps to jump-start the writing and research process.

Freewriting, Brainstorming, and Mind-Mapping

When you freewrite, brainstorm, or mind-map, you write down any idea, in any order, without worrying about making logical connections. Freewriting can take many forms, including lists, sentences, phrases, and diagrams. Freewriting lets you generate an abundance of material, which you can edit and shape when you sit down to write your first draft. When you see your ideas on paper, you can connect them with arrows to come up with a "map" of ideas that can lead you to a useful outline. See the following illustration for an example of freewriting.

A *n Example of Freewriting*

"Theodore Roosevelt's Ideas on Manhood"

Consider the illustrated example that follows. A student began freewriting by jotting down the title of Theodore Roosevelt's famous essay on manhood, "The Strenuous Life." Then, using arrows, the student noted which aspects of life Roosevelt himself thought were strenuous, that is, war, exercise, hunting, and risk-taking. Beginning with these words, the student then wrote down other associated words that popped into his head. As he looked at these words, the student discovered that the word *power* was important in all the areas Roosevelt wrote about. By linking this recurring word, the student began to see a pattern in Roosevelt's thinking. This pattern helped the student make his own analysis of what the "strenuous life" and manhood meant to Theodore Roosevelt.

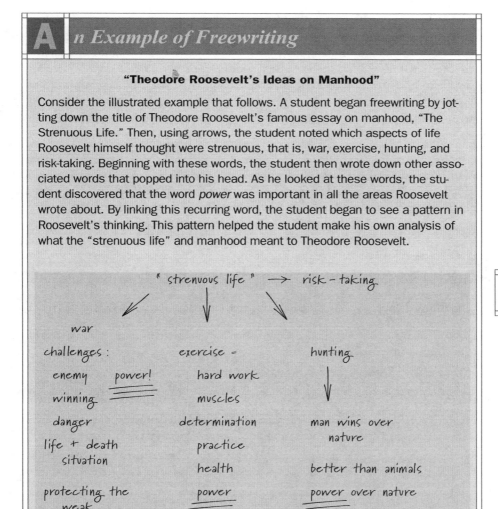

WRITING 7

Starting with Passages from Source Material

Often, typing out passages from a text helps you to analyze them. Typing forces you to think about the passage slowly and to "process" it more thoroughly than if you only underlined or highlighted it.

Outlining

It's likely that all of us learned how to make an outline at some time in our school careers. With Roman numerals, letters, and Arabic numbers, we organized our ideas into a plan that was supposed to structure our paper. Some of us, however, became proficient outliners without being able to transfer the outline structure to our actual writing.

More detailed—and potentially more helpful—than such an outline, a paragraph outline gives you a chance to think through an organizational plan for your paper, build in transitions, and begin to develop your ideas. A **paragraph outline** contains the main idea for each section of your paper and includes several sentences explaining that idea and showing ways that you can support it. A paragraph outline is useful to help organize the ideas generated by some form of freewriting.

Sample Paragraph Outline

How did Theodore Roosevelt's relationship with his sons reflect his ideas about manhood?

I. Introduction. Brief overview of Roosevelt's life. In this section, I'll tell about his marriage and give dates for the birth of his sons.

II. Roosevelt's ideas about manhood. In this paragraph, I'll talk about "The Strenuous Life," the essay where Roosevelt talks about a man's responsibilities and how men should behave.

III. Kermit. In this paragraph, I'll describe Kermit and tell what kind of a boy he was. Source will be biographies of Roosevelt.

IV. Relationship between Kermit and his father. I'll use letters from Roosevelt to Kermit about athletics at Harvard to show what Roosevelt valued.

V. Quentin. In this paragraph, I'll describe Quentin and tell what kind of boy he was. Source will be biographies of Roosevelt.

VI. Relationship with Quentin. What activities did Roosevelt share with his son?

VII. Conclusion. I'll relate my findings to the ideas that Roosevelt discussed in "The Strenuous Life" to show how the essay can be seen as an explanation of his relationship with his sons.

Visualizing a Reader

As you write, explain your ideas to a specific person. Your "imaginary reader" might be unknown to you or might be an interested friend, a sympathetic instructor, or a classmate who shares your interests.

PLANNING

Your plan need not be a formal outline with each section and subsection numbered. Some students use images and shapes to help them visualize the paper's organization. Some students create a map, moving from one point to another as they create a "road" of ideas.

Having a plan, however, will help you as you draft your paper. Here are five questions to keep in mind as you construct your plan:

1. What information does your reader need as background?
2. What are the main points you want to make in the essay?
3. How will you construct a transition between one point and the next?
4. Where will you include your evidence?
5. What might someone with an opposing view argue? Where will you consider opposing views in the paper?

DRAFTING

Any piece of college writing contains a beginning, where the reader discovers the focus of the paper; a middle section, where assertions are presented, supported by evidence; and a conclusion. These sections vary in length, depending on the length of the total paper. A two-page essay may well fit into the famous five-paragraph model: one paragraph for an introduction, three paragraphs for development, one paragraph for a conclusion.

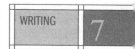

In a five- to seven-page paper, which is a popular length for college essays, the introduction may consist of several paragraphs, the development may cover several pages, and the conclusion may take one or more paragraphs.

Writing an Introduction

The first paragraphs of an essay should tell the reader, clearly and precisely, what the paper is about. Your reader should discover what question you are asking, what argument or analysis you are making in response to that question, and what sources you are using to answer the question.

A strong first paragraph also will help your reader understand the context for your question and, therefore, your paper. For example, the student writing about Theodore Roosevelt's relationship with his sons was interested in Roosevelt's self-proclaimed courage and manliness. The student learned from the course that Roosevelt's phrase "the strenuous life" served to defend many aspects of American culture, from international politics to the building of the Panama Canal. *In that context,* looking at how Roosevelt communicated his values to his children seemed interesting. A strong introduction would present this context so that the reader understands why the student is interested in answering the question about Roosevelt's relationship with his sons.

Weak introductions are vague and unfocused, such as this one for a literature paper:

> Kate Chopin's *The Awakening* can be looked at from many points of view. Many critics have examined the novel to see what it tells us about Chopin's ideas about women's lives. Indeed, by looking at the women artists in the novel, they discover some interesting things.

Except for finding out that this person will be writing on Kate Chopin's *The Awakening,* the reader will have no idea what "interesting things" critics have said about Chopin's women artists. Most important, the reader doesn't know what the writer thinks. In college, you are asked to do more than report about what other people think; you need to come up with an idea of your own.

Here is a better introduction on the same topic:

> Kate Chopin's *The Awakening* shows us the conflicts some women face when they want to express their creativity. When we look at the lives of two women artists in the novel, we can see that Chopin took a pessimistic view of the possibility of being a wife, mother, and artist.

This introduction tells the reader specifically the question being asked: What does Chopin think about the possibility of a woman's being a wife, mother, and artist? It tells the reader that in this paper, the writer both looks at two women artists and thinks Chopin's view is pessimistic. This writer has done a good job in just two sentences.

Your introduction may be one paragraph in a fairly short essay or several paragraphs in a longer essay. Some useful strategies for introductions include:

- beginning with a question
- beginning with a quotation
- beginning with an anecdote or illustration

Developing Paragraphs

A paragraph consists of a group of sentences that develops and supports an assertion. Usually, that assertion is expressed in the topic sentence. The topic sentence helps the reader to anticipate what idea you will develop in the paragraph. The rest of the paragraph develops the idea by offering evidence and supporting details. Each sentence in the paragraph relates to the main idea.

In papers that are longer than a page or two, you often cannot develop ideas fully in one paragraph. In that case, you will create paragraph **clusters** of two, three, or four paragraphs. Each paragraph within that cluster develops a subtopic of the main idea.

Within a paragraph, sentences follow one another logically. Sentences can be connected by **transitions** or by **repetition** of words. Here is one paragraph that uses both strategies:

> The controversy over home schooling focuses on the need for students to become socialized through **interaction** with other students. That **interaction,** in class and through extracurricular activities, helps students learn how to share ideas, work on teams, and respect others' needs. **Furthermore,** students in class learn that their own interests do not always dictate activities and decisions. **Nevertheless,** proponents of home schooling argue that despite the socializing potential of classroom learning, the potential for intellectual growth is severely limited.

In this paragraph, you can see that the word *interaction,* repeated in the first two sentences, connects those sentences logically. The next two sentences begin with transitional words, *furthermore* and *nevertheless,* that show the relationship of the sentence to the one preceding it.

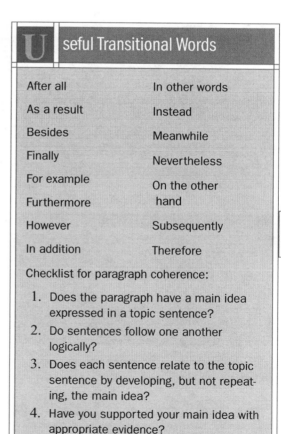

U seful Transitional Words

After all	In other words
As a result	Instead
Besides	Meanwhile
Finally	Nevertheless
For example	On the other
Furthermore	hand
However	Subsequently
In addition	Therefore

Checklist for paragraph coherence:

1. Does the paragraph have a main idea expressed in a topic sentence?
2. Do sentences follow one another logically?
3. Does each sentence relate to the topic sentence by developing, but not repeating, the main idea?
4. Have you supported your main idea with appropriate evidence?
5. Is each sentence grammatically correct?

7

Writing a Conclusion

A concluding paragraph both sums up your paper and points to its significance. Some students are used to creating a conclusion by restating the introduction. In a short paper, however, a concluding paragraph need not repeat the assertions you made in your introduction. A more creative concluding paragraph might:

- suggest the implications of your ideas
- show how your topic is part of a larger issue
- suggest how your ideas can lead to changes in your readers' attitudes, behavior, or actions

REVISING

Revising means reseeing. Often, it's easier to "resee" your essay a day or two after you've written it. Writers call that waiting period a "cool down," when they have time to change their perspective from writer to reader. Revising can happen on two levels: globally, which means that you look at organization and paragraph construction; and locally, which means you look at sentences and words. If you decide to move a paragraph on the third page to the second page, you are revising globally. If you decide to restructure sentences to eliminate unnecessary words, or if you change particular word choices, then you are revising locally.

As you read your essay, use the following five questions to help you discover where you want to revise:

Revision Checklist

1. Does the essay have a clear focus?
2. Does the essay have a logical organization?
3. Is each paragraph organized around one main point? Do you support your main points with evidence?
4. Is your style appropriate for college-level work?
5. Is the essay technically and mechanically correct?

1. *Does the essay have a clear focus?* You may have a clear idea of exactly what you intended to write about. Where is that idea clearly stated? To test whether the essay has a clear focus, read your first paragraphs and isolate the one or two sentences that give your main idea. Which sentences tell the reader what you are arguing? Which ones state the question you are answering or the problem you are trying to solve by writing this essay?

Your first paragraphs should help the reader to anticipate the structure of the essay: How will you answer your question? What sources will you examine? What texts will you discuss?

2. *Does the essay have a logical organization?* An essay should not be an interior monologue, a record of your own stream of consciousness. To test whether your essay has a logical structure, construct an outline *from the essay*

itself. Number the paragraphs; write the main point of each paragraph in a single sentence. Do these sentences follow one another logically? Does each paragraph help to support your main idea? Should some paragraphs be reordered? Are any points missing?

An essay should have transitions between paragraphs. The last sentence of one paragraph should relate to the first sentence of the next paragraph. Sometimes, you can help your reader see the relationship between those sentences by including transitional words such as *therefore, however, finally, consequently, similarly.* If you find yourself beginning each paragraph with *also,* you should recognize that you are merely listing points rather than organizing them logically.

3. *Do you support your main points with evidence?*   Sometimes, you may find a paragraph where one idea is repeated in different ways in several sentences. That paragraph lacks development. Choose the sentence that best expresses your point, make that the topic sentence of the paragraph, and, in revising, find support for the point with concrete evidence from readings or research.

You should develop your essay by making assertions and supporting those assertions with evidence from your sources. Among your tasks in writing an essay are drawing inferences from the texts you are reading, showing connections between texts, identifying differences between texts, and tracing the development of ideas from early texts to later ones. All of these tasks require that you read texts carefully and use them as evidence. When you quote a text, your reader should understand why you are quoting, how you are reading the passage, and what ideas you are taking from it.

Your essay should reflect your ability to *think critically.* **Summarizing** (distilling the content of what you have read) and **observing** (noting certain patterns that recur in texts) are only beginning stages of critical thinking. Your reader wants to see that you can ask questions about texts, find key passages, draw inferences, and formulate your own argument.

4. *Is your style appropriate for college-level work?*   Some students try to impress their instructor by using cumbersome words and convoluted sentence structure. Big words, however, are not as important as strong ideas. Instructors prefer writing that is clear, lively, and concrete. On the other hand, they don't want slang or jargon. If you have doubts about your style, ask your instructor if you may see a successful paper written for the course by another student. Pay close attention to the style; you'll see that direct and precise language conveys ideas most clearly.

5. *Is the essay technically and mechanically correct?*   If you have problems with grammar or sentence correctness, Appendix A may help you learn some basic rules.

THREE QUALITIES TO AIM FOR IN YOUR WRITING

Good writing has conciseness, clarity, and coherence. Here are some guidelines for editing your own work to enhance these three qualities.

Conciseness

Conciseness does not necessarily mean brevity; it does mean that unnecessary words are eliminated. Strong writing depends on strong nouns and verbs. Compare the following sentences:

> A majority of staff members have the capability of contributing very meaningfully to policy decisions.
>
> Many staff members can contribute significantly to policy decisions.

The second sentence eliminates long phrases and empty words. A strong, concrete subject noun (members) takes the place of a weak, abstract subject noun (majority). A strong verb (can contribute) takes the place of a weak verb (have).

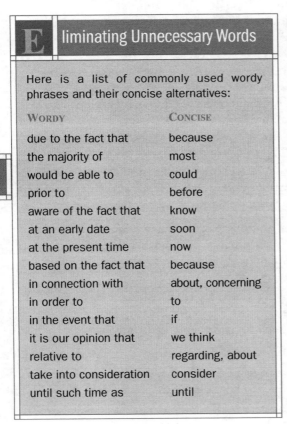

Eliminating Unnecessary Words

Here is a list of commonly used wordy phrases and their concise alternatives:

WORDY	CONCISE
due to the fact that	because
the majority of	most
would be able to	could
prior to	before
aware of the fact that	know
at an early date	soon
at the present time	now
based on the fact that	because
in connection with	about, concerning
in order to	to
in the event that	if
it is our opinion that	we think
relative to	regarding, about
take into consideration	consider
until such time as	until

Clarity

Clarity can be undermined by poor sentence structure or poor word choice. To check the clarity of a sentence, ask yourself: What is this sentence about? Do the subject and verb clearly indicate the sense of the sentence? To edit for better clarity, focus on the following:

- purpose
- subject
- verb
- construction
- word choice

Focus on the purpose. Sometimes the purpose is unclear:

It is the belief of the Accounting Department that the predicament was precipitated by a computational inaccuracy.

What is the purpose of this sentence? The writer seems to want to explain the cause of a problem. If so, the reader expects a sentence that reads: The problem was caused by this reason. Here is a revised sentence:

> The Accounting Department thinks the problem was caused by a computation error.

Focus on the subject. Sometimes, the real subject is hidden by poor construction:

> The use of this method of keeping records would promote increased efficiency.

In the sentence above, the subject is *use*. It is followed by two prepositional phrases (*of* this method, *of* keeping records) that are needed to clarify the word *use*. The actual subject of this sentence, however, is *method*. Here is a clearer sentence:

> This method of record-keeping would promote increased efficiency.

Focus on the verb. Sometimes, the real verb is hidden by poor construction:

> An investigation of all possible sources of funding was undertaken.

In this sentence, the passive verb form *was undertaken* obscures the real action of the sentence, which is the act of *investigating*. Here is a revised sentence:

> The department investigated all possible sources of funding.

Focus on construction. When the subject and verb are separated by long strings of phrases and clauses, the reader has trouble following the sense of the sentence:

> The bank, which had a long history of poor management and shaky investments, beginning in 1972 when a merger failed to strengthen its image in the banking world, and continuing to the present day, finally began to show signs of irreversible weakness during the present administration.

In this sentence, the subject *bank* is four lines away from the verb *began*. A revision would place the subject and verb closer to one another:

> The bank's long history of poor management and shaky investments began in 1972, when a merger failed to strengthen its image in the banking world. Under the present administration, the bank shows signs of irreversible weakness.

Focus on word choice. Your writing is as strong as the words you choose. Strong words are direct, lively, and precise; they are not necessarily polysyllabic, Latinate, and flowery:

> The organization endeavors to impact favorably upon the environment by promoting a recycling program to encompass all office waste materials.

A sentence with better word choice might be:

> The company's recycling program reflects its concern for the environment.

Some students worry that their vocabulary is too limited for college-level work. The best way to build a vocabulary is by reading. If you read challenging material, look up words you don't know. If you discover interesting words that you'd like to use in your own writing, keep a list with both the word and its use in context. Whatever you read, you'll grow in your facility with language.

As you write, you might struggle to find just the word you want. A quick way to jog your memory is by using the thesaurus or dictionary on your word-processing program. Click on Tools, then Language. You'll find Thesaurus as one of your options. A thesaurus is a compilation of synonyms. If you highlight any word in your own writing and click on Thesaurus, you'll find other choices that may be more appropriate. Experienced writers caution against using a thesaurus to choose a word you never have seen before just because it looks fancy. Words have connotations that often are revealed only when you know how they are used in context. The thesaurus option also includes a dictionary, so you can check the meaning of a word you may not be sure about.

Coherence

In writing, coherence means that one sentence relates logically to the next. Transitional words, when necessary, help the reader to understand the relationship among sentences. In one paragraph, all sentences develop one idea; no information is missing, and no irrelevant information is included. Here are two sentences that lack coherence:

> Because the company was concerned about contract forms, it hired a law firm to review them. There have been many changes in contract law during the last 10 years, and the company discovered that its forms were obsolete.

These two sentences seem choppy because they are not logically connected. The end of the first sentence does not lead the reader into the second sentence. The second sentence begins with an idea that is only hinted at in the first sentence. Through revised sentence structure or the use of transitions, a writer can help readers understand the logic of the writing:

> The law firm advised the company to change its contract forms. Those forms, in use for a decade, were now outdated because of major changes in contract law.

WORD PROCESSING

Computers make writing deceptively easy, because instead of typing an essay over and over as you move from draft to revision, you can cut and paste, delete passages with the press of a key, change fonts at will, and print out a piece of work that looks clean, neat and professional. Experienced writers, though, report that they edit both on screen and on hard copies. They don't rely on some computer functions—spell checkers, for example, or grammar checkers, to insure correctness.

Computers do make some tasks easier:

- You can create lists identified by bullet points or numbers. This function appears on the Tool Bar.
- You can number pages. Click on Insert, then Page Numbers for options.
- You can change spacing, margins, and fonts. Click on Format.
- You can insert endnotes or footnotes. Click on Insert, then Reference, then Footnote. When you type your information, the note will automatically be entered at the bottom of the page or the end of your document.
- You can import a passage from a text or note file into your current work. For example, if you take notes on a computer, you can highlight a passage, click on Edit, click on Cut or Copy and close your file. Open your essay, locate the place you want to insert the passage, and click on Paste.
- You can replace words throughout an essay by asking your computer to find a word and replace it with another. Click on Edit, then Replace. This function is useful if you decide that one word is more appropriate than something you have chosen to use; or if you decide that you over-use a word and want to replace it with another word.
- You can find word choices or meanings by clicking on Tools, then Language, and then on the Thesaurus or Dictionary option.
- You can edit your essay or ask someone else to edit your essay and indicate suggested changes using Track Changes, an option under Tools. This function highlights suggestions in a bright color, making them visible as you read through your essay.

Tips for Writing on a Computer

1. Save your work often. Back up your drafts during the writing process as well as at the end of each writing session. "My computer crashed" is an excuse your professors are tired of hearing.

2. Proofread carefully. Don't rely on spell checkers or grammar checkers to correct your errors. Neither tool can understand the cents of your own sentences. Or do I mean sense? Neither a spell checker nor grammar checker found "cents" to be an error. After all, it's spelled correctly and it's a noun. You need to take responsibility for correctness.

3. After cutting and pasting passages, make sure the material reads logically. Students often cut and paste without creating needed transitions or other logical connections.

4. Give your revisions a clear file name so you don't hand in an early draft by mistake.

5. Print out your work for a final editing. Experienced writers often find mistakes on a hard copy that they missed when reading on the screen.

Writing is a challenge for all writers, even professionals. No one sits down at a computer and produces a perfect piece of writing. Instead, writing is the product of much thinking, questioning, and revising. It is an ongoing process that reflects the learning and growth you will experience as you progress through college.

GRAMMAR BRUSHUP

ost of us learned principles of grammar far back in our school careers. This chapter will remind you of what you may already know, teach you some things you may not know, and serve as a reference for revising your work.

THE PARTS OF SPEECH

The parts of speech are the names of words that perform different functions in our language.

NOUN. A **noun** names a person, animal, place, object, or idea:

> Edward
> psychology
> the Empire State Building

These words all are nouns.

PRONOUN. A **pronoun** takes the place of a noun and may be singular or plural:

> *Singular:* I, you, he, she, it
> *Plural:* we, you, they

Pronouns, like nouns, may show possession. Possessive pronouns are:

> *Singular:* my, mine, your, yours, her, hers, his, its
> *Plural:* our, ours, your, yours, their, theirs

Taken from: *New Beginnings: A Reference Guide for Adult Learners*, by Linda Simon

121

VERB. A **verb** describes action, shows a state of being, or helps other verbs. These verbs show action:

> tumble
> accelerate
> invent

Verbs that show a state of being include *is, are, was*, and *were:*

> Edward *is* nine.

In this example, *is,* a form of *to be,* expresses Edward's age, not something that Edward is doing.

In the examples below, forms of *have* and *be* serve as helping verbs:

> The psychologist *has* studied extrasensory perception.
> His work *is* published regularly in professional journals.

ADJECTIVE. An **adjective** describes a noun or pronoun:

> the *unruly* child
> an *intense* argument

ADVERB. An **adverb** describes a verb, an adjective, or another adverb:

> The carpenter worked *carefully.*
> My instructor gave directions *too quickly.*

Carefully and *quickly* describe verbs; *too* describes another adverb.

PREPOSITION. A **preposition** is a word that can be joined with a noun to function as an adjective or adverb:

> The book *on* the table is my textbook.
> The man *without* a hat is my husband.

Some common prepositions include:

about	above	across
after	against	along (or along with)
among	around	as
at	before	behind
below	beneath	beside
besides	between	beyond
by	despite	during
except	for	from
in	inside	into
near	next	of

on	out	over
since	through	to
under	until	up
upon	with	within
without		

CONJUNCTION. A **conjunction** joins words, phrases, or clauses:

Political Science *and* Psychology are my favorite classes this semester.
I arrived late, *but* the lecture had not yet started.

The most common conjunctions are:

and, but, for, nor, or, so, yet

Other conjunctions come in pairs:

both—and
either—or
neither—nor
not only—but also
whether—or

Here are two examples:

Neither the state legislature *nor* the federal government opposed the new law.
Both Vermont *and* Massachusetts support recycling.

WHAT IS A SENTENCE?

A **sentence** is a group of words that contains a *subject* (a noun) and a *predicate* (a verb) and makes sense alone. Another term for *sentence* is *independent clause.* Consider two examples:

The boy laughed.
The attorney, in practice for 10 years, presented an argument in defense of his client.

The first example is a sentence because it contains a subject (the boy) and a predicate (laughed). The subject contains a noun; the predicate in this case is a verb. You know both who did something and what was done.

The second example contains the same elements: a subject (the attorney) and a predicate (presented an argument). In this sentence, the verb *presented* takes an object, *argument,* that tells us what the attorney presented.

Sentence Fragments

A **sentence fragment** is a group of words that does not make sense alone because it lacks either a subject or a verb, or because it contains a word or phrase that makes it a *dependent clause* (it is dependent on additional words in order to make sense). Here are three examples:

> Under the new law in effect since October.
> For example, courses with no midterm or final exam.
> Despite the author's argument about the comparative economic strength of both economies.

In the third example, the word *despite* signals the beginning of a dependent clause. This clause can serve as the beginning of a sentence:

> Despite the author's argument about the comparative economic strength of both economies, the book fails to present a clear forecast of future growth.

In this sentence, the subject is *book* and the verb is *fails*. This subject and verb make the passage a sentence.

Combined Sentences

To keep our writing from being choppy, we often combine sentences. The simplest way to combine sentences is by using a comma followed by a conjunction: *and, but, for, nor, or, so, yet*. For example:

> Rain drenched the garden, *and* the flowers grew.
> I will take the train, *or* I will wait for the bus.
> I tried to reach you, *but* your phone was turned off.

There is a complete sentence on either side of each conjunction.

The *semicolon* may be used instead of a conjunction to combine complete sentences:

> I may take the train; on the other hand, I may wait for the bus.

Another, more sophisticated way of combining sentences is to turn one part of the sentence into a dependent clause. A **dependent clause** may contain a subject and a verb, but it is not a complete sentence because it is introduced by a preposition (or a prepositional phrase) or an adverb (or an adverbial phrase). Consider these two examples:

1. I tried to reach you. I discovered your phone was turned off.
   When I tried to reach you, I discovered your phone was turned off.
2. Rain drenches the garden. The flowers will grow.
   After rain drenches the garden, the flowers will grow.

GRAMMAR BRUSHUP

In these two examples, the words in italics form a clause. That clause cannot stand independently; it is not a sentence.

Run-On Sentences and Comma Splices

When two sentences are incorrectly combined, the result is a run-on sentence or a comma splice. A comma alone cannot serve as a connector between two sentences. For example:

> The author argues about the strength of both economies, the book fails to present a clear forecast of future growth.

When a comma is used incorrectly to combine sentences, the error is called a **comma splice**. When the comma is omitted altogether, the error is called a **run-on sentence**.

To correctly combine the two sentences in the example, you may add the word *but* after the comma:

> The author argues about the strength of both economies, but the book fails to present a clear forecast of future growth.

Another way of combining these two sentences is by using a semicolon and a transitional phrase:

> The author argues about the strength of both economies; nevertheless, the book fails to present a clear forecast of future growth.

PRONOUN PROTOCOL

When you substitute a pronoun for a noun, your reader needs to know precisely what noun is being replaced. For example:

> The boy is 15, and he is tall for his age.

The word *he* is a pronoun in this sentence, replacing the noun *boy*.

Sometimes, the reference is not as clear as in the example. The following sentence does not show a clear referent for the pronoun *it:*

> Whenever an economic indicator points to a possible problem, it causes a reaction in government.

What causes the reaction: the indicator or the problem? This sentence needs to be restructured as follows to avoid confusion:

> Whenever an economic indicator points to a possible problem, government reacts.

GRAMMAR BRUSHUP **8**

Noun and Pronoun Agreement

Singular nouns need to be replaced by singular pronouns, plural nouns by plural pronouns:

Singular: The lecturer presented new ideas to the audience. He made sure that he defined all his key terms.

Plural: The speakers on the panel were well informed about campaign strategies, based on their own experiences.

The following sentence, however, reveals a common problem:

Each speaker was well informed about campaign strategies, based on their own experiences.

The noun *speaker* is singular; the pronoun *their* is plural. Therefore, the sentence is grammatically incorrect.

Making the sentence correct, however, poses another problem: The speakers on the panel included two women and two men. Here is another sentence:

Each speaker was well informed about campaign strategies, based on his or her own experiences.

This correction, however, is wordy.

Using a plural noun in this sentence avoids both wordiness and the problem of using pronouns that designate gender:

The speakers were well informed about campaign strategies, based on their own experiences.

HANDLING VERBS

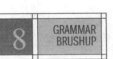

Subject–Verb Agreement

Just as nouns and pronouns must agree in number, subjects and verbs must agree in number (singular or plural) and person (first, second, or third):

Singular: The poll shows that the Democratic candidate has a 20-percent lead.

Poll is a noun in the third-person singular. Singular verbs in the third person generally end in *s*.

Plural: The polls indicate a healthy lead for our candidate.

Polls is a noun in the third-person plural. Plural verbs in the third person generally do not end in *s*.

As with nouns and pronouns, sometimes agreement problems occur, as in the following case:

Incorrect: Three polls were taken. *Each* of the polls *show* a substantial margin of victory.

Even though three polls were taken, in the second sentence, you are indicating the results of each single poll. *Each* is the subject of the sentence; because it is singular, it must take a singular verb.

Verb Parts

Sometimes, a verb is just one word in a sentence:

The boy *jumped* from the ledge.

Here, the verb is *jumped*.

Sometimes, however, the verb is more than one word:

The boy *had jumped* from the ledge before his father came to help him.

Here, the verb is two words: *had jumped*. Generally, a sentence is clearer if the words that make up a verb are not interrupted by other words.

Some instructors insist on following two grammatical conventions:

1. Don't split infinitives. An **infinitive** is a verb form that begins with *to:* to go, to see, to plummet.

   Incorrect: He decided to finally go to Europe.

   Correct: He finally decided to go to Europe.

   Finally, he decided to go to Europe.

   He decided finally to go to Europe.

2. Don't split verb parts. Some verbs consist of several words: have been ill, was going, has taken.

   Incorrect: He *could* definitely *have avoided* the mistake by doing nothing.

   Correct: He definitely *could have avoided* the mistake by doing nothing.

GRAMMAR BRUSHUP 8

PLACING PHRASES AND CLAUSES LOGICALLY

To avoid confusion, place phrases and clauses near the words they modify:

Confusing: Religious intolerance caused waves of emigration toward dissenters.

In this sentence, the phrase *toward dissenters* should modify *religious intolerance*. Here is the restructured sentence:

> *Clear:* Religious intolerance toward dissenters caused waves of emigration.

In the following sentence, the phrase *from Oxford University* describes the noun *speaker:*

> The speaker who delivered the opening address, from Oxford University, generated hearty applause.

As the sentence is constructed, it sounds as if either the opening address came from Oxford University or the speaker delivered the address while at Oxford University.

Placing the phrase next to the noun it modifies avoids this kind of confusion:

> The speaker from Oxford University, who delivered the opening address, generated hearty applause.

Modifiers must refer to a word in the sentence; if they do not, they are called **dangling modifiers.** The sentence below has a dangling modifier and needs to be reconstructed:

> Drawing upon campaign experiences, the audience listened attentively to the speaker.

However, it was the speaker, not the audience, who drew upon campaign experiences. Here is a revised sentence:

> Drawing upon campaign experiences, the speaker captivated the audience.

PUNCTUATION

Comma

The **comma** is a useful form of punctuation because it helps you write clearly by separating parts of a sentence from other parts. The main uses for the comma are:

- to work along with a conjunction that joins two complete sentences

  The book is difficult, but I understand most of it.

- to separate items in a series

  The author discusses social, cultural, and personal influences on behavior.

- to set off an introductory word or phrase

  Usually, there are no obstacles to success.

- to set off a nonrestrictive phrase or clause from the rest of the sentence

    Ronald Reagan, a Republican President, made substantial economic reforms.

In the last example, the phrase a *Republican President* is **nonrestrictive:** It is not necessary for the reader or the sense of the sentence. The writer assumes that the reader knows who Reagan is and cites Reagan's political affiliation simply as additional information.

If the reader does need the information in the phrase or clause, then the phrase or clause is **restrictive.**

    The speaker who advised Reagan provided useful background information about the current crisis.

In this sentence, readers need to know *which* speaker the writer is referring to; he is, specifically, *the speaker who advised Reagan.* That information, which is necessary for the sense of the sentence, is included in a restrictive, or necessary, clause.

Two other uses for commas are:

- to set off direct quotations

    "Bring me the book," he demanded.

    (Notice here that the comma goes *inside* the quotation marks.)

- in dates and addresses

    On June 4, 1992, my sister graduated from college in Washington, D.C.

Semicolon

Semicolons serve two main purposes:

- to separate items in a series when one or more items contain a comma

    The panel included John Allen, last year's award winner; Preston Smith; and this year's award winner, Marian Copley.

- to join two sentences when no conjunction is used to connect them

    The reception convened at 10; nevertheless, a few people still came late.

Remember: Nevertheless cannot join two independent clauses unless a semicolon is used. Neither can other transitional words, such as:

furthermore	then	however	therefore
likewise	thus	similarly	

Quotation Marks

Quotation marks enclose the exact words of a speaker or writer. Notice how a quotation by novelist Katherine Anne Porter is used in different ways by different writers. First, the quotation is unbroken:

> As Katherine Anne Porter wrote, "Most people won't realize that writing is a craft. You have to take your apprenticeship in it like anything else."

In the next example, breaking the quotation makes for a more conversational tone:

> "Most people won't realize that writing is a craft," said the novelist Katherine Anne Porter. "You have to take your apprenticeship in it like anything else."

Next, excerpts from the quotation are used:

> Katherine Anne Porter called writing "a craft" that requires an "apprenticeship . . . like anything else."

In this example, notice the use of three dots to signify the omission of words from the original quotation; these dots are called an **ellipsis**.

In the fourth example, the end of the quotation is left out:

> Katherine Anne Porter saw writing as "a craft" and advised beginning writers "to take your apprenticeship in it. . . ."

Here, notice that there are four dots at the end of quoted material: Three dots signify an ellipsis; one dot is the period for the sentence.

Quotation marks are also used to enclose the titles of short poems, short stories, magazine or newspaper articles, essays, television episodes, and chapter titles:

> Yesterday's editorial, "Medicare Medicine," offered some concrete suggestions for reform.

Place commas and periods *inside* quotation marks; place semicolons and colons *outside* quotation marks. *Remember:* The end punctuation in the original quotation is dropped in favor of the punctuation you need for the correctness of your sentence. Suppose you wanted to quote the following sentence by Robert Louis Stevenson: "The difficulty of literature is not to write, but to write what you mean." Here is one possible sentence:

> "The difficulty of literature is not to write, but to write what you mean," said Stevenson.

In this example, the end punctuation of the quotation, a period, is dropped. A comma, necessary for your sentence, is inserted instead. Notice that the comma goes *inside* the quotation marks.

USING THE ACTIVE VOICE

Nouns and verbs are important parts of speech. More than other words, they convey the sense of what you want to say. When you use the **active voice**, the subject of the sentence acts; the verb describes that action:

> The candidate announced his platform last week.

In this sentence, the subject, *candidate*, took action: He announced his ideas.
When you use the **passive voice**, the subject of the sentence is acted upon:

> The platform was announced last week.

In this sentence, the subject *platform* is not taking action; it is acted upon. But by whom? Who announced the platform? The sentence does not tell us.
Because passive construction omits the real subject of the sentence, its use makes writing confusing and weak. Sometimes, students use the passive construction when they feel uncomfortable about making their own argument.

POSSESSIVES

The people or things that nouns represent are able to possess or own. An apostrophe followed by an *s* indicates possession:

> Robert's lecture was more interesting than John's.
> James Joyce's *Ulysses* was the text for my English class.

Pronouns also are able to show possession, but possessive pronouns are not formed by adding an apostrophe and an *s*. See "The Parts of Speech" for a list of possessive pronouns.

COMMON USAGE ERRORS

GRAMMAR
BRUSHUP 8

This section focuses on commonly confused words; it is designed to help you choose the correct word for your sentence.

ACCEPT, EXCEPT. *Accept* means to receive or agree to; *except* means *but:*

- ▪ The applicant decided to accept the position.
- ▪ Everyone except John went on the trip.

AFFECT, EFFECT. *Affect,* a verb, means to change or influence; *effect,* a noun, means result:

- ▪ The war affected women's job opportunities.
- ▪ The effect of the war can be seen in the current workforce.

AGGRAVATE, IRRITATE. *Aggravate* means to make worse; *irritate* means to annoy:

- The noisy children aggravated my headache.
- The noisy children irritated their grandfather.

ALL READY, ALREADY. *All ready* means prepared; *already* means previously:

- We were all ready to go on the trip.
- The tickets already had arrived.

ALL RIGHT. *All right* is always two words:

- Our plans were all right with my parents.

ALLUSION, ILLUSION. *Allusion* is an indirect reference to something; *illusion* is an image or appearance:

- The horror film contained allusions to *Frankenstein* and *Dracula*.
- When the monster appeared, the victims at first thought they were perceiving an illusion.

A LOT. *A lot,* meaning *much,* usually is too colloquial an expression for a college essay; *alot* is incorrect.

AMONG, BETWEEN. *Among* is appropriate when the emphasis is on distribution rather than individual relationships; *between* is used to denote a one-to-one relationship, regardless of the number of items; it can be used when the number is unspecified or when more than two items are enumerated:

- I had to choose a partner from among my best friends.
- Finally, I chose between Sue and Mary.

AMOUNT, NUMBER. *Amount* refers to quantities that you cannot count; *number* refers to objects you can count:

- A large amount of food is needed for the starving people of Uganda.
- A number of charitable organizations have decided to contribute.

8 GRAMMAR BRUSHUP

ANYONE, ANY ONE. *Anyone* means any person; *any one* means any single person or thing:

- Anyone can attend the conference.
- Any one of the speakers can answer your question.

BAD, BADLY. *Bad* is an adjective (it must describe a noun); *badly* is an adverb (it must describe a verb, an adjective, or another adverb):

- The bad apple was moldy.
- The pianist performed badly on Friday night.

BESIDE, BESIDES. *Beside* means next to; *besides* means in addition to or moreover:

- The moderator sat beside the main speaker.
- Besides making a clear argument, he gave strong examples.

CAN, MAY. *Can* refers to the ability to do something; *may* refers to permission to do something or to the possibility that something may occur:

- Because he was trained in carpentry, Bill can build a house.
- Bill may build a house on our property.

COMPLEMENT, COMPLIMENT. *Complement* means to complete or enhance; *compliment* is a flattering remark:

- Hiring an accountant complements our support staff.
- The professor complimented my latest essay.

CONSCIENCE, CONSCIOUS. *Conscience* allows us to distinguish between right and wrong; *conscious* means aware of or alert:

- His conscience told him not to cheat.
- He was conscious of his parents' influence.

CONTINUAL, CONTINUOUS. *Continual* refers to the repetition of an activity; *continuous* means without interruption:

- His continual failure on math tests caused him to hire a tutor.
- Yesterday's continuous rain caused flooding.

COUNCIL, COUNSEL. *Council* means a group of people; *counsel* can be a noun, meaning advice, or a verb, meaning to advise:

- The mayor's council established a youth club.
- The club's director counseled members.

CRITERIA, CRITERION. *Criteria* is the plural of *criterion,* meaning basis of judgment:

- The most important criterion for hiring a teacher is the ability to make ideas clear.

GRAMMAR
BRUSHUP   8

DATA. *Data* is the plural of *datum,* meaning fact:

- The data collected by the researchers support adopting a new method of experimentation.

Note: Because *data* is a plural noun, it takes a plural form of the verb.

DIFFERENT FROM. The preposition *from* is the correct word to use with *different:*

- My version of the report is different from yours.

DISINTERESTED, UNINTERESTED. *Disinterested* means unbiased; *uninterested* means not interested:

- We brought the problem to a disinterested mediator.
- The mayor was uninterested in solving the problem himself.

EXPLICIT, IMPLICIT. *Explicit* means fully expressed; *implicit* means implied:

- The contract explicitly stated our responsibilities.
- Close analysis sometimes reveals the implicit meaning of a poem.

FARTHER, FURTHER. *Farther* refers to physical distance; *further* means more or additional:

- You need to go farther down the road to find the restaurant.
- He argued further to convince me to accept his position.

FEWER, LESS. *Fewer* refers to things you can count; *less* refers to things that are not countable:

- He brought fewer supplies to the laboratory than I did.
- I had less difficulty completing the lab experiment.

GOOD, WELL. *Good* is an adjective; *well* can be either an adjective (meaning in good health) or an adverb (meaning in a good manner, skillfully):

- We had good weather for the picnic.
- The boys played volleyball well.

IMPLY, INFER. *Imply* means to suggest; *infer* means to draw a conclusion from something:

- His behavior implied his attitude toward the group.
- We inferred that he wished he were not participating.

ITS, IT'S. *Its* is a possessive of the pronoun *it; it's* is a contraction of *it is:*

- The wind knocked the statue off its pedestal.
- It's unusual to have such a storm.

LAY, LIE. *Lay* means to put something down or to place an object (the past tense of *lay* is *laid*); *lie* means to recline (the past tense of *lie* is *lay*):

- Be careful when you lay the crystal bowl on the table.
- My cousin lay on the beach for the whole vacation.

LIKE, AS. *Like* should be followed by a noun (or noun phrase); *as* should be followed by a clause containing a subject and verb:

- The child looks like his father.
- The musician played the Bach fugue as it ought to be played.

LOOSE, LOSE. *Loose* means unfastened; *lose* means to misplace:

- The awning became loose and began to fall.
- Watch your belongings so you don't lose anything.

MEDIA, MEDIUM. *Media* is the plural of *medium,* which refers to a means or mode:

- The media reported the bombing in great detail.
- Television, though, seemed the most suitable medium to convey enough information.

PRECEDE, PROCEED. *Precede* means to go before; *proceed* means to move forward:

- The main speaker preceded the rest of the panel.
- The committee will proceed on my application as soon as it is complete.

PRINCIPAL, PRINCIPLE. *Principal* means the director of a school or the first (or highest) in rank; *principle* means rule or theory:

- The principal attraction of New York City is its theaters.
- Cheating goes against my principles of ethical behavior.

STATIONERY, STATIONARY. *Stationery* means writing paper; *stationary* means fixed in place:

- My stationery is imprinted with my name and address.
- The old warship remained stationary in the harbor.

THAN, THEN. *Than* can be a conjunction or a preposition, referring to a comparison; *then* is an adverb referring to time:

- The student would prefer to take a written test than to take an oral exam.
- After we complete the questionnaire, then we can leave.

GRAMMAR
BRUSHUP   8

WHO, WHOM. *Who* is a subjective pronoun (it replaces a subject in a sentence); *whom* is an objective pronoun (it replaces an object in a sentence):

- I saw the actor who performed last night.
- Let me know to whom I should send this letter.

WHO'S, WHOSE. *Who's* is a contraction for *who is* or *who has; whose* is a possessive adjective:

- Who's attending the concert tonight?
- Whose tickets were left in the reception room?

YOUR, YOU'RE. *Your* is a possessive adjective; *you're* is a contraction for *you are:*

- Your talk was the best on the panel.
- You're going to be invited to another conference.

This brief grammar review may help you to correct some problems as you write your college essays. Most students find it helpful to have a grammar handbook on their bookshelf. See "Additional Resources" for some popular and widely used handbooks.

ADDITIONAL RESOURCES

Hacker, Diane. *A Writer's Handbook*, 4th ed. Boston: Bedford Books, 2000.

Harris, Muriel. *Prentice Hall Reference Guide to Grammar and Usage,* 6th ed. Upper Saddle River, NJ: Prentice Hall, 2005.

Troyka, Lynn Quitman. *Simon & Schuster Quick Access Reference for Writers,* 3rd ed. Upper Saddle River, NJ: Prentice Hall, 2000.

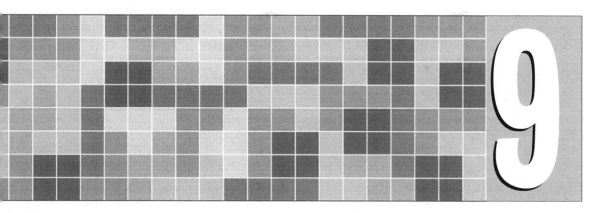

Why Teams?

GOALS

■ Understand advantages of the team approach to work.

■ Grasp importance of "buy-in" for team effectiveness.

■ Relate team concepts to your own work opportunities and challenges.

Although analogies tend to hide as much as they reveal, let's begin our conversation about teams by considering sports teams. Perhaps we can learn basic lessons from basketball, football, baseball, and other team sports that can enlighten and inform our approach to work teams.

What's your ticket? Basketball? On the court, five players form a team. One person, of course, could dribble the ball downcourt and shoot (making basketball a one-on-one sport similar to tennis singles), but the sport has evolved as a team endeavor for at least five reasons:

1. A team offers the possibility of more talent on the floor. All parts of the game move more quickly due to the specialized skills of individual players and the mutual cooperation of team members.

Imagine the limitations of one player compared to the team. That person would have to do it all, including jumping, shooting, rebounding, playing defense, and so forth. At least two disadvantages of this approach come to mind. First, the person

Taken from: *Learning Team Skills*, by Arthur H. Bell and Dayle M. Smith

probably cannot be equally good at each of those sports skills. A great re-bounder, for example, is not often a great ball-handler or dribbler. Second, the player who tries to do it all quickly becomes exhausted.

Let's translate this basketball analogy into the practical world of business and other organizations. In business and school endeavors, you require a broad range of talent to understand problems, recognize opportunities, and carry on the many processes necessary to meet the organization's goals. Even the smallest company needs someone adept at financial management, some-one attuned to personnel recruitment and development, someone to oversee operations, someone who is good with the public and press, and yes, some-one to sweep the floors at night. This team understands the importance of allowing each member to do his or her job. Team members are careful not to trespass unnecessarily onto one another's job responsibilities. In short, they trust one another to carry out each of their specialized tasks. The com-pany as a whole works well because each member of the team performs well.

INSIGHT 1	The team approach brings together the specialized skills of many individuals to resolve problems, seize opportunities, and meet organizational goals.

Your Turn

Call to mind a team on which you served in business or school. List the specialized strengths of each of the team members. Was the team missing any particular skills it needed to reach its goals? If so, how did the team make up for this skill deficit?

2. Each player can count on backup in case of a stumble, a bad game, or an injury.

A team provides an insurance policy of sorts for unexpected interrup-tions and disabilities. Even when one of the team's stars is unavailable for play, the concerted efforts of other team members can often make up the difference and achieve success.

In the same way, a team in a business or academic setting ensures that important goals can be met regardless of the ups and downs of individual team members. Too much is at stake in such environments to risk failure over one member's sudden ill health, family emergency, job transfer, or other unexpected circumstance. The Broadway slogan for this ongoing effort continues to be, "The show must go on." The cast—or team—pulls together to fulfill its mission even if key members are missing in action.

Teams provide a backup system that ensures continuity and mission fulfillment even if particular team members are unable to perform.	**INSIGHT 2**

Your Turn

Think about a time when a team on which you served was "left in the lurch" by the sudden absence of one of the key members of the team. Did your team survive this change? If so, how did your team compensate for the missing member? What was the ultimate result?

3. Individual eccentricities are tempered by the team for the good of the game.

In basketball, some players love to shoot the ball. Even when they miss repeatedly, they try and try again. If their failure to consistently make baskets begins to harm the team's efforts and success, team members take it upon themselves to change the "ball-hog's" behavior. When the team refuses to pass the ball to the ball-hog, the message comes through loud and clear: Quit shooting all the time and become more of a team player. In this way, individual idiosyncrasies are suppressed for the good of the team effort.

Similarly, on business and school teams, the wild ideas of some team members get tested by the judgment and experience of the rest of the team. If the team as a whole rejects the wild ideas of one member, those ideas usually fade away and play no role in the eventual report, project, or other activity developed by the team. This self-censoring function of teams is a valuable aid to upper management. Without the idea filters naturally provided by teams, upper management could easily face a plethora of documents, all written by individuals, and all expressing highly individual ideas about company problems and opportunities. It would then be the difficult task of upper management to sift through the set of often bizarre ideas in search of a few that made sense. Teams take much of this burden from upper management by squelching unworkable ideas from the outset.

Peer pressure on teams operates to enforce common sense judgments and ideas. Extreme or impractical ideas are usually rejected by the team before such ideas find their place in the work output of the team.	**INSIGHT 3**

Your Turn

Think about a time when one of your team members expressed an idea that was judged to be "crazy" or "way off track" by the rest of the team. How did other team members let this person know that the idea did not meet the approval of the team? How did the person react? What was the ultimate result for the person and the team?

---

4. Motivation increases as team members take pride in one another and try not to let each other down.

When members of a basketball team win their league championship, they do not come to the microphone to speak about "motivation from my million dollar salary" or "special treatment I was given by the coach." Instead, they almost always talk about the inspiration they received from their teammates; the effort all members gave so as not to let each other down; and the powerful influence each member felt by seeing other team members working so hard for victory.

That same kind of team motivation occurs in business and school environments. When a meeting is called for 9:00 A.M., you try to be on time, not merely because your boss expects promptness, but because you respect the time of your fellow team members. You do not want them sitting around waiting for you to arrive. When an approaching deadline requires that the team work late, you do your part in seeing the project through to completion. You are willing to go the extra mile not only because you want the project to be successful, but because you do not want to let your teammates down.

This is not to say that we automatically become close friends with all team members we serve with over the course of a business or academic career. Some team members don't earn our respect and it is hard to feel much obligation, responsibility, or liking for them. But other team members—perhaps the majority we encounter—are hard-working, well-intentioned coworkers with whom we feel bonds of camaraderie. In these cases, a significant factor in our motivation to do a good job and see the project through to success stems directly from our feelings toward other team members. Esprit d'corps on a team, in fact, can be one of the most powerful motivators in professional life.

INSIGHT 4

Teams whose members respect and like one another gain the advantage of motivation internal to the team. Members of the team want to perform not only for external rewards, but for the internal rewards of partnership, mutual respect, and friendship engendered within the team.

Recall a team made up of people you liked and admired. How did these positive feelings toward other team members influence your performance on that team? Would you have performed differently if you had little liking or admiration for your fellow team members?

5. The task of beating the opponent requires the combined talents of five players.

Finally, teams are required in sports because opponents are strong and shrewd. In other words, external challenges have much to do with the necessity for forming teams. In the case of basketball, it would be folly for a single player to go up against an opposing team of five players. Teams form in response to the challenges they face.

Let's take business examples of this same principle. If the "opponent" to a new product is millions of consumers who don't know about the product, a company wisely assembles a marketing team to take on this significant challenge. If a competitor comes out with a similar product to your own but priced considerably less, your company will probably act quickly to put together a response team made up of representatives from marketing, research and development, accounting, operations, and other specialities to determine how this challenge can be met and overcome.

Powerful challenges must be met by powerful responses. Such power often comes in the form of a talented, motivated team.

INSIGHT 5

Remember a time when your company or school organization faced a significant challenge or problem and, in response, formed a team on which you served. In what ways was the membership of the team determined by the nature of the challenge or problem? In your opinion, were members well-chosen for the responsibilities they had to perform? How successfully was the challenge or problem met by the team?

TEAMS AND BUY-IN

In the best of all worlds, companies would be made up of individuals, work groups, departments, and divisions all equally committed to reaching common company goals. In such a world, the head of finance would not mind giving up 50 percent of his department's budget if that sacrifice would help the Marketing Department do a better job for the company.

Anyone who has worked even a few days in an organization of any size quickly realizes that politics play a major role in determining the behavior of individuals and groups. The head of finance, for example, probably had to battle long and hard against other department heads for his share of the company budget. He will battle even harder to keep other departments from taking his budgeted money or otherwise intruding on his turf. In many companies, work groups and departments seem to be more concerned with their own growth and financial support than with the overall welfare of the company. This competition for resources pits all divisions in the company against one another in an ongoing political wrangle that consumes enormous energy and attention.

In such a political minefield, the steps and missteps of one division alone may be doomed to disaster. "That's a report from marketing," the head of accounting may bluster. "They've skewed everything to support their own needs." The head of marketing may be just as suspicious of any data or other information sent forward exclusively from accounting. How does business get done in such a charged environment where the left hand doesn't trust what the right hand is doing?

The simple answer is teams. By assembling representatives from the various political entities within the company, upper management ensures that the work product of the team will be generally acceptable to all company members. "After all," the head of marketing explains, "we had one of our people on that team. Our interests were represented." Other department or division heads feel similarly. In short, the buy-in assured by the membership of the team extends to its work product. A report from the team, for example, will be greeted with much more credibility by the company as a whole simply because that document arose from the combined efforts of somewhat opposed interests.

INSIGHT 6	Even though teams and teamwork may be more cumbersome and time-consuming than individual action, the team approach may nevertheless be justified, in large part, for the buy-in it facilitates in politically charged organizational environments.

Your Turn

Think about a time when you served on a team made up of individuals representing different and perhaps opposed interests within the company or organization. Was it difficult for the team to make decisions? If so, why? Did the team complete its work? If so, was that work widely accepted by the company or organization?

TEAMS AND CENSORSHIP, PRO AND CON

As discussed earlier, a team provides an early-warning system and an effective suppression mechanism for member ideas judged by the team to be impractical or outlandish. Filtering out such ideas at an early stage saves money and organizational energy. Imagine the damage a wrong-headed idea could do if allowed to proceed forward in the development of a project or other company activity.

On the other hand, teams must exercise caution that they do not become guilty of what Harvard professor Irving Janis has called Group-Think. This phenomenon occurs when a group refuses to hear ideas or information in conflict with the majority opinion. The group may put too much stock in the strength-in-unity notion, to the point that all dissent is ridiculed or angrily dismissed. Influential group members may urge other team members to adhere to the party line for the sake of group harmony.

Perhaps the classic case study of GroupThink occurred at Morton Thiokol Corporation in the days just prior to the Challenger disaster. Although one engineer, Roger Beaujolais, raised serious concerns about the safety of "O"-ring functions at low temperatures, his dissent was discounted by Morton Thiokol project managers and ignored by NASA administrators. These managers and administrators felt pressure from their superiors and from the press, including Dan Rather's reporting on the nightly news, to launch the often-delayed shuttle. Safety concerns aroused by the "O"-ring matter did not fit in with NASA's overarching agenda. The team in this case squelched dissenting information that could have saved the mission as well as the lives of the astronauts involved.

GroupThink can be prevented in teams by getting all members to agree to several procedural guidelines:

- Rules of order (such as Robert's Rules of Order) should not be used to silence dissenting opinions.
- Pressure for consensus should not be applied in such a way as to prevent the expression of minority perspectives.
- Each team member should be a critical evaluator of team processes. In doing so, team members must call attention to symptoms of Group-Think that occur during team discussion.
- The team leader must not impose a preordained perspective or foregone conclusion on group members.
- The group must welcome outside information and opinion, especially when such input disagrees with the dominant direction of team discussion.

INSIGHT 7	In suppressing worthless and impractical ideas, the team must be careful not also to suppress valuable dissent.

Your Turn	
Bring to mind a time when you or another team member disagreed strongly with the direction of discussion and decision making taken by your team. How was that disagreement presented? How did other team members respond? What finally happened?	

TEAMS AND CROSS-TRAINING

An additional defense of teams arises from the need for cross-training in organizations of all kinds. When specialists gather as members of a team, a certain amount of cross-fertilization takes place. Like actors in a play, each team member learns at least a portion of the "lines" of other team members. For example, an advertising specialist on the team shares her approach to product marketing with the human resources (HR) representative. Even though the HR representative does not then become an instant expert on advertising, he or she nevertheless has important insights into the art of advertising and can add to discussion and decision making on the topic. If the advertising team member had to miss a meeting, others on the team would be able to carry on, thanks to their cross-training.

Companies and other organizations maximize the contributions of their employees by such cross-training. Especially in economically stressed times, companies may not have the luxury of hiring specialists as needed for every project underway in the company. Upper managers must rely on employees to use not only their first areas of expertise, but also their background knowledge in secondary areas (achieved through cross-training) to keep projects on target and on time.

Cross-training within teams can be facilitated in at least two ways:

- Take regular cross-training breaks from usual team activities. For example, you can devote an hour every few meetings exclusively for sharing core aspects of each member's expertise and techniques. Rather than overloading any one meeting with too much cross-training data, one or two team members can share their perspectives and knowledge at each cross-training occasion. Put in common terms, a cross-training session can be labeled, "How to Think Like a . . . (marketing, finance, operations, etc.)."

■ The team can invite outside expertise to visit team meetings with the goal of sharing techniques, skills, and concepts as an upgrade to the existing knowledge and skill base of team members.

Cross-training makes each team member more valuable to the team and ensures against knowledge and skill gaps during the life of the team.	**INSIGHT 8**

Your Turn
If you have received valuable cross-training as a part of your membership on a team, tell about that cross-training and how you used it. If you have not received cross-training in this way, write briefly about the kind of cross-training you would like to receive and how it could help you contribute to the team.

TEAMS AND FOLLOW-UP RESPONSIBILITIES

Like most assemblies of individuals, a team has a life span ranging from a matter of days to several years. No matter how long the team survives, someone must remain active and available as its spokesman, interpreter, and perhaps defender. Here's an example of follow-up responsibilities after a retailing team finished its work. Someone had to

■ present team findings to several levels of management
■ draw together team documents, data, and meeting notes
■ answer questions about what the team decided, meant, suspected, and recommended
■ meet with other teams who wanted to learn from the success of the previous team or continue its work in some way

Although these duties often fall to the team leader, they can be assumed by other team members. A high-performing team can distribute these follow-up responsibilities among its members partly to lighten the load on the team leader and partly to prevent team history from being rewritten in the retelling by just one member.

The work of a team is not over after the team's last meeting. Many important follow-up responsibilities can be distributed among team members.	**INSIGHT 9**

Recall the aftermath activities of a team on which you served. What kinds of things happened after the team's last meeting? Who took responsibility for those tasks and opportunities? Did the person(s) do a good job? If not, what improvements in follow-up responsibilities can you suggest?

TEAMS AND THE SOCIAL ASPECT OF ENTERPRISE

Finally, teams have the advantage of being more enjoyable than most work accomplished all alone. Here's the opinion of one manager in the computer industry after a 6-month period of service on a 6-member team within her company.

> We met at least once a week. Even though we didn't know one another before our first meeting, we quickly gelled into a comfortable and stimulating work group. I looked forward to seeing my teammates each week for at least four reasons. First, I wanted to find out how their individual portion of our work was going. Second, I needed perceptive people to hear about the work I had accomplished and give me meaningful feedback. Third, we all needed other people with whom to share our joys and frustrations about the project. Finally, we just got along as people. Although we didn't spend a lot of time on social talk, there was the inevitable chat about kids, pets, hobbies, life stresses, good restaurants, interesting movies, and so forth. For all those reasons, I found team membership much more energizing and fulfilling than simply laboring away by myself in my cube.

INSIGHT 10   Most people have a natural tendency to seek out the company of others. This tendency can help to make teamwork more motivating and fulfilling than the same work undertaken alone.

Compare a time when you accomplished a project or task by yourself with a time when you accomplished a similar project or task as a member of a team. Which form of work was most fulfilling to you? Which was most efficient? Why?

Summing Up

Teams offer many advantages as an organized way to accomplish tasks. First, work teams have all the positive qualities of sports teams in extending available expertise, coordinating knowledge and resources, and utilizing internal modes of motivation. Second, teams provide a means of achieving buy-in in politically charged work environments, where opposing interests may resist accepting the work product of any one constituency in the oganization. Third, teams act to censor worthless ideas before they negatively influence the development of decisions and projects. Fourth, teams encourage cross-training, with resulting advantages to the company in case particular specialists are unavailable. Fifth, teams provide more people to handle follow-up responsibilities than in work accomplished by a single individual. Finally, teams are often fun work experiences. Such enjoyment and satisfaction promotes employee loyalty, motivation, and commitment.

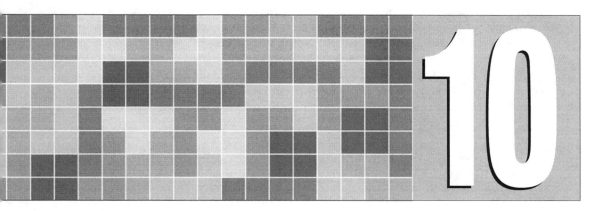

Assessing Your Team Experience and Insights

GOALS

- Assess characteristics of effective team membership and leadership.
- Discover evaluation instruments that can lead to productive discussion of team issues.
- Develop personal priorities for improvement in team skills.

The poet Robert Burns wished that "the gift God would give us/To see ourselves as others see us." His sentiment echoes that of Socrates: "Know thyself." In both cases we are being counseled to delve beneath the surface layers of self-congratulation and image enhancement to learn what really

Taken from: *Learning Team Skills*, by Arthur H. Bell and Dayle M. Smith

makes us and others "tick" as team leaders and members. The instruments and exercises contained in this chapter can prove helpful in moving beyond subjective assessment ("What I think about myself") to more objective analysis ("How I appear to others"). Like the personality test contained in *Developing Leadership Abilities* (Bell/Smith, Prentice Hall, 2002), Chapter 2, these instruments provide information that may indicate major tendencies, strengths, and weaknesses in our individual portfolios of team skills. These test indications are best used as a starting place for self-reflection and development rather than as a judgment of any kind on one's present or future potential as a team member or leader. The results of these exercises are best used as the focus for in-depth discussion by all team members, including the team leader. In some cases, you may want to complete the instruments anonymously so that answers can be discussed without any threat to individuals on the team.

Exercise 1	What Do You Expect of a Team Leader?

Directions: Put the following qualities associated with team leadership in order of your perception of importance, 1 through 11, with 1 being highest. Then compare your ranking with that of 7 years of surveys recently published in *Best Practices*[1] magazine.

I believe a team leader should be (in order of importance):

Dependable_____

Straightforward_____

Broad-minded_____

Intelligent_____

Forward-looking_____

Honest_____

Imaginative_____

Courageous_____

Fair-minded_____

Inspiring_____

Competent_____

_____
[1] "Establishing the Credibility Factor," *Best Practices*, January 1999, p. 121.

Here are the percentages of thousands of survey respondents who ranked the importance of these qualities:

Honest 87%
Competent 74%
Forward-looking 67%
Inspiring 61%
Intelligent 46%
Fair-minded 42%
Broad-minded 38%
Courageous 35%
Straightforward 33%
Imaginative 32%
Dependable 31%

We each have different expectations of a team leader. The same leader can fulfill the expectations of some members of the team while disappointing other members. A team can usefully discuss its expectations of leadership and communicate those expectations to the team leader.	**INSIGHT 11**

Your Turn

Choose two or more qualities that you ranked significantly higher than the survey respondents. Explain why you believe the qualities you selected are of special importance for an effective team leader.

When the Team Makes a Mistake — Exercise 2

Directions: Write down three mistakes for which a team could easily be forgiven or that could be used without penalty as learning experiences, such as not keeping detailed minutes of their team meetings. Once you have completed your three items, try to find them on the list of actual team mistakes gathered from managers and supervisors by researcher Deborah Harrington-Mackin; all mistakes in her list were judged as forgivable by these business professionals.

(continued)

| Exercise 2 | **When the Team Makes a Mistake (continued)** |

I believe teams can be easily pardoned for making the following mistakes:

1.

2.

3.

The following is Deborah Harrington-Mackin's[2] list of forgivable team mistakes. A team's mistakes can be accepted and forgiven by management if:

- the mistake doesn't have significant negative impact upon the company
- it is a first-time mistake, not part of a pattern
- team members were working outside the team's usual area of responsibility
- the team member was following explicit instructions or proper procedures
- the team member was working with shared equipment that was not always available
- the team learns from the mistake and is able to say how it will be avoided in the future
- the mistake occurred within the scope of the team's authority in pursuit of the team's goals
- the team was really trying to do things right
- the team's actions were consistent with the policies and rules of the company
- incorrect information was given to the team
- the team was taking initiative and reasonable risks
- procedures weren't clearly defined by management
- different skill and ability levels of team members caused erratic results
- there were extenuating circumstances
- the situation was outside the team member's control
- the error was not caused by negligence or lack of action
- there were unavoidable time constraints
- there was poor training

---

[2] Harrington-Mackin, Deborah. *Keeping the Team Going.* New York: American Management Association, 1996, p. 15.

Knowing that your team can and will make pardonable mistakes frees each member of the team to take risks, explore options, and "push the envelope" of imagination.	**INSIGHT 12**

	Your Turn

Recall a past job, perhaps a summer job, in which your boss at the time was critical of each mistake you made as a new employee. (If you have not had this work experience, recall a person in your life who has been too critical of your missteps.) How did you respond to the threat of criticism hanging over your head? Did it help your work performance in any way? Did it hinder that performance in any way?

Who Pulls Your Strings as a Team Member?	**Exercise 3**

Directions: Each member of the team, including the team leader, should complete the following assessment, then compare and discuss results with one another. From its discussion of the results of this instrument, the team can accurately appraise the various types and degrees of influence perceived by the team.

For each worker category, circle the number that best represents your estimate of influence this worker category has on your performance as a team member:

Category	Very High	High	Moderately High	Some	Little	Very Low
CEO/President	6	5	4	3	2	1
Top managers	6	5	4	3	2	1
Mid-level managers	6	5	4	3	2	1
Team leader	6	5	4	3	2	1
Team members	6	5	4	3	2	1
Subordinates	6	5	4	3	2	1

Team members often seem as if they are acting in response to an unseen boss. Learning who that perceived boss is can help team members distinguish their real priorities from imagined ones.	**INSIGHT 13**

Your Turn

Think about a time when you had to guess what your boss was thinking about you, your job, and company operations. (This approach to management is called MBM—Management by Mystery.) How did this uncertainty affect your work performance and attitude toward your job?

Exercise 4   Does the Team Control Its Own Destiny?

Directions: Circle the "a" or "b" option you most agree with for each pair of questions. Then transfer your answers to the interpretive scoresheet. Your cumulative totals under the respective columns will indicate the degree to which you believe the team to be in control of its own destiny or controlled by forces external to the team.

1. a. Team members must often deal with issues they do not understand and cannot control.
   b. Team members understand most issues they deal with and have substantial control in their decisions regarding those issues.

2. a. The value of the team's work is usually determined by the hard work and insights of the team members themselves.
   b. The value of the team's work usually depends on how well others in the organization do their work.

3. a. A good team leader is born, not made.
   b. Depending on the situation, any member of a good team can perform well in the role of team leader.

4. a. Teams fail most often due to internal strife and lack of focus.
   b. Teams fail most often because they lack organizational power and support.

5. a. The amount of support given to a team in an organization depends primarily on the intelligence and fairness of top management.
   b. The amount of support given to a team in an organization depends primarily on how well the team makes its case for deserving support.

6. a. The success of a team is often due as much to good fortune or luck as to good work.
   b. The success of a team is almost always due to the quality of its work.

7. a. Teams that make careful plans for their activities usually succeed.
   b. Teams do better to remain flexible because changes in the marketplace and in organizational priorities usually can't be anticipated.

Does the Team Control Its Own Destiny? (continued)   Exercise 4

8. a. Being a valuable team member depends most of all on one's previous level of power in the organization.

    b. Being a valuable team member depends most of all on one's ability to listen well and respond intelligently.

9. a. The work of competent teams is usually rewarded in the organization.

    b. Organizational rewards go most often to teams with the right contacts inside and outside the organization.

10. a. Team skills can be learned by almost all employees.

    b. A significant percentage of employees could never learn to be good team members.

Scoresheet

Perception of External Control Over Team	Perception of Internal Control Over Team
1a _____	1b _____
2b _____	2a _____
3a _____	3b _____
4b _____	4a _____
5a _____	5b _____
6a _____	6b _____
7b _____	7a _____
8a _____	8b _____
9b _____	9a _____
10b _____	10a _____
Totals _____	_____

INSIGHT 14

The issue of control is crucial for any team. Team members who feel that they have little to say or do about their own destiny may show signs of discouragement and lack of initiative in working on team projects.

Your Turn

Recall a time in your work or academic life when you had little control over the activities and duties expected of you—you had to do them but had little choice over what, where, or when. How did this lack of control affect your performance and attitude?

Exercise 5	How Effective Is the Team Leader?

Directions: Using the scoresheet provided, circle the number that comes closest to your opinion for each statement. A total of all your circled scores will provide a single number measurement of the leader's effectiveness, at least in your opinion. The lower the final total score, the more effective the team leader is in your view.

1. The team leader supports my efforts on the team.
2. The team leader usually goes along with decisions of the team.
3. The team leader accepts differences of opinion among team members.
4. The team leader makes good use of time spent in team meetings.
5. The team leader is a good listener to problems I face as a team member.
6. The team leader makes sure that I am fairly rewarded for my work on the team.
7. The team leader helps the team resolve its internal conflicts.
8. The team leader helps team members develop and improve.
9. The team leader leaves many important decisions up to the team.
10. The team leader treats all team members fairly.

Scoresheet

	Strongly Agree	Agree	Slightly Agree	Slightly Disagree	Disagree	Strongly Disagree
1.	1	2	3	4	5	6
2.	1	2	3	4	5	6
3.	1	2	3	4	5	6
4.	1	2	3	4	5	6
5.	1	2	3	4	5	6
6.	1	2	3	4	5	6
7.	1	2	3	4	5	6
8.	1	2	3	4	5	6
9.	1	2	3	4	5	6
10.	1	2	3	4	5	6
Totals	____	____	____	____	____	____

Cumulative total of all scores: ____

Team members should take this assessment anonymously and present scoresheets to the team leader for review and discussion. Once these perceptions are known to the team leader, goals can be set for both the team leader and team members to achieve more effective relations with leadership.

Although team relationships depend on more than the leader's action, this key figure has much to do with the way team members think about themselves, their work, and the team itself. By understanding their feelings about the team leader, team members can make the most of the leader's strengths and find ways to address his or her weaknesses.	**INSIGHT 15**

Your Turn

Think about a time when you worked for or served under a leader you did not like or respect. Did you communicate your feelings to this person in any way? How did your feelings toward the leader influence your work performance and personal satisfaction in the position?

Assessing My Participation in Team Meetings | Exercise 6

Directions: Each team member and the team leader should fill out the following assessment as soon as possible after a team meeting. Results should then be discussed openly as a direct means of improving team relationships and interaction.

1. Where I sat during the meeting. Sketch your seating position in relation to other team members.

2. How this seating position influenced my participation.

3. Types of participation during the team meeting. Place numbers in each blank according to the following scale: 1—Agree; 2—Not sure; 3—Disagree.
   _____ I spoke up to initiate new ideas.
   _____ I spoke up to disagree with other speakers.
   _____ I spoke up to agree with other speakers
   _____ I spoke up to offer additional information.
   _____ I spoke up with questions.
   _____ I spoke up to clarify points for others.
   _____ I spoke up to summarize points for others.
   _____ I spoke up in a humorous way related to the point at hand.
   _____ I spoke up in a humorous way unrelated to the point at hand.
   _____ I did not speak up.
   _____ Other forms of participation: (specify)

(continued)

Exercise 6	**Assessing My Participation in Team Meetings (continued)**

4. My attitudes toward participation. Place numbers in each blank according to the following scale: 1—Agree; 2—Not sure; 3—Disagree.

____ I felt I expressed myself clearly and persuasively.

____ I felt I expressed myself clearly but not persuasively.

____ I felt that I did not express myself clearly or persuasively.

____ I felt that the team usually let me have my say.

____ I felt that I was usually cut off by other team members before having my say.

____ I felt that I spoke up too often.

____ I felt that I wanted to speak up more often, but did not.

____ I felt that I spoke up too little.

____ I felt that I communicated an impatient attitude toward the meeting.

____ I felt that I communicated a discouraged attitude toward the meeting.

____ I felt that I communicated an upbeat, energetic attitude toward the meeting.

INSIGHT 16	The usual forum for team gatherings is in a meeting. A team member's physical position in the meeting room and ways of participating in the meeting itself can tell much about the team member's relationship to the rest of the team and that member's contributions to the work of the team.

Your Turn

Call to mind the last meeting you attended. In your view, was it a good, bad, or indifferent meeting? Write out how you reached your judgment about the meeting. What aspects of the meeting were important to you in arriving at your judgment?

Summing Up

Talking about what's right and what's wrong with a team can often be difficult for team members and the team leader. A variety of exercises offer insightful questions that should be answered by the entire team. These answers can form the basis of a productive discussion of team policies, procedures, processes, and problems.

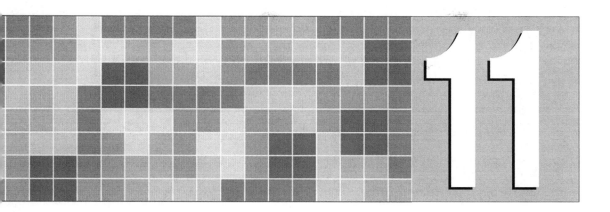

Building a Balanced Team

GOALS

- Grasp the importance of balance among member types for a productive team.

- Learn the main components that work together to create team balance.

- Become acquainted with techniques for building and restoring team balance.

Do you remember the process most of us used in elementary school to select team members for playground sports? Two captains (often self-selected!) would take turns choosing players for their teams. If you were one of the last chosen, that process was often painful indeed. Just as often, the teams ended up with various forms of imbalance: the boys against the girls, one set of friends against another set of friends, and so forth.

Teams in companies and other organizations cannot afford imbalance based on bias, whim, or accident. Just as a major league sports team endeavors to fill each position with talent, so a company tries to build teams whose members have complementary skills and backgrounds.

Taken from: *Learning Team Skills*, by Arthur H. Bell and Dayle M. Smith

THE IMPORTANCE OF BALANCE

You can imagine the difficulties a company would encounter if it turned an important marketing project over to a team made up exclusively of accountants. It is likely that every aspect of the project would be judged solely and narrowly by its cost. Just as disastrous would be the assignment of financial reform in the company to a team made up of advertising specialists. In these examples, the presence of an accountant or an advertising person on the team is not in question; both would probably play a valuable role. Only when the team is composed of one employee type do difficulties often arise.

Consider the many ways in which teams can achieve balance:

- by mixing team member personality types
- by mixing team members according to their expertise and experience
- by mixing team members according to their place in the organization's hierarchy
- by mixing employee ethnicities
- by mixing employee genders

In all cases, the purpose for such balancing is not political correctness but improved bottom-line results for the team. The balance sought for any specific team depends on the purpose or project at hand, the audience to whom the team will report, and the company culture itself. Therefore, no single formula can be given as an ideal recipe for the balanced team. Instead, this chapter points out options and advantages you may want to consider when building a team in your organization. We focus especially on the advantages of gender balance.

INSIGHT 17	Balance in the membership of a team gives the company the differing perspectives of several stakeholders. Variety of opinion makes for more complete discussion of issues and, eventually, better decision making.

Your Turn

If you believe you have served or now serve on a balanced team, jot down any advantages and disadvantages that came as a result of the team's diverse membership. If you have never served on a balanced team, think about a recent team experience. Describe the kinds of members that, if added, would have made your team more balanced.

CAUSES OF TEAM IMBALANCE

Although imbalanced teams arise for many reasons, four causes in particular appear to account for most imbalanced teams.

The team as the boss's clones. In many companies, bosses have such high opinions of themselves that they appoint team members strictly in their image. For many years, IBM struggled with this cloning phenomenon on its sales teams: All IBM sales representatives seemed to look, act, dress, and think in remarkably similar ways. Certainly, in the last decade, IBM has acted aggressively to achieve the advantages of diversity in its workforce and on its key teams.

The team as the usual players. The old business adage asserts that "20 percent of the employees do 80 percent of the work." Unfortunately, some companies take this folk wisdom so literally that they keep appointing only that 20 percent to company teams.

The same people seem to appear on major company teams year after year and, with no surprise, probably tend to make the same kinds of decisions (or mistakes) year after year.

The team as those most suited for the task. At first glance, this form of imbalance makes a certain amount of sense. For example, it would seem logical to give a research project to a company team made up of researchers, but an imbalance of any one employee type yields less than satisfactory results. The team could no doubt profit from the addition of a member from the finance group or marketing department. These members could help researchers see the "big picture" and avoid intellectually interesting but impractical decisions.

The team as one personality type. Some companies make the right move in balancing teams with employees of differing backgrounds, only to make the greater mistake of choosing members all of whom share the same personality profile. For example, imagine a team composed entirely of obsessive planners, each with their Palm Pilot crammed with dates, deadlines, and schedules. Their team project will almost certainly be delivered on time, but may be sorely lacking in creativity and fresh thinking. The same general point could be made for teams composed entirely of any of the other personality types discussed later in this chapter.

Uniformity in membership usually has little advantage to a team. Diverse personality types, expertise, experience, and other differences among members tend to enrich discussion and improve decision making.	**INSIGHT 18**

As a speculative exercise, think of some work- or school-related project that might well be accomplished by a team. Describe the characteristics of at least five members—your "dream team"—that you would assemble to serve on that team. Explain why you aimed at the balance you describe.

HOW AND WHEN TO PLAN FOR BALANCE

Like balancing a car tire, the balancing of a team is better undertaken before the journey begins, so to speak, than when you're already on the road. Once you have formed a team, there is great stigma attached to removing a team member for any reason. Therefore, make it your priority to choose team members wisely from the outset of a project. Many managers follow these approximate steps in shaping the membership of a team:

- Write down the specific goals you want to achieve through your team.
- List any constraints (such as personnel availability, budget factors, and company policies or procedures) that will limit your choice of team members.
- Describe skill or expertise categories (not specific people) that should be represented on the team.
- Describe personality types that will help the team function optimally.
- Nominate in writing several people, if possible, for each of the skill or expertise categories you have described. For each person on this list, write down an educated guess about his or her basic personality type.
- Select team members who fulfill the desired skill or expertise categories and provide a useful distribution of personality types in relation to your project goals.
- Inform these individuals in a motivating, morale-building way of their membership on the team. (You will want to make yourself available for individual conferences to deal with questions and concerns.)
- Plan carefully for an inspiriting first meeting of the team, at which basic information regarding goals, team leadership, available resources, milestones, deliverables, and evaluation measures are thoroughly discussed.

INSIGHT 19   Productive teams rarely happen by chance. The effort a manager puts into the selection of team members is repaid many times over by the team's cooperative proceedings and significant achievements.

Think about a time when you found yourself as a member of a team that was apparently assembled without forethought or planning. If the efforts of the team were not successful, explain reasons for this failure. If the efforts of the team were successful, explain any adjustments team members had to make to deal with the lack of planning in the forming of the team.

THE LIMITS OF PERSONALITY TESTS

Team members typically exhibit personality tendencies that can be placed at some point on four continua:

Member —— Self
Thinker —— Empathizer
Planner —— Juggler
Closer —— Researcher

Experts in personality testing caution against an overly simplistic interpretation of personality types or test results. Human beings are complex bundles of intellectual and emotional potential that resist any single label. As you may have guessed, stress levels and other life circumstances can dramatically influence one's dominant personality type. For example, a Juggler (someone who likes to have many balls in the air at once and live in the excitement of the moment) may, during times of stress, revert to a rigid Planner mentality, complete with a daily "to-do" list of things to accomplish. A Thinker, who usually values proof, rationality, and logic can, under the impact of stress, exhibit qualities of the Empathizer.

The key to evaluating the personalities of team members (or potential team members) lies in knowing your people as thoroughly as possible. If you have not worked with them personally, talk at length with their previous supervisors and coworkers to learn about their work habits, attitudes, needs, and career goals.

Personality tests are only a starting point for the accurate description of your own personality or someone else's. Use the results of such tests carefully and in combination with other evidence to develop an appropriate balance of personality types on a team. **INSIGHT 20**

Your Turn

Do you believe that your personality changes in significant ways during times of stress? If so, what are those changes?

MAKING THE MOST OF GENDER BALANCE

In the 1990s, several influential books (including Deborah Tannen's *You Just Don't Understand* and *Talking from 9 to 5*,[1] and Kathleen Reardon's *They Don't Get It, Do They?*[2]) have argued that many aspects of women's verbal and non-verbal communication in business are distinctly different from those of men. Moreover, these authors assert, women's communication habits sometimes put them at a disadvantage for leadership roles, team participation, promotion, recognition, and full participation in decision making in corporate life.

For our purposes, the goal of every team leader and member should be to understand possible communication differences between genders so that the contributions of both genders can be maximized. In some descriptions of team processes, the topic of women's modes of communication has been reduced to a latter-day version of Henry Higgins' complaint of Eliza Doolittle in *My Fair Lady*: "If only a woman could be more like a man!" Teams and team leaders who have a similar attitude toward women members are missing the unique contributions women bring to the team table. As Tannen, Reardon, and others point out, women's communication habits in business exist for reasons. To understand those reasons is to put ourselves as team members and leaders in a better position to make the most of the communication patterns of both men and women. In short, women and men who serve together on teams must learn to listen to themselves and to one another, then to make adjustments in communication styles to achieve fairness, make the best use of team resources, and successfully execute the organization's mission.

Let it be said at the outset that the following observations are by no means applicable to all women in business environments. No researcher of women's communication behaviors has claimed universality for the results of quite limited studies. In the words of Deborah Tannen,

> I do not imply that there is anything inherently male or female about particular ways of talking, nor to claim that every individual man or woman adheres to the pattern, but rather to observe that a larger percentage of

---

[1] Tannen, Deborah. *You Just Don't Understand.* 2d ed. New York: Quill, 2001; *Talking from 9 to 5.* 2d ed. New York: Quill, 2001.
[2] Reardon, Kathleen. *They Don't Get It, Do They?* New York: Little, Brown, 1995.

women or men as a group talk in a particular way, or individual women and men are more likely to talk one way or the other.[3]

Tannen's research, joined by dozens of supportive studies, makes the point that women do appear to communicate differently than men in work environments, including teams. Most often women have been judged negatively for this difference, and they have been instructed (often by women) to "talk the talk" (i.e., the male talk) if they want to rise to positions of power in companies and be taken seriously in teams. This effort to recreate women's communication patterns in men's images ignores the very real contributions women bring to the team through their ways of communicating. As a counterbalance, then, to the pervasive argument that women should learn to speak more like men, we offer brief interpretations of 20 gender communication patterns. These interpretations are intended to point out the value of women's communication patterns *as they are* without repair or alteration for modern teams.

Gender-based patterns of communication, whether those of men or women, can be useful in a variety of business circumstances and are equally of value.	**INSIGHT 21**

Your Turn
Give your own impressions of ways in which communication may differ somewhat depending on the gender of the communicator.

CHARACTERISTICS OF MEN'S AND WOMEN'S COMMUNICATION HABITS

1. Men are less likely to ask for information or directions in a public situation that would reveal their lack of knowledge.

Man: I don't need to stop at the gas station for directions. I can find the right street.

Woman: Why not stop and ask? It will save us time.

---

[3] Tannen, Deborah. *Talking from 9 to 5*, p. xxi.

The willingness of women to seek help in such situations can prove useful to what Peter Senge has called "the learning organization,"[4] including its learning teams. The reluctance, out of pride or embarrassment, of independent men on a team to seek assistance is counterproductive. The language habits of women in this case can be extended throughout the team as a way of encouraging openness to new information, reliance on team members as resources, and a constant readiness to ask questions and learn.

2. Women perceive the question, "What would you like to do?" as an invitation for discussion and negotiation. Men perceive the same question as the stimulus to a direct answer.

> Woman: We have to arrange a holiday party. What would you like to do? [She is expecting conversation about past holiday parties, anecdotes, personal memories, and possibility thinking.]

> Man: We have to arrange a holiday party. What would you like to do? [He is expecting places and times to be named.]

Women's willingness to delay decision making pending a multidimensional review of background information and influences is sometimes portrayed as a deficit, especially for would-be leaders of teams. However, that same communication tendency can be valued as an antidote to a team's tendency to rush to judgment or to ignore relevant input. On modern teams, leaders are cast less and less in the role of quick-draw decision maker and more in the role of seer, with wisdom and patience implied. The gender communication approach of women in this case fits well with the requirements of team leadership, where instant answers and quick decisions are often impossible or foolhardy.

3. Women misunderstand men's ultimatums as serious threats rather than one more negotiation strategy.

> Man: This is nonnegotiable. [A bluff.]

> Woman: Fine, then. Have it your way. [She accepts the bluff as reality.]

This may be a way of saying that women tend to attach meanings to words and assume that male speakers do as well. In this example, the woman speaker believes that the man knows what "nonnegotiable" means and chooses that word sincerely to describe his position. If the man knows that his position is negotiable but chooses to dissemble, are we to praise his strategy and recommend it to both genders? In George Orwell's fine phrase, "The great enemy of language is insincerity." Women have much to teach about integrity in saying what you mean and meaning what you say.

---

[4] Senge, Peter. *The Fifth Discipline: The Art and Practice of the Learning Organization.* New York: Doubleday, 1994..

> What men and women say is not always what they mean. Listen to subtle expressions of attitude and emotion and pay attention to nonverbal signs to determine the complete meaning of a statement.

INSIGHT 22

Your Turn

Describe a time when a person's words to you revealed only a small portion of the complete meaning they were trying to communicate. How did you go about discovering the full intent of their communication?

4. In decision making, women are more likely to downplay their certainty; men are more likely to downplay their doubts.

> Woman: In making this recommendation, I think I've covered every base—at least the ones I'm aware of.

> Man: I make this recommendation with complete confidence.

This language tendency on the part of women is sometimes portrayed as an inability to stand strong as a confident decision maker. It can just as easily be regarded and valued as a reluctance to bluff the audience or to assume a posture of confidence that is neither felt by the speaker nor supported by the facts. Women, by their language of qualification as exemplified here, may be providing a necessary caution against the male tendency toward exaggeration and bravado. In effect, women are telling it like it is: "I'm not entirely sure about my conclusions and I'm not going to pretend otherwise. To do so would be lying to you and, ultimately, empowering myself at your expense."

5. Women tend to lead by making suggestions and explaining those suggestions in terms of the good of the team. Men are more likely to lead by giving orders, with explanations (if any) based on rationales related to project goals.

> Woman: Let's proceed by dividing into teams. I think we can make the most of our individual talents by working with one another in smaller groups.

> Man: We're going to break into teams to divide up the workload and meet our deadlines.

Modern teams obviously require both approaches to planning and decision making as a way of dealing with rapidly changing business conditions. For every occasion when the team must be nourished and encouraged there is also a circumstance when someone has to make decisions without consensus (or relying on a trust bond that already exists within the group). The important point is that neither style is dysfunctional; both can be useful on teams to serve different but complementary goals.

6. Women tend to apologize even when they have done nothing wrong. Men tend to avoid apologies as signs of weakness or concession.

> Woman: I'm sorry, but I have to read you this e-mail that just arrived from the boss.

> Man: Listen up. The boss just sent this e-mail.

In this case, only the most rigid literalist would interpret the phrase, "I'm sorry" as an apology for a mistake of some kind. These words instead reveal a recognition that the listener's feelings may be bruised by the ensuing message, and that the speaker is not unaware of or unresponsive to those feelings. In this way, the communication patterns of women tend to insert emotional buffers into sometimes turbulent business life. What on the surface may appear to be unjustified apologizing is, at a deeper level, an effort to humanize the team and soften harsh effects.

INSIGHT 23	Apologies and equivocations do not necessarily indicate guilt or a perception of wrongdoing on the part of the speaker. These phrases may be a way of attempting to deal gently with an uncomfortable moment or situation.

Your Turn

Consider your own use of apology phrases such as "I'm sorry, but . . ." or "Excuse me" beyond their literal meanings. Try to paraphrase exactly what you are attempting to communicate by the use of these phrases.

7. Women tend to accept blame as a way of smoothing awkward situations. Men tend to ignore blame or place it elsewhere.

> Woman: I probably didn't welcome our Japanese visitors exactly as I should have, but I tried to be gracious and sincere.

> Man: I met the Japanese visitors at the airport. Next time someone should tell me when and how to bow.

Teams require accountability, but it is hardly present in the male language pattern illustrated here. The woman is clearly accepting responsibility both for what went right and what went wrong in her efforts to greet the Japanese visitors. The man, by contrast, seeks to avoid personal accountability and instead to pass it on to a vague "someone" in the organization. When less-than-ideal situations in business occur, the language habits of women may be more likely to depict accurately the accountability involved.

8. Women tend to temper criticism with positive buffers. Men tend to give criticism directly.

> Woman: You're doing a great job on this report, but you may want to look at page eight one more time. At least see what you think.

> Man: Fix page eight, then let me reread your report one final time before we send it upstairs.

An awareness of the listener's feelings is not a bad thing for team relationships. In this woman's example, the speaker tries to preserve the relationship while changing the behavior. The man seems more willing to sacrifice or at least risk the relationship for the sake of behavior. That choice leads directly, on many teams, to low morale and excessive turnover of membership.

9. Women tend to insert unnecessary and unwarranted "thank you's" in conversations. Men tend to avoid thanks as a sign of weakness.

> Woman: Thanks anyway, but I don't think I want to trade my parking place with Jack.

> Man: No, I don't want to trade for Jack's spot.

The facade of thanks is only part of a complex architecture of courtesy and civility that women may tend to prefer in the team environment. By contrast, the apparent tone of the male response portrays the team environment as an arena for confrontation, victory, defeat, and perhaps bullying.

Every manager must deliver constructive criticism, often hourly or daily. Your own way of delivering such criticism may be influenced by your gender.	**INSIGHT 24**

Your Turn

Write down how you prefer to receive criticism of your work behavior when such criticism is necessary. Then describe how one or two recent supervisors have chosen to deliver performance evaluations or other forms of constructive criticism. Did their approach to delivering criticism meet with your approval? If so, how did you feel in receiving the criticism and what was the result? If not, how did you feel in receiving the criticism and what was the result?

10. Women tend to ask, "What do you think?" to build consensus. Men often perceive the question to be a sign of incompetence and lack of confidence.

> Woman: What do you think about dividing my office into a work area and a waiting area?

> Man [thinks]: It's her office. Can't she decide what she wants to do?

Let's assume that the woman in this case knows full well what she wants to do with her office. Her question is not a solicitation of permission (although the man takes it as such) nor a sign that she can't make her own decisions. Instead, it is another demonstration of the tendency we have already observed in women's language patterns to gather input and weigh opinions before acting.

11. Women tend to mix business talk with talk about their personal lives and expect other women to do so as well. Men mix business talk with banter about sports, politics, or jokes (many of them sexually oriented).

> Woman: I don't mind traveling to Cincinnati, but it will mean finding overnight care for our baby.

> Man: If I do go to Cincinnati, I'm taking an afternoon off to see a ball game. That's the least they can do.

This question is worth asking: Which gender is expressing most truthfully and accurately the impact team and business responsibilities have on personal life? Let's assume that the man in this case is a father and that he, no less than the working woman, has family matters to consider in arranging his business trip. He too must make provision for children, pets, and so forth. The point is that the woman tends to discuss with others how business duties influence her personal life. The man is reluctant to do so. Businesses probably operate best knowing what problems, obstacles, and burdens their employees face. By knowing an employee's circumstances, the business can adapt for win-win solutions.

12. Women feel that men aren't direct enough in telling them what they (women) are doing right. Men feel that women aren't direct enough in telling them what they (men) are doing wrong.

> Woman: I don't know how you feel about my work. [This is a request for more feedback.]

> Man: Just tell me right out if you don't like what I'm doing. [This is a request to avoid mixed signals.]

Feedback is a business buzzword that refuses to fade, perhaps because of its importance to employee motivation and quality management, including that of teams. Both genders in this example are asking for feedback, but the woman's way of asking is more in line with the 360-degree-feedback systems currently used for performance evaluations at all levels of teamwork. The woman's communication pattern allows for the possibility that feedback may include both positive and negative aspects, that is, the full range of evaluation. The man's communication pattern closes the door to praise almost entirely and solicits only negative feedback.

Soliciting the opinions of others ("What do you think?") often is not an invitation to provide specific answers so much as an invitation to join in discussion and to offer an emotional response of some kind.   **INSIGHT 25**

Your Turn

Recall a recent conversation with a member of the opposite sex in which you seemed to have different goals for the conversation or in some way "talked past" one another. As you reflect on that conversation, what do you believe the conversational expectations of the other person were? What were your conversational expectations?

---

13. Women bring up complaints and troubles with one another as a means of arousing sympathy and building rapport. Men bring up problems only when they want to hear solutions.

> Woman: Our problem at home is just not having enough time with each other. I get home just as Bob is leaving for his job.

> Man: We haven't been out to a show for months. Where do you find babysitters?

Sharing problems is not just an effort to build rapport and arouse sympathy. In addition, and perhaps more crucially, it is an effort to understand pain and thereby alleviate it. The woman's communication pattern assumes that the group may have insights and experiences that will enlighten the nature of the pain or frustration at hand. The man's communication pattern is cynical about the ability of the surrounding group to provide indepth perspectives or resonant ideas. The woman wants help in understanding the problem; the man wants help in postponing the problem.

14. Women's humor tends to be self-mocking. Men's humor tends to be razzing, teasing, and mock-hostile attacking.

Woman: So I said in my charming way, "You forgot to plug it in."

Man: So I said, "Did you notice anything strange about the cord lying on the floor?"

Freud wrote at length about "tendency humor"—our effort to disguise in humor what we really want to communicate, but dare not directly. The tendency of the male communication pattern illustrated here is to emphasize the person's stupidity or foolishness. By contrast, the person making the comment is to be seen as superior and smarter. The woman defuses this potential power play in her softened version of the verbal transaction. She recognizes that the person may feel insecure and awkward about the incident, and so consciously lowers her own status by self-mocking humor to avoid a threat to the relationship.

15. Women tend to give directions in indirect ways, a technique that may be perceived by men as confusing, less confident, or manipulative.

Woman: You can handle this account any way you want, but taking him out to lunch might be a possibility. Or meet in his office. Whatever you think. Lunch, though, might be the way to go.

Man [thinks]: Is she telling me to take him out to lunch or not? Is she setting me up for an I-told-you-so if I don't do it her way? And what is her way?

Teams make much of empowerment, which can only take place when the decision maker has options. In this example, the woman's communication pattern is conducive to empowerment because it leaves the decision maker free to choose, learn, and grow within a range of options. The man's apparent preference for a command style of management may allow short-term efficiencies, but does not encourage empowerment with its allied benefits of creativity, motivation, and loyalty.

INSIGHT 26	Humor often disguises messages that others are trying to share with us. Seeing through the humor to the underlying message can be a good way of determining the true nature of your relationship with the other person.

Your Turn	
Think of someone in your work or social life who uses humor, perhaps in a mocking way, to say something to you and other people. Write down an approximate translation of what that person is usually trying to communicate by such humor. Why do you believe the person uses humor to disguise those messages?	

16. When women and men gather in a team setting, women tend to change their communication styles to adapt to the presence of the men. Women also practice "silent applause" by smiling often, agreeing with others often, and giving more non-verbal signals of attentiveness than do men.

Audience adaptation is highly recommended in virtually all communication guides and textbooks. The apparent fact that women change their communication behaviors based on their audience is not a sign of uncertainty, deceit, or weakness. Instead, it is an effort to relate successfully.

17. Women in positions of team leadership tend to be less accustomed to dealing with conflict and attack than are men.

Woman: Why is everyone mad at me?

Man: This is an unpopular decision, but I've got to make it.

As consensus builders, women respond quickly and vocally to signs that consensus is failing and that relationships are threatened. For generations this behavior has been interpreted negatively: "If you can't stand the heat, stay out of the kitchen." It can just as well be interpreted positively for the purposes of modern teams. Women are no less tough for recognizing and responding to conflict and attack. It can be argued that they are all the more tough for their willingness to confront and deal with those forces rather than stoically or stubbornly ignoring them.

18. Women tend to be referred to more often by their first name than are men, sometimes as a sign of respect for women and sometimes as a sign of presumed familiarity or intimacy.

Man: Get Smith, Underwood, Connors, and Jill to go along with you on the sales call.

The use of the woman's first name in this example may or may not be a subtle way for the man to minimize the woman's professionalism. He may feel more gallant in calling women by their first names. As a team leader, however, he should choose one form of address or the other and apply it consistently to both genders.

19. Men tend to be uncomfortable with female peers, particularly those who may threaten their power.

Working for a woman is uncomfortable for many men, primarily because they misunderstand the communication patterns explained throughout this chapter. The male employee may complain about the woman boss's seeming lack of direct supervision and mixed messages, whereas the woman boss may simultaneously complain about the male employee's unwillingness to discuss problems openly, to work well with others on the team, and to share ideas.

20. Men tend to perceive a group of women in conversation as wasting time or hatching a plot of some kind. Women tend to perceive a group of men in conversation as doing business or working out power relations through bonding and joking.

These impressions from a distance of gender-exclusive groups tell volumes about the core misunderstandings between male and female members of a team. Interestingly, women credit men with more positive activities (doing business, etc.) than is the reverse (wasting time, hatching plots). Are women more sanguine about their fellow team members than are men? Do women tend to see the corporate glass as half full and men to see it as half empty?

INSIGHT 27	One's comfort level in working for or with members of the opposite gender can help or hinder career success. It is important to understand one's feelings about the role of gender in interpersonal relations.

Your Turn

Briefly describe in writing your own experiences and feelings about working for a member of the opposite gender. If you prefer, describe the attitudes of someone who has strong feelings (pro or con) about working for a member of the opposite sex. Explain their attitudes to the best of your ability.

Summing Up

Balancing the personal qualities, expertise, experience, and other factors of team members is important in achieving a harmonious team that discusses issues fully and reaches decisions only after gathering a wide range of data. An evaluation of personality types can be useful in establishing this balance, but such personality information should not be applied too narrowly or literally. In attempting to balance the influence and interaction of men and women on a productive team, a team leader or manager must bear in mind many communication differences associated with gender. Communication on the team can be improved if all members are aware of and respect the value of these communication differences.

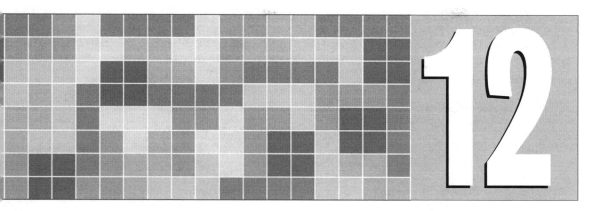

Becoming a Team Member and a Team Leader

GOALS

- Discover how to establish teams within an organization.
- Prepare for effective membership skills on a team.
- Learn techniques for leading teams.

In the best of all worlds, successful teams are already a well-established tradition within your company. There's a place waiting for you on a team. In that case you may want to skim this chapter, because it assumes that this is not the best of all worlds, and that you may have to work for—even create—your own place on a productive team.

Taken from: *Learning Team Skills*, by Arthur H. Bell and Dayle M. Smith

HOW TO KNOW IF YOUR ORGANIZATION NEEDS TEAMS

Let's say that you are now associated with a company or organization that makes little or no use of teams. Is there a reason why it should? Yes, if it experiences any of the following circumstances:

- Projects, documents, and other major tasks are done by one or two individuals, then distributed for significant revision by others in the company. (A team could speed this process by putting all those involved into the development loop from the beginning.)
- Political factions vie for resources and distrust the work product of any one faction. (If departments or divisions within the company do not share turf comfortably, a team comprised of members from each of these groups may ease tensions and give more credibility and acceptance to work products developed by the team.)
- Employee turnover is high because workers know few other people in the company and have little reason to stay beyond the paycheck. (Human relationships are fostered in a team environment—and those relationships can dramatically decrease employee turnover.)
- The company's work product requires input from several specialized skill areas. (A team can combine these skill areas and afford a measure of cross-training in the process.)

INSIGHT 28	The team approach to work is more appropriate in some organizational environments than in others. To decide whether teams are advantageous to it, a company must evaluate its work goals and culture.

Your Turn	
Think of a company or organization (perhaps one to which you now belong) where the team approach to work appears to be a good idea. Discuss reasons to support your opinion.	

PUTTING TOGETHER YOUR CASE FOR A TEAM

If you find yourself having to propose team-based work to your manager, here are the bases you will want to touch in preparing to make your case.

1. Make a list of projects, documents, presentations, and other company tasks that could be accomplished with higher quality in less time and at

lower cost by a team. (If no such tasks are available in your company, the chances are slim that management will see the need for teams.)

2. With your manager's approval, circulate your list of possible team projects to a wide cross-section of those likely to be chosen for company teams. Survey their interests, including questions about any reservations they may have about team work. (For example, some workers may wonder how they will be evaluated for raises and promotions if they serve on a team. Will their individual effort count, or will they be judged along with the entire team?)

3. Compile the results of your findings in a concise report addressed to management. You should accompany your report with a cover memo summarizing your case for teams (see the examples that follow in this chapter).

You may be addressing executives who have already had good experiences with teams in other companies or have heard good things about teams from peer companies. In that case, your memo and report will probably gain easy acceptance. If your senior management is sour on teams from past experience, you may find that your memo and report lead to a number of meetings with management, where you will have to sell your idea more thoroughly.

Upper management must often be convinced of the need for teams by the potential team members themselves.	**INSIGHT 29**

	Your Turn
Assume that you wanted to form a team within a company or organization that you know well. Describe in specific steps how you would go about getting authorization to form the team.	

A SAMPLE COMMUNICATION TO MANAGEMENT REGARDING TEAM FORMATION

To: Morton Evans
Executive Vice President
XYZ Corporation

From: (you)
Subject: Advantages of Forming Work Teams

I'm pleased to attach my report, "Attitudes and Opportunities regarding Teams at XYZ Corporation." It makes the case that employees working in teams can accomplish corporate assignments more quickly, more affordably, and with more quality than under the present sole-worker arrangement. The report also summarizes a survey of 100 employees, 92 percent of which believe that team-based work would be good for the company, good for their development as employees, and good for product improvements. After you have had a chance to read this report, I would appreciate an opportunity to meet with you to learn about your perspective on the establishment of work teams at XYZ and to talk about ways that any obstacles to teamwork can be removed. Thank you in advance for your interest in what I believe to be a promising development for the company.

Your communication, of course, may be worded differently as you try to match your argument to the nature and needs of your audience. In any case, it's a good idea to write down your argument even if you plan to deliver it orally to your boss. The process of writing down your ideas gives you a chance to see how well they hang together, how well they are supported, and to what degree they can be streamlined to make your point with more impact.

INSIGHT 30	Written or oral requests for the formation of teams must show why the team approach to work has advantages over other approaches.

Your Turn	

What three points (you may have more) would you make in a memo to upper management in your efforts to win approval of the formation of a work team? Use any company or other organization you know well.

PREPARING FOR TEAM MEMBERSHIP

The boss says "yes." You realize from your survey of employees, however, that their eagerness to participate in teams is not matched by their preparation to do so. You may feel that you need a brush-up of team member skills yourself.

Here, then, is the outline of a boot camp of sorts for those who want to work well as team members. This list can serve as the backbone of a training program in your company for potential team participants.

Before becoming a member of a team, an employee must know how to

- listen to others
- work without close direction

- give and take constructive criticism
- participate in efficient discussions
- understand the nature of consensus decision making
- work well with others
- share credit and blame as a group rather than as an individual
- consider the welfare of the team in your words and actions to outsiders
- contribute expertise without flaunting it

The skills necessary for a strong team member may be somewhat different than the skills required for a strong sole contributor to an organization.	**INSIGHT 31**

Your Turn

Using the qualities just listed, evaluate your own abilities as a team member. Where do your strengths lie and where do you need improvement? For the area(s) of improvement, tell how you could go about becoming more skilled.

PREPARING TO LEAD A TEAM

Every team established by management will probably have a leader, usually drawn from among the ranks of the team members themselves. Some companies obey a seniority principle in selecting team leaders. Others award the position to the highest paid or most degreed worker in the group. The wisest companies, however, pick the person who has the best leadership skills. If you intend to be that person—or to be able to recognize him or her on your team—here's a concise summary of the qualities most often sought in team leaders. This individual must be able to

- withhold personal ideas and judgment long enough for others on the team to have their say
- listen with interest and respect even to ideas and opinions that differ significantly from their own
- direct traffic in discussion without playing favorites
- draw out quieter members of the team and hold back more vociferous members as necessary
- keep discussion moving in a fruitful direction, with an eye toward reaching stages of agreement that will eventually underpin a decision
- build consensus rather than forcing close votes

- focus the team, as often as required, on its short- and long-term goals
- defuse conflict among team members by distinguishing between ideas and personalities, redirecting comments, and using humor as appropriate
- be an advocate for the team in its negotiation for resources, personnel, facilities, and support
- be a liaison for the team with upper management
- be a cheerleader for the team, with a firm belief in the ability of the team to achieve its goals

A team leader doesn't need to have "the right stuff," if that phrase implies some kind of heroic courage and wisdom. Good team leadership is much more a matter of learned skills applied consistently—doing things right.

INSIGHT 32 | The skills necessary for strong team leadership go beyond those required for strong team membership. A team leader should not be chosen simply because he or she has been a good team member.

Your Turn

Using the leadership qualities just listed, evaluate your own abilities as a team leader. Where do your strengths lie and in what area(s) do you need improvement? For the areas named for improvement, tell how you would go about becoming more skilled.

ACTIVITIES FOR THE FIRST TEAM MEETING

So far so good. With the help of your company's training department, you've prepared team members and team leaders. You're now ready to kick off your first team meeting—a marketing team, let's say, with responsibility for investigating and recommending new sales opportunities for the company.

Your first team meeting is crucial in setting the agreed-upon ground rules, goals, and methods of operation for the team. It's a good idea to allow team members to get to know one another before any substantive issues are discussed or decided upon. The typical "let's each introduce ourselves" approach gives each member a chance to speak briefly, but does not allow opportunity for relationships to develop. Therefore, consider one of the following icebreakers:

1. Team members are divided into pairs, with person A interviewing and gathering notes on person B, and vice versa. After 20 minutes or so of such paired conversation, person A introduces person B to the team, then person B

introduces person A. The process continues until all team members have been introduced. The team leader should include himself or herself in this activity so as not to seem aloof from or superior to other team members. In the case of an odd number of team members, one group of three can form, with person A interviewing person B who interviews person C who interviews person A.

2. Each member of the team is given a few minutes to call to mind a brief "impress us—depress us" set of experiences to tell the group. For example, a member might decide to talk about recently having twins on the "impress us" side, then tell about the cost of diapers on the "depress us" side. Another team member may point to some impressive achievement in the company, then talk about a recent depressor such as a speeding ticket or car problem. This good-natured activity gives members not only a chance to tell something positive about themselves but also to poke a bit of self-directed humor at something less positive. In virtually all teams where this activity has been tried, a great deal of laughter accompanies the disclosures of team members. If time allows, team members can ask questions after each person's turn at speaking.

3. Each member takes a minute or so to tell what he or she would do if they won the lottery. Because this activity takes the focus off business, it gives members a chance to get to know one another as people. This form of self-introduction invites a mixture of humor and serious disclosure and can be accompanied by questions from the group.

No matter what icebreaking activity you decide to use, make every effort to avoid the drill sergeant approach to the first meeting, in which one person drones on while team members sit silent and become increasingly sullen about the team experience.

| Team members must get to know and trust one another before open discussion of work issues can be successfully undertaken. | **INSIGHT 33** |

Your Turn

Recall the first meeting of a team on which you served. How did team members get to know one another? If the members knew each other before joining the team, how was the first meeting spent? Looking back, would you have used this time differently in any way if you had been the team leader?

WRITING AN INFORMAL AGENDA FOR TEAM MEETINGS

As a general rule, team meetings do not follow the same rigid agenda or rules of order used by standing committees of companies and other organizations. It's rare indeed to find a team that abides strictly by Robert's Rules of Order in conducting discussion and making decisions. On the other hand, teams require some organization for their meetings and a reasonable degree of prior notice about the topics to be discussed.

Several days before the team meeting, the team leader should contact team members to gather suggestions for agenda items, announcements, and other matters for the meeting. The team leader compiles these ideas into an informal agenda that should be sent to each member with enough advance notice to allow calendaring the meeting and preparing for the topics to be discussed. Of course, many teams have a fixed time each week or other period for their meeting.

The goal of this informal agenda is to keep discussion from becoming chaotic or imbalanced. Devoting most of the team meeting to a relatively trivial item wastes not only the meeting at hand, but also pushes forward more and more weighty topics to future meetings, where insufficient time may be available to give them their due. An informal agenda structures and paces the work of the team without imposing a rigid schedule or process that detracts from the nature and advantages of the team approach.

Here is an example of an informal agenda for a meeting of a marketing team composed of six members:

Weekly Meeting for February 8, 200_, 10:00 A.M. to 12:00 P.M.,
Conference Room 323.
Marketing Team: A. Williams, C. Trent, G. Chung, H. Evans, E. Ramirez.
Contact for questions and input: G. Chung, ext. 9824.

Scheduled topics for discussion:

1. Discussion and possible decision on partnering with C-tronics—30 min. Overview of issues: C. Trent

2. Review of advertising media recommendations—30 min. Overview of issues: H. Evans

3. Investigation of vendor marketing models—60 min. Overview of issues: E. Ramirez

By this simple agenda, sent to participants several business days before the meeting, the team leader—G. Chung in this case—sets up the team meeting for success in several ways. First, the burden for introducing each of the main topics is taken off the team leader and distributed to the team members themselves. They have ample notice from the team leader to prepare their remarks for the meeting. This distribution of responsibility has the added value of building the participation and leadership skills of the members. Second, the topics for the meeting are published so that members can think about them before the meeting, not just during the meeting. Finally, a time limit is recommended (though not insisted upon) for each topic so that more important or more complicated topics receive an appropriate amount of time for discussion. If the team discovers at the meeting that a particular topic is taking more time than anticipated, the members can agree to redistribute the time limits suggested on the informal agenda.

Teams usually do not require a formal agenda, but they can gain advantages from an informal description of topics and responsibilities distributed well in advance of meetings.	**INSIGHT 34**

Your Turn
Think about a team on which you now serve or have served. Does the team make use of an agenda of any kind? If so, describe and evaluate it. If not, explain why an informal agenda would or would not be appropriate for your team.

TAKING NOTES OR MINUTES FOR TEAM MEETINGS

In the same way that agendas for team meetings are usually less formal than agendas for traditional committees, so the notes or minutes for team meetings are less formal in format but not less accurate in description and detail. A team usually does not have a non-team member (such as a secretary) present to take notes. Nor does one of the team members opt out of discussion for the sake of keeping the minutes. Instead, team members can take turns writing up the nature of discussion and decisions for distribution to all members after the meeting. The goal of these less formal notes is to record what the team considered and decided, not to present a blow-by-blow description of who said what to whom. Team minutes are usually distributed within 48 hours of the meeting. In some organizations, teams keep their notes or minutes confidential so that interim team opinions are not misinterpreted by the rest of the organization as final judgments. In other companies, teams use their minutes as a way of keeping the rest of the workforce, especially upper management, informed of their activities on a week-by-week basis.

Here is an example of minutes for the marketing team's February 8 meeting (see previous agenda):

Minutes for weekly meeting for February 8, 200_, 10:00 A.M. to 12:00 P.M.,
      Conference Room 323.
Marketing Team: Attending were A. Williams, C. Trent, G. Chung, H.
      Evans, E. Ramirez.
Please direct questions, comments, or corrections to G. Chung, ext. 9824.

Topics discussed:

1. Possibility of partnering with C-tronics on magazine advertising: C. Trent presented an analysis of pros and cons. Discussion focused on C-tronics's low name recognition for our customer base. Decision postponed until after a presentation by a C-tronics representative scheduled for February 15.

2. Advertising media recommendations: H. Evans reviewed team findings for television and internet advertising. Team unanimously agreed to recommendation contained in supplement A.

3. Investigation of vendor marketing models: E. Ramirez presented four vendor models for discussion. Team concluded discussion of models 1 and 2; discussion of the remaining models was sent forward to the next weekly meeting.

Meeting notes taken by: A. Williams

INSIGHT 35   Teams require a permanent record of their topics, discussion, and decisions.

Your Turn

Think of a team on which you now serve or have served. Describe and evaluate any system of notes, minutes, or other record keeping used by your team. If your team uses no such system, describe a form of notes or minutes that you believe would be helpful to your team and organization.

KEEPING THE TEAM INFORMED BETWEEN MEETINGS

The team leader makes pertinent information available as it arises between meetings. However, the responsibility for gathering and distributing such information should not fall to the team leader alone. Each team member has the ongoing task of keeping in touch with the rest of the team between meetings, sending insights as they occur rather than saving them up for a meeting, and gathering information that may prove useful to the team. In this way the team avoids meetings characterized by lectures that transfer knowledge to team members, and instead makes it possible for knowledge to be discussed. Only by getting knowledge between meetings can the team reserve the meeting time itself for an evaluation of that knowledge.

The work of a team does not begin and end with its meetings. Team leaders and members make an effort to acquire and distribute insights and information between meetings so that meeting time can be used for discussion and decision making.	**INSIGHT 36**

Your Turn

Think of a team on which you now serve or have served. Describe what members typically do between meetings with regard to the work of the team. Make any recommendations you wish for ways in which that between-meeting time could be better used to the team's advantage.

Summing Up

Teams become valuable to organizations only when team members are prepared for team participation and leadership. The skills that make for a successful team often require training; the competencies that make for a productive single contributor in the organization may be quite different from the abilities that make for a good team member or leader. By using informal meeting agendas and notes or minutes, teams organize their work and record progress.

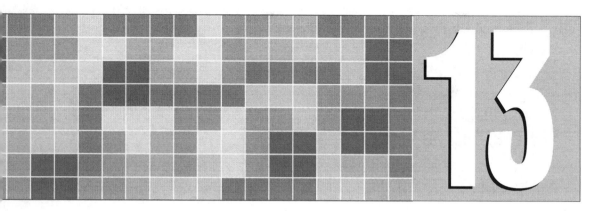

Understanding and Resolving Team Problems

GOALS

- Recognize team problems in their early stages.
- Understand the causes of such problems so they can be prevented in the future.
- Learn techniques for resolving a variety of common team problems.

Trouble in team paradise? Not all teams function smoothly and effectively in business or other organizations. Simply gathering a group of workers together and calling them a team does not guarantee they will act as a team or that the company will gain the benefits of teamwork.

Understanding the problems teams face is often difficult. When teams aren't working well, companies usually don't rush to *The Wall Street Journal*

Taken from: *Learning Team Skills*, by Arthur H. Bell and Dayle M. Smith

to tell their woes. Instead, they quietly bury their mistakes, dissolve their teams, and return to previous ways of organizing work. This chapter faces the reality that teams frequently encounter a variety of problems, some of them so serious that the company gives up on teams entirely. A better option, and certainly a more cost-effective one, is to understand the primary causes of team problems and assemble tools and techniques to resolve those issues.

A CASE HISTORY OF A TROUBLED TEAM

A West Coast executive tells this story of his company's experience with troubled teams:

> We followed a high-paid consultant's advice and organized our work processes around teams. Perhaps we expected too much too soon. The fact is that work flow and decision making slowed dramatically, as teams got used to working with one another and had meetings, meetings, meetings to deal with even small decisions. After about 6 weeks the company grapevine was carrying the message loud and clear: This team thing just doesn't work. We convened our executive committee to make a decision whether to struggle on with the team organization or to go back to our traditional work roles and reporting order.
>
> Before we made that decision, however, we took time to investigate what had gone wrong with our teams. We discovered three problems: We hadn't trained employees to work as team members, we hadn't revised the pay and bonus structure in the company to reward teamwork, and we hadn't realized that new ways of working would yield new kinds of results, not the same deliverables we were used to. Instead of scrapping the teams, therefore, we invested money and time in a 2-month intensive training program for all employees, top to bottom. We haven't ironed out all the wrinkles, but we're definitely seeing progress in the form of morale, innovation, and flexibility to meet changing market conditions.[1]

This corporation survived its turbulent period with teams and now continues to reap the benefits of a motivated, team-based workforce. The lesson? Don't assume that teams will run smoothly on their own. Prepare your employees for what they can expect and contribute as team members and monitor teams carefully for the first signs of trouble.

We can follow that general advice as an organizing principle for this chapter. First, we will discuss five ways in which employees can be taught to work well as team members. Second, we will investigate the 10 most common problems faced by teams across industries and organizations. Finally, for each of these problems, we will suggest techniques and tools for repairing problems and preventing their recurrence.

---

[1] Personal conversation, October 1, 2001.

A team problem is an opportunity to make the team stronger. Team members, the team leader, and upper management can all participate in that opportunity.	**INSIGHT 39**

Your Turn
Recall a recent team experience that in some way was unsatisfactory to you. Was the problem treated as an opportunity for improvement? Explain your answer.

TEACHING PEOPLE HOW TO BE TEAM MEMBERS

Putting several people together in the same room and giving them a common task in no way guarantees that they will work together effectively to accomplish that goal. Usually the reason has little to do with the intelligence, loyalty, or intentions of the people involved. Too often they simply don't know how to be members of a team. This may be especially true of fast-track, competitive workers who have little patience with group discussion, consensus building, and shared decision making. Even the company's brightest and best employees may have difficulty making the transition from independent contributors to team contributors.

Here, in no particular order, are five lessons that employees must learn well if they are to function effectively as members of a team.

1. Team members must know how to listen. This statement may seem like an innocuous truism comparable to "birds must know how to fly," but sometimes the most obvious truths are the most ignored. As people rise in power, recognition, and compensation within an organization, they often become so enamored of their own insights, opinions, and perspectives that they prevent others from getting a word in edgewise. You may have worked for a boss who lost his or her ears in this way. When you walked into such a boss's office, you knew in advance that you wouldn't get a chance to tell much of your story or make your point. The boss would immediately launch into a sermon that you could only bring to an end by nodding agreement.

Listening requires acknowledgment that the other person may have something worthwhile to say. Even if the content of the person's words is not particularly memorable or valuable, a good boss (or team member) listens anyway. People often communicate much between the words by their eye contact, body language, pauses, sighs, hesitations, and other meaningful signals.

One technique for practicing better listening habits is the "20 breaths" test. When the person begins talking to you about something of importance, see if you can listen to that person for 20 of your own breaths before inserting your own perspectives or objections. (You could also look at your watch, of course, and try to listen for 60 seconds. The problem here is that the person will see you glancing at the clock and draw the conclusion that you are more interested in the time than in what's being said.)

2. Team members must know how to contribute concisely. As people rise in position and importance within an organization, they often feel they have a license to bore—that is, to talk as much as they want to in meetings. They ramble on, repeat their point more than once, and ignore the stifled yawns (silent screams) of their audience. This talent for too much talk isn't exclusively reserved for managers on the rise. Lower-ranking employees, especially those who want to impress their superiors, also can hold forth much longer than anyone wishes. This unfortunate behavior can be death to a team environment. No one wants to be stuck with one or more "big talkers" for the weeks or months that a team may be active.

The answer to this dilemma is not to shut people up—a poor practice on any team—but to remind people to get to the point (once, thank you).

3. Team members must understand the nature of team discussion and decision making. We each have different tolerance and expectation levels for group discussion. Some of us get antsy if an issue can't be presented, discussed, and resolved within a matter of minutes. Others, perhaps those who like committee work, seem content to let discussion meander for hours without any sign of resolution. These differences in discussion habits can rip a team apart. All team members have to have approximately the same model in mind for how—and how long—a topic is discussed; how consensus is achieved or at least attempted; and how group decisions are made without creating winners and losers on the team. These skills and group experiences are a matter of training. Lacking such development, workers will probably persist in their individual approaches to discussion, sure that everyone else on the team is doing it wrong.

4. Team members must know how to criticize ideas without criticizing personalities. "I think you're wrong" is the kind of phrase that sets tempers on edge among team members. "I don't agree with your point" changes the focus to the idea at hand rather than the person espousing the idea. Again, a short training session can make all workers aware of this simple but crucial adjustment in thinking and perspective.

5. Team members must be able to rely on others for help. "Lone rangers" are alive and well in companies and other organizations. These are the rugged individualists—corporate survivalists, really—who depend only on themselves to fulfill all aspects of their job responsibilities. Although these people may make productive employees in some work environments, they make lousy team members. Just as children learn early on to play together

and share toys, so team members must be socialized at some point (obviously in a more sophisticated way) to work together and share resources.

> The knowledge and skills required to be an effective team member do not come naturally to most people. We learn to become team members just as we learn many other professional roles.
>
> **INSIGHT 40**

> **Your Turn**
>
> Based on your team experience, which of the five training suggestions in this section seems most important to you? Explain why.

FIVE COMMON TEAM PROBLEMS AND TOOLS FOR REPAIR AND PREVENTION

Now that we have prepped our potential team members by training them to listen, contribute concisely, discuss patiently, criticize objectively, and rely on one another, we can set the team in motion and see how it spins. If we observe a wobble or worse, the fault probably lies in one of the following five team maladies:

Unsuitable Personalities

Not everyone is cut out to be a team member, even with prior training. If most team members agree that one or two individuals are causing the team to founder, investigate their opinion and act promptly to deal with (probably remove) the problematic individual. (We aren't talking here about the individual whose opinions differ from those of the majority on the team; this person can be valuable as a devil's advocate or the "loyal opposition." A problematic team member is one whose character or personality subverts the trust level and basic processes shared by other team members.)

The Fink

This individual offends other team members by "talking out of school"—that is, gossiping to outsiders about privileged discussion among team members. In unguarded discussion, all team members occasionally say something that they would not like quoted to certain other individuals, perhaps a boss, outside the team. To have their words shared and often distorted without their consent is an intolerable rift in the trust level that team members must assume for frank discussion.

Inveterate finks must be removed from teams. Accidental finks (those who are trying out fink behavior for the first time) can be saved for team service by having their behavior called to their attention, preferably by the boss. "If I want to know what Alice thinks," a boss can say to the wanna-be fink, "I will ask Alice. Don't start harmful rumors." That kind of frank response usually alerts a fink to his or her objectionable behavior.

INSIGHT 41	"Talking out of school" as a team member ends up hurting both the team and the person spreading rumors about the team.

Your Turn

How do you respond when someone approaches you with hot news about an otherwise confidential matter at work?

The Stone

This is the individual who rarely speaks up in team discussion, seldom volunteers for responsibility, and seems to have no opinion when it comes to decision making. The silence of the Stone can arise from basic shyness (not uncommon for new employees), annoyance at being put on the team, plain laziness, or other causes.

Discover what's going on inside the Stone by means of an individual, heart-to-heart conference. If the cause of this individual's silence is shyness, work with other team members in making the individual feel more a part of the group. If the individual dislikes serving on the team, find something else for this person to do. No team should have to endure an unwilling member. If the Stone is simply kicking back and letting others do the work, give the individual a significant work assignment and make its accomplishment part of the person's performance evaluation.

The Objector

An objection can no doubt be raised to any statement uttered by a human being. Do you object? The problem with the Objector is that this person has no other discussion technique beyond objection. Sometimes the Objector has developed this discussion habit as a way of attracting attention, albeit largely negative attention, or the Objector may simply have a speculative mind that needs exercise by playing the pros and cons game with every imaginable assertion.

Within moderation, Objectors serve a valuable function for the team by preventing GroupThink and other rushes to team judgment, but when this individual puts up roadblocks to team discussion at every opportunity, something must be done. Perhaps the team itself can have a discussion with the Objector (if he or she doesn't object!) in an effort to understand the person's one-track approach, or the team leader can privately make the Objector aware of how this behavior undercuts the work of the team.

The Petty Tyrant

This individual is a verbal bully. Through sarcasm, ridicule, temper tantrums, and other emotional displays, the Petty Tyrant makes his or her mood the real agenda for every team meeting. Discussion is held captive by this person's interpersonal aggression. As a general rule, the personality defects that allow a Petty Tyrant to behave in this way are not amenable to quick fixes by a chat with the team leader or intervention by the team itself (although both approaches are always worth a try). It's often necessary to remove the Petty Tyrant, but seldom necessary to apologize to the team for doing so.

Silence, constant objection, and tyrannous domination of others are behaviors that make teamwork impossible.	**INSIGHT 42**

Your Turn
Call to mind someone from your experience with teams who fits one of the previous descriptions. How did the team respond to this individual? How did you respond? What finally happened?

The Word Machine

Jerry Seinfeld's famous phrase, "yada yada yada," typifies the Word Machine. The Word Machine manages to turn a simple thought into a long harangue through three verbal devices. First, the Word Machine creates a series of paraphrases for the same idea: "I went to lunch because it was noon and I needed to eat, which is pretty much what I do every day around 12 o'clock, because we get an hour or so off work at that time for, you know, the midday meal." Second, the Word Machine tells not only what things are but what they aren't: "I stapled the pages together. I didn't use a paperclip or tape or a manila folder or those spiral bindings you can get at the copy shops." Finally, the Word Machine accompanies every expression of thought with a record of personal information or emotion: "I got here at 8:00 A.M., even though I'm not really a morning person, probably because I had to get up early with my kids for all those years and I finally said to myself, 'Enough of this greet-the-dawn routine,' so now I just work out some kind of flextime so that usually I don't have to get here early, like I did this morning."

The Word Machine doesn't mean to be annoying. In most cases, he or she simply likes to chatter and assumes (against all nonverbal evidence) that others don't mind listening. Intentions aside, the Word Machine can be dangerous to team processes if other team members begin to dread meetings; if a significant percentage of valuable team time is taken up by such gabble; or if the team fails to discuss topics thoroughly because of constant distractions from the Word Machine.

Talking to the Word Machine seems somehow redundant, akin to carrying water to the lake. Because a good shaking is out of professional bounds, the team leader can meet privately with the Word Machine and say something along these lines: "You're a very nice person and we all like you. Do you realize that you talk much, much more than any other team member? You've got to let others have their fair share of our discussion time." As an alternative to this conversation, a team leader can make a copy of the Word Machine discussion in this book and leave it in the Word Hog's office mail.

INSIGHT 43   Saying too much too often is as ruinous to team proceedings as failing to contribute at all.

Your Turn

Certainly you have worked with someone who simply talks too much. Why do you think this person is so talkative? How can this tendency be controlled?

The Stalled Team

Even the most promising of teams have times when work bogs down and progress comes to a halt. The causes of such unexpected stalls usually can be determined only by a careful review of the business circumstances and team processes existing at the time. In general, however, teams experience periods of frustrating stagnation for one or more of the following reasons.

1. Team members are exhausted from an overly ambitious work schedule. Their inability to press on with work is a way of telling people in the company that they need a break of some kind.

2. Team members have experienced some kind of disappointment or dead end. Perhaps one of their decisions, for example, has been soundly rejected by upper management. In this case, the stall they are experiencing stems from a lack of motivation to press ahead with work that apparently is not respected or approved in the organization.

3. Team members have a problem of some kind with the team leader. Members sometimes "go to ground" in not-so-subtle protest against what they perceive as overly dominant leadership, favoritism on the part of the leader, or perhaps too little leadership.

4. Team members have a problem with one another. The stall reflects their common judgment that team processes have broken down.

TOOLS FOR REPAIR

Like a stalled car, a stalled team can either be jump-started by an outside energy source of some kind or turned on again by repair of its own internal workings. If the new start comes from an outside source, it is usually in the form of a meeting with one or more senior managers who are not part of the team but are nonetheless responsible for its progress. At this meeting (or series of meetings) the senior manager expresses confidence in the team, reviews their positive accomplishments in the past, and investigates through active listening and probing questions, the circumstances (as team members perceive them) causing the current stall. The senior manager leads the team to a solution that, preferably, the team itself helps to shape. An imposed solution usually has less power to restart a team; participative buy-in to the solution is a critical component of a workable answer to the team's problems.

If the jump start comes from within the team itself, it can take the form of a retreat of some kind, in which the team gets away from its usual surroundings and work issues to approach its problems in a fresh way. Some teams arrange an off-site day at a resort location or other meeting place where natural beauty, creature comforts, and the opportunity to relax combine to renew team creativity and the willingness to seek solutions. At such a retreat the team leader can ask each team member to talk about what's going right and what's going wrong on the team. Discussion should move toward consensus and then toward a team-generated action plan.

| A stall should not be taken as a permanent condition of the team. Stalls can be overcome by external or internal measures. | **INSIGHT 44** |

| **Your Turn** |
| Recall a time when a team on which you were a member reached a stall or dead end of some kind. Did the team recover? If so, how? |

The Out-of-Control Team

This is the team that exceeds its envelope of authority and begins using resources and making decisions in areas where it has no business operating. Some teams make this mistake because their original charter was never made clear by management. Other teams grow power hungry within the company and attempt to gobble up other job categories and budgets that can add to their influence in the organization.

TOOLS FOR REPAIR

No matter what the cause, the runaway team must be called back into check without deflating the high energy level and motivation that characterizes the team. A senior manager can meet with the team leader to reinforce the boundaries of the team's authority and responsibility. The team leader is then given the chance to communicate these limits persuasively to members of the team. If that communication fails, the senior manager must step in again, this time in a meeting with the entire team. The senior manager can praise the team for its gung-ho spirit, but also insist that those energies be focused on the specific work assignments given to the team. Members of the team should leave that meeting feeling appreciated for the effort and reeducated about the scope of their work.

INSIGHT 45	Because they are usually composed of talented, influential individuals, teams have implicit power within organizations. When they misuse that power and exceed their authority, teams become an organizational liability.

Your Turn

If you have observed or served on a runaway team, briefly tell its story and outcome. If you have never observed or served in this way, tell what you would do as a team member if your team showed signs of becoming a runaway group.

The Bickering Team

No senior manager likes to have to deal with a whining, backbiting group of individuals whose single interest seems to be "who did what to whom" on the team. The bickering team, like squabbling children, seems to cry out for parenting, and yet when a senior manager steps in, he or she is immediately accused of listening to only one side of the story or taking sides unfairly. Before senior managers enter the fray, therefore, they should get the team to distill the nature of its problems. If the team itself can define the root causes of its bickering, a senior manager can usually guide the team to find its own solutions.

TOOLS FOR REPAIR

If the team can't diagnosis its own ills successfully, a senior manager should meet privately with each member of the team. After hearing each person's gripes (often an unpleasant series of interviews), the manager will have a rather clear picture of what's going wrong in the team. Solutions can include reassigning certain team members, changing the leadership of the team to a person all members can accept, or exerting disciplinary authority by telling team members to act professionally if they hope to be rewarded professionally in the organization.

People squabble for hundreds of reasons. No matter what the cause, their interpersonal friction can seriously interrupt the work of teams.	**INSIGHT 46**

Your Turn
Call to mind two people who didn't get along at work. What was the source of their antipathy? Was the matter ever resolved? If so, how?

The Leaderless Team

In some companies, a stigma attaches to people who stick their necks out in taking over leadership responsibilities. As the Japanese saying goes, "The protruding nail must be hammered down." Democratic culture can be so influential in these organizations that teams attempt to do without a leader entirely. A senior manager often discovers this situation in trying to determine how the team is progressing. When the manager contacts one team member, the manager is passed along to another member with the explanation, "Well, I can only speak for my own activities on the team." The truth soon emerges that no one speaks for the team as a whole, nor does anyone know quite what the team has done, is doing, or will do.

TOOLS FOR REPAIR

A senior manager may be sorely tempted to simply appoint one member of the team as leader, in effect saying to the members, "Look, just do what Ruth tells you to do." This solution, of course, is only the beginning of bigger troubles for the team. The senior manager's designation of Ruth as leader is the kiss of death to her authority in the team. She quickly becomes the last person team members will listen to or follow. A better solution lies in working with the team so that it chooses its own leader and participates, with the senior manager's input, in defining the roles the leader will play on the team. Finally, if the spirit of individual rights is so strong on the team that no leader can be agreed on, the senior manager may have to join the team and impose a reasonable degree of leadership. This option is quite literally a case of "if you can't beat them, join them."

INSIGHT 47	Too little leadership can be as devastating to business processes as too much leadership.

Your Turn	
Tell about a time when you wanted more leadership from some individual in your business or academic life. Why do you think that person did not lead in the way you wished? How did the situation finally turn out?	

HOW PEOPLE INDICATE THAT A TEAM IS IN TROUBLE

Indications that a team is in trouble frequently are not spelled out for a manager or for the team members themselves. The SOS message comes in more subtle ways. Team leaders, team members, and upper managers can watch for 10 symptoms of the troubled team:

- The work product is shoddy and deadlines are continually missed.
- Members miss meetings using suspicious excuses.
- Members treat a minor achievement as if it were the culmination of their entire work. They reveal their lack of interest in accomplishing the true goals of the team by celebrating victory too soon.
- Members gossip about and talk down their fellow team members to outsiders.
- Individual members seem to be cutting their own deals, advancing their personal agendas, and setting their own goals without regard for what the team as a whole should be doing.
- The team leader appears constantly involved with putting out small fires of controversy among team members or, just as bad, trying to hide the squabbles on the team from outside view at any cost.

- Members complain that they were under duress of some kind and were compelled by social pressure or implied threats to go along with the will of the majority.

- Particular members keep asking for individual praise for their work on the team and refuse to find any satisfaction in recognition for the entire team.

- Some members withdraw and sit sulking on the sidelines of the action taking place in the team.

- One or more members constantly play the "blame game" by attributing any team failure, however small, to ineptness on the part of the leader or other team members.

These signs, singly or in any combination, tell a good manager that trouble is brewing on the team. Early intervention can prevent major blowups, including terminations, resignations, and even lawsuits.

People do not sit idly by while the team ship begins to sink. They let outsiders know about team troubles by their words, actions, and nonverbal communications.	**INSIGHT 48**

Your Turn
If you have served on an ineffective team, tell specific ways in which you or other team members let others know about what was wrong with the team. If you have never served on an ineffective team (lucky you!), tell about signs or signals you have observed from others who did serve on such teams.

A LIGHTER LOOK AT THE CHALLENGE OF MANAGING A TEAM

Sometimes the fault with a team lies not with the team itself, but with the management style (or lack of style) of the senior manager responsible for the team. *Today's Team Facilitator* magazine takes a tongue-in-cheek swipe at managers who are themselves the source of the team problems about which they complain.[2]

---

[2] Cited in Skopec, E. *How to Use Team Building to Foster Innovation.* Chicago: NTC, 1998, p. 97.

If you want to make sure your team fails, the article proposes, simply do the following:

- Don't listen to any new idea or recommendation from a team. It's probably not a good idea because it's new and different.
- Don't give teams any additional resources to help solve their problems in their area. Teams are supposed to save money and make do with less. Besides, they probably will just waste more time and money.
- Treat all problems as signs of failure and treat all failures as reasons to disband the team and downgrade team members. Teams are supposed to make things better, not cause you more problems.
- Create a system that requires lots of reviews and signatures to get approval for all changes, purchases, and new procedures. You can't be too careful these days.
- Get the security department involved to make it difficult for teams to get information about the business. Don't let those team members near company databases. You don't want them finding out how the business is really run.
- Assign a manager to keep an eye on the teams in your area. Tell each member that he or she is there to help facilitate (teams like that word). But what you really want these managers to do is control the direction of the teams and report back to you on any deviations from your plan.
- When you recognize or change policies and procedures, don't involve team members in the decision or give them any advance warning. This will just slow things down and make it difficult to implement the changes.
- Cut out all training. Problem solving is just common sense anyway, and besides, all that training really accomplishes is to make a few consultants rich.
- Express your criticism freely and withhold praise and recognition. People need to know where they have screwed up so they can change. If you dole out praise, people will expect a raise or reward.

Again, this is all satiric advice—the precise opposite of what a good team manager should do.

| **INSIGHT 49** | The way teams are managed has much to do with the way they look upon themselves and the success with which they function. |

Your Turn

Call to mind a team on which you served. To whom did the team report? Describe how this person managed (or mismanaged) the team.

Summing Up

The fact that teams experience problems from time to time does not mean that the team concept itself is a failure or that particular teams are doomed. The first signs of such problems gives team members, the team leader, and senior management an opportunity to discover the causes of the difficulty and resolve it in a way that strengthens the team for increased productivity.

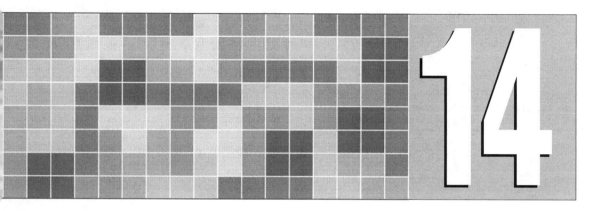

Completing Collaborative Projects Through Teamwork

Taken from: *Learning Team Skills*, by Arthur H. Bell and Dayle M. Smith

"A camel is a horse designed by a team." "Too many cooks spoil the broth." Those two sayings communicate a common distrust about teamwork. Do you share that distrust, based on your experience with teams to date? This chapter shows, step-by-step, how to avoid the common pitfalls associated with the group development of a major document or presentation. A team has much to gain by mastering skills in collaborative work: Documents and oral presentations undertaken collaboratively are often more thoroughly researched, carefully designed, and efficiently written than similar projects taken on by a single writer. Moreover, such projects spring from a broader cross-section of the organization, which usually translates into greater buy-in from the company for the work product itself.

WHY TEAMS OFTEN HAVE TROUBLE WITH COLLABORATIVE PROJECTS

This chapter will investigate why many team members resist collaborative projects that involve developing a lengthy report, proposal, or presentation. Along the way we will discuss the importance, even the necessity, of the collaborative approach to many company communications. Then we will describe the step-by-step stages that teams can use in creating a major document or presentation. Finally, we will suggest practical techniques for team leaders who must supervise the collaborative efforts of their team members.

"It's easier to just do it myself." During your work or academic experience to date, you may have said these words about a team project that was hopelessly bogged down in disagreements, missed deadlines, and conflicting approaches. You may have had a team experience, for example, in which the eventual work product was supposed to be a report. Even though you related well to all other members of the team, complications in the project seemed to spring up from the very beginning. No one knew quite how to proceed or, just as bad, everyone had a different idea of how to get started and insisted their idea was the only good idea. When work finally got underway, some team members did too little and some did too much. Ill will crackled in the meeting room. Pieces of prose from individual team members didn't flow smoothly together to make a consistent document. Each team member wrote in a somewhat different style and could not be persuaded to write in any other manner. Finally, as in most cases of team collapse, one or two team members simply took charge of the project and did it themselves. Perhaps you were one of those brave souls. The team gave a collective sigh of relief to complete the project, but not one of the members found the collaborative process fulfilling or efficient.

Collaboration is a learned skill. Lacking that skill, team members may well find collaborative work inefficient and nettlesome.   **INSIGHT 58**

Your Turn

Call to mind a group project or other collaborative attempt that did not go well. Analyze the causes for its failure.

The frustrations and reservations you may have already experienced with the collaborative approach are usually due to one or more of the following factors:

Lack of Experience

Especially for new employees, the concept of developing a document or presentation as a team is quite new. Their experience through high school and college focused primarily on completing such work alone. Unauthorized assistance, in fact, was considered cheating. No wonder that many team members come to their first collaborative experience with little to offer and much to fear.

Lack of a Common Model

At the first team meeting with team members inexperienced in the collaborative approach to projects, it's not uncommon for each team member to describe, and even insist upon, his or her own way of developing a document or presentation. Listen in, for example, on these team voices:

Ralph: I think we all know approximately what we want to say. Let's just start on page one and write until we have a rough draft completed. That's the way I always did it in college. And I got good grades, by the way.

Manuel: That won't work, Ralph. Obviously the first thing we have to do is make an outline. All my teachers told me to begin with an outline, and that's what all the books say as well. Then we can divvy up parts of the outline and get this thing done.

Susan: How can we make an outline before we agree on our ideas, Manuel? Shouldn't we have a few meetings to agree on the basic ideas for our report before we even think about writing?

Linda: Wait a minute. A few meetings? We've got a deadline for this project and we can't just sit around talking. Let me try to write up the whole thing this weekend. Then you can all revise what I've done and put in any extra material you have. Don't worry, I'm a fast writer.

It's easy to see that such disagreements can quickly undermine the team's effort and eventual success. In such circumstances, the most senior or most powerful member of the team usually weighs in and has his or her way with the writing process. Grumbling, the rest of the team members give in and half-heartedly participate in the frustrating development process, but none does his or her best work. Some team members simply opt out of the process entirely or attempt to get reassigned.

Lack of Understanding About Relating to One Another

Inevitably in the process of team collaboration some team members will criticize and even discard the ideas or work samples of other group members. Unless the team knows how to work through such periods of disagreement, tempers will flare and work will grind to a halt. An important part of the collaborative process, therefore, involves successful group dynamics. On one hand, the team should not fall into GroupThink, described in Chapter 1 as the pressure to accept ideas solely to maintain group harmony. On the other hand, the team should not destroy itself by personal attacks, counterattacks, and hurt feelings. The team should seek a middle road where ideas and drafted work are evaluated fairly with a consensus view toward what's best for the emerging project.

INSIGHT 59	Simply knowing the main pitfalls to collaborative projects is the first step in avoiding those mistakes.

Your Turn	
Think about a time when you were less than happy as a member of a collaborative team. Describe the source of your unhappiness. What eventually happened?	

WHY COLLABORATIVE PROJECTS ARE GOOD FOR TEAMS AND GOOD FOR BUSINESS

The struggles of a team to work together on a collaborative project would matter less if business could get along without collaborate work—but it can't for at least five reasons.

First, participation in collaborative projects strengthens the work team itself. The value of collaborative writing, for example, lies not only in its end—a document completed on time—but in its means. Employees, often from different work units, join as team members and learn to work together toward a common goal. They experience the value of sharing expertise and accepting feedback. In short, they build the team spirit so crucial for corporate success.

Second, collaborative projects involve a political process. Few large corporations are pure dictatorships with the CEO barking out strict orders for employees to follow. Instead, many if not most companies organize according to what Douglas McGregor has called Theory Y principles (see Chapter 8), including participative decision making and shared work goals. In this kind of business, a manager doesn't put an engineer, a technical writer, a personnel officer, and a computer specialist on a collaborative team solely for the sake of their differing areas of expertise. The manager assembles this collaborative team to forge alliances and satisfy constituencies within the company. The engineering division, for example, may want to have its say in the document under development by the team; the inclusion of an engineer on the collaborative team assures that division that its interests will be represented.

Thus, when a collaborative team succeeds in working productively, different sectors around the company reap political dividends. Seeing this example of effective interaction on the team, divisions within the company become more cooperative and less likely to suspect the motives of other divisions. The collaborative team is the tip of an iceberg that extends deep into the political structure of the company.

A third reason business needs collaborative teams is that this approach to work reduces risk factors. Few companies can afford the risks involved in turning over a major document or presentation project to one individual. Even the most talented individual can be dead wrong at times. The company could face disaster if an incorrect or one-sided report goes forward from one individual without the checks and balances provided by other team members. Another risk is the dependence of a major project on the continued employment, health, or work habits of one individual. The team approach to collaborative development assures that the project will proceed, even if an individual on the team leaves the company or becomes ill.

Collaborative work incorporates more expertise—the fourth reason for its importance to business. No one person knows it all. Most important business documents and presentations discuss more than one point of view and come to a balanced conclusion. For those points to emerge, they must be represented on the team. Using the collaborative approach to document or presentation development, a safety specialist's expertise can temper a design expert's enthusiasm for a new product. A technical writer's skill can convey, in readable form, the precise data offered by a statistician.

The final reason collaboration is needed in business is that the process often makes the best use of company resources. When a contract is at stake or a government deadline looms, a company can't afford to have a solitary writer laboring for weeks on a project. The cost of assigning a team to develop a major project is justified if the result is winning the contract, meeting the deadline, or satisfying the client. Choosing a team for the project presumes, of course, that the team members know how to work together to get the job done. If they don't, one skilled writer-researcher might indeed do a better job than a disorganized, bickering team.

INSIGHT 60	Teams serve valuable functions for business far beyond their usefulness as a means of organizing work. Only effective teams, however, can fulfill those functions.

Your Turn	
Call to mind the last team of which you were a member. What purposes did it serve for the larger organization beyond its specific goals and deliverables?	

STEPS IN THE COLLABORATIVE PROCESS FOR DOCUMENTS AND PRESENTATIONS

The collaborative process follows these major steps:

- generate ideas
- organize information
- draft
- revise and edit

In the collaborative process, each of these important stages must be adapted to include the participation of the entire team. It won't do, in other words, to assign major parts of the development process to separate team members ("You think of the ideas. I'll do the writing") any more that two singers can divide a song into lyrics and melody. What follows, therefore, is a step-by-step plan for involving all team members in all stages of the development process for documents and presentations. These steps can be altered to suit varying business circumstances, as the needs of your purpose, audience, and resources dictate.

Step 1: Assemble a Team with Appropriate and Complementary Expertise

Too often, teams are formed on the basis of friendship, volunteers, or simply who's available. None of these approaches guarantees a group of writers with complementary skills and expertise. As a team leader in charge of assembling a collaborative team, consider both professional and personal qualities in deciding which team members will work best together.

The purpose of and audience for your project will determine what professional qualities various team members should bring to the team. For example, the writing of a flight training manual requires expertise from an experienced aviator, a training expert, an instructional writer, and probably a skilled illustrator. The writing of an annual report, by contrast, might well require one or more senior managers, a high-ranking financial officer, a professional writer, and others.

A variety of personality tests (including the well-known Myers-Briggs Type Indicator) can be used to determine the personality profiles of potential team members. Even if managers do not use such assessments, they can try to combine complementary types on the collaborative team. They might put a detail-oriented worker, for example, on the team to balance the influence of a bright but disorganized member. A writer with a lively, journalistic style might be brought aboard to keep a statistician from burying the project in numbers.

Step 2: Meet to Discuss What, When, Why, Where, How, How Much, and Who

What are we developing? In its first meeting, each member of the team must help answer this question. Let's say, for example, that a senior manager has assigned the team the task of writing a report on employee benefits. In this case, the team can decide the precise form of the document (in terms of length, organization, and format). From the beginning, all team members must reach agreement on the essential nature of the task: Is the report to be descriptive, giving details of past, present, and future employee benefit plans, or is the report also to be prescriptive, with recommendations for changing employee benefits in some way? Unless the team answers such initial questions, it cannot proceed productively to other stages in the development process.

When? Just as college assignments usually come with a deadline, so business tasks are tightly constrained by time. The development team must keep time limits in mind when making decisions about the topic range and research scope of the project. Length alone cannot be used to accurately determine how much time a project will take. Projects with short page counts, in fact, sometimes take much longer than more wordy documents. The French philosopher and mathematician Pascal captured this truth in a memorable line to a friend, albeit in French: "I'm sorry I haven't written a shorter letter, but I didn't have time."

Why? It isn't enough for senior management to have a reason for doing projects. Each member of the collaborative team must understand the business reasons and urgency for the project at hand. Team members who understand why they are writing a document, for example, have a much better chance of avoiding unnecessary digressions and blind alleys.

Where? The team must agree on the physical logistics of the collaborative process from the beginning. Where are team members physically located in the building? What communication links or useful software exists? Will the group meet in person or electronically, or both?

How? As we discussed earlier in the voices of Ralph, Manuel, Susan, and Linda, members come to the team with different approaches to the collaborative process. Therefore, they must discuss the process itself, with the goal of reaching a workable consensus. For example, all team members could review the steps set forth in this chapter or another book. Based on that review, the team could discuss and decide on the best way to accomplish the task before it.

How much? Money influences virtually every business decision. Collaboration, like all important business activities, costs the company money. (The salaries alone of four team members working for 1 week on a report could total $10,000 or more.) Instead of ignoring financial realities, the collaborative team should carefully assess how much the company wants to spend (in salaried time, research expenses, and support resources) to accomplish the project at hand. Operating within a budget may mean trimming the team's development plans for the project, but it's better to deal with financial limitations from the beginning rather than confront them later, when the project languishes overextended, half-finished, and underfunded.

Who? In this last agenda item of the first team meeting, the team designates a coordinator and perhaps other roles for team members. Sometimes, of course, the team coordinator is appointed in advance by senior management. If not, it's often better to wait until the end of an initial meeting to decide who will serve as leader or coordinator. In discussing the what, when, why, and other questions, the team has a chance to see each member in action. The team is then in a better position to choose as coordinator the member most likely to keep the team on track, on time, on budget, and not on each other's nerves.

INSIGHT 61	Thinking about the resource and time limitations placed upon a team's work is better undertaken at the beginning of the project than at a later stage.

> ### Your Turn
>
> For a team project on which you are now working or have worked recently, specify at least three resource limits and/or time constraints placed on your work. How did your team cope with these constraints?

Step 3: Meet in Person or Electronically to Generate Ideas

Most collaborative teams brainstorm their topics in face-to-face meetings. At these intense gatherings, team members try out ideas on one another. They listen, react, and avoid the temptation to settle on certain ideas too early in the process.

Especially when team members are separated by distance or scheduling conflicts, they can nevertheless generate ideas and bounce them off one another by means of the many groupware programs now available for collaborative work. The goal of idea generation is to produce not merely enough, but more than enough, useful ideas for the collaborative process. The team strives for as many and as far-reaching ideas as possible during the idea generation stage. Winnowing those ideas (selecting some, discarding others) comes later in the organization stage.

Step 4: Organize Ideas into a Working Outline

Some collaborative teams develop a working outline in a face-to-face meeting. Group members propose, challenge, argue, and compromise on each item in the growing outline until the full scheme lies before the team. Other teams choose to let each member form an organizational outline independently. Members then bring their outlines to a common meeting or share them electronically. In either case, the team reviews the various organizational approaches and puts together the best version—the working outline—from the many versions offered.

Step 5: Evaluate the Working Outline with the Help of Stakeholders

Before pursuing the hard work of research and writing that leads to the first draft of a document or presentation, the team takes time to evaluate the working outline with care. What does the boss or other significant audience member have to say about the outline? Does it satisfy the requirements and expectations of the company? Does the team have the talent, time, and resources to complete the project as outlined? Are all members of the team clear about the meaning of each item in the outline and the relations between those items (i.e., the logic of the outline)?

Step 6: Discuss and Undertake the Research Process

The team now investigates the full range of available research materials to elucidate and support the ideas and statements on the working outline. The coordinator of the team probably assigns portions of the outline to each team member for research. Members bring back their results to a common meeting or make them available to all members electronically.

Step 7: Discuss and Undertake the Drafting Process

Some collaborative teams operate by gradual accumulation. Individual members begin to draft small pieces of the project even during the research process. The team then decides which of those pieces fit well into the overall document and in what ways they should be expanded and connected.

Other collaborative teams require that each member turn over a carefully organized compilation of his or her research to one or two members who are responsible for actually drafting the document. In most cases, the drafters are the most proficient writers in the group—those with a special talent for style, clarity, and flow.

Rarely does a collaborative team compose each sentence of the first draft together. There are simply too many decisions to be made word-by-word in the drafting process for each team member to suggest and argue alternatives. Such discussion can be accomplished better at the revision stage.

The first draft, once completed, should be regarded by all team members as an exceedingly tentative document. In the understandable excitement of nearing the end of the project, too many collaborative teams consider the words of the first draft as text cast in granite. A better approach is to distribute the first draft electronically so that each team member can work through it to note his or her suggested changes.

INSIGHT 62	Few teams have success in beginning the drafting process too early in their collaborative work. Writing becomes quite difficult when you are unsure what you want to say.

Your Turn	
	Is it your habit to create an outline before drafting a document or presentation? How do you go about testing your outline to make sure it flows logically and makes your point? What use do you make of the outline in the drafting process?

Step 8: Evaluate the First Draft with the Help of Stakeholders

All team members now carefully review the completed first draft, looking for qualities of logic, persuasion, support, style, and format. There's no better occasion than this to see if the document suits its audience. If, for example, the project is being completed for senior management, the team may want to schedule a meeting to show these executives the first draft and talk through its major points. The team notes carefully all questions, criticisms, and comments from stakeholders as part of the agenda for the revision process.

Step 9: Revise the Draft for Consistency and Impact

No document is right until it is right for its audience. The team makes adjustments in logical flow, persuasive argumentation, level of diction, paragraph length, tone, format, illustrations, and all other aspects of the project with one goal in mind: to carry out the intended purpose of the document.

Step 10: Edit to Achieve Error-Free Text

Revision differs from editing in the way that farming differs from gardening. The team's revision efforts focus on larger matters of placement and style; those matters often require major renovation, reworking, or deletion. Editing, by contrast, takes a magnifying glass to each word, sentence, paragraph, footnote, and heading of the document. The team relies on iterative editing sessions by different pairs of eyes to catch every typo, misspelling, punctuation mistake, and other error.

These 10 steps describe a path, but not the only path, for the collaborative development of a document or presentation. If your team decides to skip one or more of the steps, take a moment to discuss what you're skipping and why.

Stakeholders, especially the primary audience to whom a document or presentation is addressed, should be involved as reviewers at early, middle, and late stages of the collaborative process.	**INSIGHT 63**

Your Turn

Bring to mind a collaborative project on which you worked. Specify the main stakeholders for that project. Tell how you involved them during the development process. If you did not involve them, tell why.

GUIDELINES FOR THE TEAM LEADER OF A COLLABORATIVE PROJECT

As team leader you have the challenging task of keeping the project moving forward with all members contributing to its development. Here are several distress signals from team members, with brief advice on how to deal with them:

"No one even listens to me." Your job as team leader is to make each team member feel valuable to the project and respected by team members. Inevitably, of course, some team members will contribute more than others, but the team leader should do everything possible (including personal conferences and assigned duties) to prevent malaise, withdrawal, or resentment from disrupting the work of the team.

"Who made you the boss?" Occasionally, a frustrated team member will directly challenge your role as team leader. In such cases, let others in the group speak for you, or you can remind the complaining team member that you have the support of other team members.

"What are we waiting for?" In any process involving the work of several people, occasional delays will occur as one team member waits for another to complete his or her work. Make sure that your team understands both the inevitability of glitches in the team process and the importance of completing work on which others depend.

"Where do you get off telling me I'm wrong?" We are all sensitive to negative criticism about the way we speak or write. That sensitivity carries over to the workplace, especially when one team member criticizes our work as "too wordy," "unclear," or "disorganized." We respond defensively—"Well, then, do it yourself!"—instead of understanding and possibly profiting from the interchange. As team leader, you should emphasize that criticism is directed at the work itself, not the person who wrote it. Conducting revision and editing sessions in a good-humored way goes far in alleviating the potential hostility that can develop when team members spar over language choices.

"I don't understand your changes." Especially as deadlines approach, the team leader and other members of the team may change the work of other members. If a team member requests an explanation, it's important for the team leader to provide one. Never simply say that a passage is "better my way." Doing so breeds ill will on the team and fails to teach the objecting team member preferable alternatives.

Team leaders are inevitably the recipients, if not the targets, of complaints and frustrations from some team members. These leaders can help the team function harmoniously and efficiently if they strategize in advance on how to deal with the most common complaints and criticisms.

INSIGHT 64

Your Turn

If you have led a collaborative effort of any kind, what types of complaints or criticism (if any) did you receive from team members? How did you respond to such comments? If you have not led a collaborative effort or received no complaints or criticism in your leadership role, what have been your main frustrations in serving on a collaborative team? What could the leader have done to address those problems?

Summing Up

Most teams are responsible for a deliverable of some kind, usually in the form of a report or presentation. Teams can be hobbled by the inexperience and resistance of their members in collaborating successfully on this kind of project. When team members and the team leader understand their roles in working together, the pitfalls of collaborative work can be avoided. Ten steps are recommended as a guide to the collaborative development of a document or presentation.

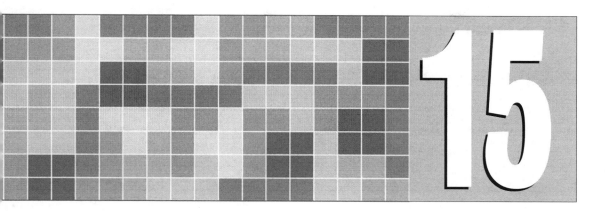

Developing Intercultural Teams

GOALS

- Recognize the increasing importance of intercultural and international teams in corporations and other organizations.

- Understand and adjust to the assumptions and practices of intercultural participants in teams.

- Make the most of the potential of intercultural teams to solve problems and seize opportunities.

Almost every major company you can name—Sears, Boeing, General Electric, IBM, and yes, McDonald's—has international branches that employ native workers. When these companies want to address a multinational problem or opportunity, they commonly assemble a team made up of members from their various branches throughout the world. Team members from India, Japan, France, Brazil, China, and the United States suddenly find themselves in a room—or in a teleconference—as members of an important team charged

Taken from: *Learning Team Skills*, by Arthur H. Bell and Dayle M. Smith

by the company to deal with a global issue of some kind. In a nutshell, that's the intercultural challenge facing more and more work teams in this new century—a challenge that may face you now or in your career future.

SHARED INFORMATION WITHOUT A SHARED CULTURE

Your team members on an intercultural team probably have access to the same company data that you do. As you sit around the meeting table, however, you soon realize that sharing data is not the same thing as sharing culture. Each person at the meeting brings quite different expectations about how and when to speak at the meeting, how to relate to the team leader and other members, when to socialize and when to talk business at meals, how to dress, and even when to arrive at team meetings.

These are all aspects of culture that we each carry with us, often unconsciously. Some things feel right and some things wrong, as judged by our cultural background. The goal of this chapter is not to ask you to set aside your own culture or become a devotee of another person's culture. Rather, the goal here is to become aware of the influence of various cultures on team processes. Once team members recognize the role of cultural difference operating within their team, they can deal constructively with those differences and often gain a competitive advantage because of them.

INSIGHT 65	Intercultural teams are a fact of business life. Their progress can be impeded if members are not skilled in making cultural adjustments.

Your Turn

If you have worked abroad, briefly describe the cultural adjustments you had to make to function effectively in that region of the world. If you have not worked abroad, describe the cultural differences you have observed in a visitor or work associate new to this country. What did they do differently from American businesspeople? What behaviors would you advise them to change if they plan to work for a prolonged period in the United States?

WHAT'S AT STAKE IN UNDERSTANDING CULTURAL DIFFERENCES

In earlier chapters we have seen how much the work of a team depends upon relationships forged among team members and with the team leader. In an intercultural team, the formation of these relationships depends, to a remarkable degree, on the willingness of all team members to

- be flexible and accepting of differences in values, beliefs, standards, and mores—even if they do not understand or personally believe in these differences
- be sensitive to verbal nuances and nonverbal behavior, as intercultural team members attempt to express their feelings as well as their thoughts
- be knowledgable about the religious, cultural, business, social, and dietary practices of other cultures
- be open in sharing aspects of your own culture at the same time you are learning about the cultures of your teammates

American team members sometimes have problems seeing beyond their own cultural assumptions in attempting to relate well with intercultural team members. By putting the spotlight on the following 10 assumptions, we can recognize them for what they are: American values and beliefs that may differ substantially from the perspectives of other, intercultural members of our team.

Assumption 1: Change Is Good

In the United States, change is often associated with progress, development, growth, and advancement. Many older world cultures do not share this basic belief. Instead, they view change as essentially disruptive and destructive. They value stability, preservation, tradition, and heritage.

Assumption 2: Time Controls Us

American businesspeople race against the clock and take time constraints seriously. Not to observe time commitments in the United States is a grave sign of disrespect or unprofessionalism. This is not so in much of the world. In many other cultures, business and other activities are not so rigidly controlled by time. "All in good time" is a common, relaxed attitude toward business projects in many cultures.

Assumption 3: We Are All Created Equal

Americans view equality as an important civic and social goal, but in most of the world, rank and status—often a part of one's birthright—are viewed as a natural part of everyday life and the source of one's authority. To many individuals in other cultures, personal progress out of their "class" is not a worthwhile goal. They have grown up knowing who they are and where they fit in the various strata of their society. Some, in fact, draw a sense of security from such knowledge.

Assumption 4: I Am an Individual with Special Interests and Needs, Including a Right to Privacy

Even though we are now a nation of more than 300 million people, each of us clings to some degree to the assumption of individualism, with attendant rights to be respected. In other cultures, where space is at a premium in homes, offices, and workplaces, and where large numbers of people are treated similarly, the American assumptions about individual rights and individual privacy are seen as merely quaint.

Assumption 5: We Are Self-Made People

In the United States we take cultural pride in making it on our own. We accept inherited wealth, but give the individual little personal credit for wealth secured from a parent. In other cultures, the self-made man or woman may not garner the respect accorded in the United States. "Old money" and old family or social connections may count much more for business influence than a person's track record of personal achievement.

Assumption 6: Competition Makes Us Feel Alive

Americans value competition and stress it as a desirable quality from the classroom to the sports field to the boardroom, but in societies that value cooperation, the intense competitiveness of the United States is not easy to comprehend. These societies place much more emphasis on the building of harmonious relationships among people, partnering with others to achieve common goals, and resisting the temptation to get ahead at the expense of others in the community or culture.

Assumption 7: The Future Looks Bright

People in the United States constantly work, plan, and strive for a better future. We set short- and long-term goals for our professional and financial lives. Much of the rest of the world, however, views an attempt to alter or improve the future as futile (and, in some cultures, even sinful). "What will be, will be" is a common attitude beyond our shores.

Assumption 8: Work Is the Only Game in Town

Americans work more hours per week than any other trading nation. Our work days and activities are scheduled weeks or even months in advance. We value work and the rewards of work so highly that many of us become workaholics. Many cultures do not share this obsessive attention to accomplishing productive labor; instead, they value a modicum of work balanced by a day strolling or meditating, frequent holidays with family and friends, and summer vacations much longer than their U.S. equivalents.

Assumption 9: We Tell It Like It Is

Americans are often viewed as being blunt to the point of rudeness. Our direct approach to people and situations may be difficult to understand for an individual who comes from a society where saving face is important or one in which an indirect method is used for conveying bad news or an uncomplimentary evaluation. Americans typically have little patience with people who hint at what they want to say rather than coming right out with it. From their vantage point, members of other cultures may have trouble trusting and respecting Americans who appear to have so little regard for the feelings of others.

Assumption 10: What Counts Is the Bottom Line

Americans are perceived around the world as being deeply materialistic. We talk about and care about our upscale appliances, cars, TVs, computers, and homes as our just rewards for hard work. Other cultures may view such materialism as spiritually shallow—the sad obsession of people who have not found deeper, less materialistic things to concern themselves with in life.

In this brief overview of some (but certainly not all) American assumptions and values, we have not attached labels of right or wrong to anyone's beliefs. Pointing out that much of the world does not share the American value system does not suggest that one group is correct and the other incorrect. Instead, we can use this knowledge of cultural difference to prepare ourselves for understanding and accepting intercultural team members on their own terms rather than assuming they are just like us.

Americans preparing for membership on an intercultural team can begin by examining their own assumptions and behaviors.	**INSIGHT 66**

Your Turn
Choose one aspect of American culture that you feel would not export well to another area of the world (of your choice). Explain why people in that area would have difficulty accepting the American cultural aspect you have chosen.

Team Manners for Intercultural Meetings

Most cultures are more formal than the United States in meeting behaviors, written documents, and oral presentations. Team members in the United States should be careful to use titles when addressing their team partners in Europe and Asia. It is almost always wise to use a surname and/or title when addressing a colleague in the work setting. A German professional may even be addressed as "Herr Dr. Professor" (three titles!).

In written communications with intercultural team members, opening sentences are usually introductory in nature rather than getting right to the point, in typical American fashion. Brief comments about a previous trip, the beauty of the locale, or other noncontroversial topic are quite appropriate as icebreakers for both written and spoken communications. Sensitive topics such as payments, behavior of company representatives, and errors or delays in shipping should be handled with deft timing, sensitivity, and tact.

In intercultural team conversations and meetings, American members should be careful to avoid terms that reflect superiority, power, or a lack of personal interest. This applies particularly to the giving and receiving of business cards from your intercultural associates. Throughout most of Asia, for example, it is expected that you will receive someone's business card with both hands, take a respectful moment to read it carefully and perhaps comment in a complimentary way on the person's title or company, then place the card in a special holder (rather than cramming it into an already over-stuffed wallet or purse). When giving your business card, you should extend it (again, with both hands) so that the print is readable from the perspective of the person receiving the card. This ritual almost always takes place upon first meeting your intercultural associate, not (as is often the case in American business practice) after a working relationship has been established.

Above all, take time to read about the cultural preferences, rituals, and habits of your intercultural associates before you meet them for the first time. You may even have the time and ability to master a few words in their native languages—a compliment to them, no matter how poorly you speak the words. Several good books on intercultural manners and mores are included in the Recommended Reading section at the end of this book.

INSIGHT 67	We tend to react in spite of ourselves to unusual verbal or nonverbal behaviors exhibited in meetings and other business occasions. Even though we understand that cultural differences explain these unusual behaviors, we often allow our attitudes and relationships to be shaped by our initial, judgmental reactions.

Tell about a time you were irritated or surprised by a verbal or nonverbal behavior on the part of a person new to U.S. culture. Did the person mean to offend you by the behavior? How can you avoid similar problems when you visit a culture that is new to you?

GRASPING THE DEEPER ASPECTS OF CULTURAL DIFFERENCE

If you intend to understand your intercultural team members in more than a surface way, you will inevitably have to come to terms with several profound cultural differences:

The perception of space. Animals, both wild and domestic, guard their territory. This concern for territoriality also exists in nations and cultures. To protect and define our territory we put up flags, fences, rows of bushes, signs, and so forth. The norms that govern our defense of territory are dictated by culture. Americans typically define an area of about 3 feet of open space around their personal territory (i.e., their bodies) as a comfort zone.

If you are a member of an intercultural team with participants from countries such as Mexico and Italy, you should expect them to intrude upon this culturally defined envelope of personal space. Your Italian member, for example, may be speaking with great excitement about a company development. As he does so, he moves to within a few inches of your face. You instinctively back up. Both of you experience an awkward and confusing intercultural moment. "Why is he moving so close to me?" you wonder. "Is he attacking me or is this a come-on of some kind?" Your Italian associate is just as confused. "Why is this person moving away from me? Am I saying something objectionable?"

Consider larger distributions of space from a cultural perspective. Look, for example, at the arrangement and division of space in a U.S. corporation. The president, in splendid isolation, occupies a large office on the top floor with corner windows. By contrast, French or Middle Eastern managing directors more commonly sit among their subordinates so they can observe all activities. Consider your Japanese associate who values a small, gem-like home characterized by elegant proportions and appointed with only the items needed for daily use. Contrast that attitude—and catch his looks of confusion—when he visits his first suburban American home measuring in the thousands of square feet and filled to the bursting point with possessions of all kinds.

INSIGHT 68   "Getting in my face" is considered a sign of hostility in the United States. It requires patience and practice to overcome these feelings when working on an intercultural team where social space is treated differently than in the United States.

Your Turn

Recall the last time that someone violated your personal space. Why did he or she do so? How did you react? What was the outcome of the situation?

The perception of time. Your intercultural team members may think of time quite differently than you do. In the United States, we save time, make time, spend time, waste time, and invest time. We distinguish between ordinary time and quality time. We become easily irritated when others do not observe time as obsessively as we do. Be prepared, therefore, for members of other cultures where punctuality is not a highly valued aspect of professional life; where "ripeness" of projects is more important than meeting deadlines; and where flexibility in scheduling and a casual attitude toward meeting times is the sign of a seasoned executive.

Friendships. As you get to know your intercultural team members over time, recognize that friendships are viewed differently from culture to culture. In the mobile U.S. society where people change jobs and locales frequently, we have all become accustomed to making new friends easily and quickly. New neighbors, church members, and work associates almost immediately become part of our social circle. When we attempt the same approach to friendship in other cultures—Germany, Japan, or Finland, for example—we may encounter a cultural surprise. Our acquaintances do not expect to become our friends. Friendships develop slowly and carefully in many cultures. In Welsh villages, for example, the "new couple" in town may have lived there 20 years or more—and still awaits full acceptance into the social life of the community. Be patient with intercultural team members, therefore, if they do not appear to warm up to you as quickly as you may have supposed they would. Instant friendship is often a new cultural experience for them.

Agreements. Perhaps most perplexing of all in working with intercultural team members is the question of "Do we have a deal or don't we?" To a U.S. businessperson, an agreement completed with a signed contract is almost sacred, but to many businesspeople in the Middle East, China, and elsewhere, a signed contract is just a piece of paper. More important by far in these cultures is the underlying relationship of trust established between parties over a series of meals. The signed contact, as many U.S. contractors have discovered to their dismay, is considered in many cultures to mark the beginning rather than the culmination of negotiation.

Ethical practices. These matters are among the most thorny for intercultural team members adjusting to one another's assumptions and business practices. What your intercultural team associate considers business as usual (including the giving of bribes or "commissions," as your team associate phrases it) may strike you as highly unethical. Certain comments or overt actions in a U.S. office between a man and woman may be termed sexual harrassment—actions that your intercultural team member views as harmless sport. It takes great skill to apprise your intercultural team members of the customary ethical codes and practices of your business environment without making them feel they are villains or worse. Difficult as it may be, this ethical education is crucial: You cannot afford to have a team representative acting on the basis of moral assumptions that are untenable and legally hazardous for your company.

"When in Rome, do as the Romans do" is hardly an adequate guideline when basic matters of ethics and social justice are involved. When you confront assumptions or behaviors that offend your personal ethics or code of conduct, carefully review your options so that, if possible, you can achieve your business purpose without sacrificing your own integrity.

INSIGHT 69

Your Turn

It is easy to think of the rest of the world as morally corrupt in contrast to a supposed law-and-order society here in the United States. Choose some part of the world, then put yourself in the shoes of a business visitor to the United States for the first time from that region. What aspects of American social or business life might that visitor find ethically or morally objectionable?

Male-female relationships. In interviews with intercultural teams, the topic that receives the most comment from team members is the matter of how men and women should relate in the workplace. Male-female relationships are a sensitive aspect of most cultures. If you visit a work associate in the Middle East, local custom dictates that you do not inquire about the health of his wife or daughters. Similarly off-limits are your inquiries into the whereabouts of wives as you are hosted by your male associates in Tokyo.

Americans have the most difficulty when they confront the spoken or unspoken assumption in intercultural team members that women are naturally subordinate to men in the order of things. The social, political, and moral dimensions of this issue come to a head when a U.S. businesswoman joins an intercultural team composed largely of members from cultures that suppress women. What is the woman to do? On the one hand, she could simply avoid contact with cultures who do not share her own culture's attitudes toward women. That option, however, may be professionally and economically hazardous for a woman's career. Although her specific choices will differ according to the culture and situation at hand, three trends have emerged in recent years:

1. Businesswomen are visiting sexually hostile cultures in increasing numbers. The American businesswoman in a Middle Eastern business meeting is no longer seen as an oddity.
2. When businesswomen anticipate problems due to sexual assumptions, they prepare in advance by establishing their professional status with their foreign clients through correspondence, telephone conversation, and mutual acquaintances. When they arrive in the foreign culture, these early contacts help these women arrive as "people" rather than as women.
3. Women sometimes make initial business contacts in the company of male associates, who then withdraw as the business relationship develops.

Attitudes toward women in business are quickly changing around the world as women assert themselves as professionals no less qualified than men to do business. It remains sad, however, when American-born Japanese businesswomen who speak fluent Japanese purposely speak only English when they visit Japan on business so that they will not be treated like a Japanese woman (i.e., given little professional respect).

| **INSIGHT 70** | Women face an ongoing struggle throughout much of the world to be accepted on a par with men for business purposes. When women confront suppression and prejudice, they can strategize to overcome these factors. |

Your Turn

If you are a woman, describe a time when you were devalued as a professional because of your gender. What did you do about the situation? If you are a man, describe a time when you observed a woman placed or kept in a subordinate role primarily because of her gender. What did you do about the situation?

COMMUNICATION IN THE INTERCULTURAL TEAM MEETING

People take for granted that verbal language differs from culture to culture, but your team members may be less aware that nonverbal language also varies dramatically across cultures. Mixed signals due to a misreading of nonverbal cues has proven a barrier in many intercultural team meetings.

Nonverbal signs and cues can range from touching and sniffing to gestures and body movement. The attitude in the United States toward the nonverbal area of touching another work associate is vastly different from that of many other cultures. It is not unusual throughout Europe and the Middle East to see two men walking arm in arm or with an arm encircling a shoulder. At a meeting, a work associate in these countries may place a hand on the forearm of the person sitting nearby and keep that hand there while talking.

Expected business posture also differs substantially from culture to culture. Discussion in a team meeting in the United States might find members in very relaxed postures. A man may even have a foot propped on a nearby chair or planted on a tabletop. Not so in Korea, the Middle East, China, Japan, and much of Europe. There, sitting "at attention" is a sign of respect to your team leader and fellow members. Showing the soles of your feet to your Saudi associates would be an insult indeed. Keeping your hands in your pockets while addressing your German or Austrian boss would be a sign of disrespect.

Perhaps most difficult to adjust to are cultural differences having to do with eye contact. In the United States we show concern when the other person does not look us in the eye or seems otherwise evasive. Is there a lack of honesty or integrity here, we wonder? But in Japan, a business leader may infer a lack of respect if a subordinate does give direct eye contact. When serving on an intercultural team, do not impute U.S. conclusions to eye contact behaviors exhibited by members of other cultures. This particular nonverbal difference is the first to be noticed and remains the hardest to change for intercultural team members attempting to adjust to U.S. ways.

Among the most difficult intercultural differences to adjust to are touching, posture, and eye contact behaviors. We tend to have knee-jerk reactions to what we perceive as abnormal behaviors in these categories. We may experience difficulty in preventing these reactions from interfering with our relationships with intercultural team members.	**INSIGHT 71**

Your Turn

Tell about a time when you noticed an unusual nonverbal behavior on the part of a visitor new to this country. How did you react? Why?

Summing Up

Intercultural teams are an increasing reality for U.S. businesspeople. The success of the team will depend in large part upon the willingness of team members to adjust to the many cultural differences they observe in one another. Learning to see a colleague as different but not "less than" is the key to productive team relationships. Members come to understand that they can respect and live with cultural differences in others even when they do not accept those values, practices, or worldviews for themselves.

CHAPTER 16

Moving Toward Your Goals

Y ou drive the transitions in your life and are the agent of your own success. A realization such as this can be both freeing and frightening because it implies no restrictions on where you can go and what you can do with your life. The other side of this freedom, though, is that it does not allow you to blame others for any slips or shortfalls along the way.

As you begin to actively manage changes in your life, you can shape each one into a transition that leads you closer to your goals. Change can be defined as merely some event or condition that is different or new. However, when you begin to set goals for your life, you will look at change events differently. Goal setting:

- gives you a direction
- defines areas in which to focus your energy
- requires you to take stock of your situation in some sort of methodical way
- provides a basis for decision making

The process itself has many elements: expectation, goal setting, assessment, plans, resources, and then action.

Taken from: *Transition Management: A Practical Approach to Personal and Professional Development*, Fourth edition by Sandra L. McKee and Brenda L. Walters

Expectation

You should have great expectations of your own life. If you expect little that is satisfying or meaningful, you will have little. Expectation is different from wishing and hoping; it is more in the realm of planning and acting. The way you think about your own potential determines the expectations you have. Your expectations define your dreams and your dreams generate your goals.

Though there will always, of course, be different degrees of success with each act and each transition, the critical point is that you start thinking of *yourself* as a success now. Until you do this, you may accept limits on what your life truly can be, limits on your expectations. Thus, the first element in the development of a satisfying life is to perceive the possibility in potential.

Shape Perceptions

When you perceive yourself as a successful person and start adding new skills and behaviors that support that perception, you begin the transition to new successes. Every change you make, every new talent you discover, and every new skill you acquire alters your potential. Thus, even if you have not seen yourself as particularly successful in the past, one change can forever shift your path to a new direction.

One of the key steps to beginning to perceive yourself as successful is to take stock of every important event in your life in terms of the successes. By looking at your life as a history of accomplishments instead of shortcomings, you can begin to change old patterns of criticizing, complaining about, or making excuses for everything that has not gone right. When you begin to accept responsibility for your role in the hardships and mistakes of the past, you also are entitled to claim the personal victories as well. Sometimes, learning gained from a past mistake or insight gleaned in the midst of a miserable experience becomes an important building block for the challenges of the future.

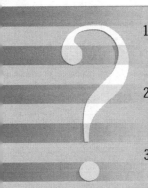

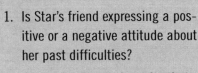

1. Is Star's friend expressing a positive or a negative attitude about her past difficulties?

2. Are there ever good results that eventually come out of a mistake or a failure?

3. Why are some mistakes called "good learning experiences"?

Raised in an angry family that regularly complained how the world had cheated them, Star grew up with little optimism or expectation of joy in life. After she left home, she went to work. She was surprised at how many of the people she met truly enjoyed their lives and felt good about the future. One day, her close friend in the office confessed to her, "You know, Star, I used to get upset over every bad thing that happened in my life, every mistake, every disappointment, every failure. But I know now that those rough times are just passing through. Not much point in getting too excited about them."

Wishing and hoping are not a cure for misery or pain; however, thoughtfully assessing your strengths and options and then acting on them will take you toward what you desire. As soon as you accept a less than satisfying life, you limit your expectations. This is called *resignation*, or in more casual terms, *settling*. Wanting and wishing are passive activities and require no real work or commitment on your part. *Expecting* means that you live your life as if the future you desire *will* happen—not *might* happen—and you direct effort toward that expectation.

Admittedly, expectation can lead to disappointment; that may be why so many of us have abandoned it as a guide for our lives. Many of the life-changing events you are expected to transition through are hard, but "any route you choose in life (and they are all your choice) comes with difficulty as a built-in feature at no extra charge. The real question you have to ask yourself is not what is difficult, but what rewards do you want out of life?" (Phillips, 2000).

When you see yourself as successful, you begin to see transitions, and the adaptations that go along with them, as bringing you ever closer to the life you desire. You perceive an event not as either a success or failure, but as a degree of contribution to your future. A willingness to adapt to new situations is a reflection of your belief that your life is moving in a positive direction. It is an ongoing process of moving, of not just finding a foothold, but making a place for yourself on the other side of life's events.

People who do not see themselves as successful may view any movement or change as necessarily bad and resist making healthy transitions. Their expectation for their future is low. When this happens, they usually become stuck, stuck in old ways of thinking that no longer work in their lives, stuck in the past of what might have been or once was, or even stuck in a pattern of predictable pain, and miss entirely the potential in the new. Once you see the future through the eyes of positive expectation, you will be expanding the way you relate to both old and new aspects of your life.

When David and Alicia got married, their lives changed. They could no longer relate to the world in the same way they did when they were single. They had to make allowances for new priorities, new goals, and new ways of relating to the world. Although there was great joy in doing so, it still required some adjusting.

1. What do you think was the biggest adjustment David and Alicia had to make?

2. What role do you think their expectations about marriage will play in making their marriage a success?

3. What do you think will happen if either fails to make a good transition and continues with the same activities and priorities as when single?

16.1

1. Describe an upcoming life event in terms of your expectation about it.

_____

_____

_____

2. Now, describe what a successful transition to the other side of the event would be like.

_____

_____

_____

_____

By seeing yourself as successful, you develop a healthy approach to life transitions, which enhances your potential for future success. When you expect a satisfying life, you base your behavior on that expectation. Characteristics of that behavior include:

- flexibility
- a desire to learn
- awareness
- a willingness to take unfamiliar avenues
- a choice to stretch past any boundaries you might have perceived
- a belief that you can manage difficult spots in life

Positive expectation is a way of approaching life as if it were a river and you are cruising effortlessly down the waterway. With this attitude, you generate less resistance and prepare eagerly for whatever eventuality you come on. You free yourself to dream, and out of the dreams come goals to make those dreams happen.

Goal Setting

Goals, like diamonds, have many facets: they must grow out of your dreams, reflect your values and priorities, and always leave room for flexibility and new options.

Dreams

Integrating your dreams into your life helps you frame a *new destiny*. A person's destiny is the end product of what he or she believes can happen and then lives or acts out. The course of history can be, and has repeatedly been, changed by people who believed strongly enough in a dream and who let that belief drive all their actions. An example is the opening up of the former Soviet Union to the rest of the world. That action began with one person who chose to think and live a different destiny. He increased the potential for a successful change for an entire nation.

Very young children see the world as full of promise and delight. Every event is a celebration; every spring a wonder; every door a threshold to a new adventure. But, somewhere along the way some children "get smart." They learn the disappointment of the dream that does not come true. After many disappointments, they learn not to set their sights too high. Their chance for happiness becomes limited by their acceptance of a limited potential. Then, in their minds—perhaps even in your own mind—the world becomes not okay; it becomes a place of unfulfilled expectations.

The "logical" conclusion for us as adults becomes, then, that dreaming is a foolish waste of time. But without the dream of what can be, we have no road map for the journey to our own happiness. We then give the power over our future away to some unguided "fate" that buffets us about with the changing circumstances of the day.

Dreams can become goals; goals can become actions that lead to a positive, satisfying life. Your dreams are the threshold to your potential.

In Activity 16.2, you are asked to put away any negative "reality" limitations that you have learned from your past and, instead, to dream. Your dreams are important, as are the many transitions you will go through to reach them.

ACTIVITY   **16.2**

Write down the dreams you have about what your future could be. Divide the dreams into professional dreams and personal dreams.

Professional dreams:

_____

_____

_____

Personal dreams:

_____

_____

_____

Priorities and Values

Remember the old adage that says, "Be careful what you wish for; you might get it." At first that seems like such a foolish warning. Why wouldn't someone want what he wished for? Look at the diagram for a model of just this idea.

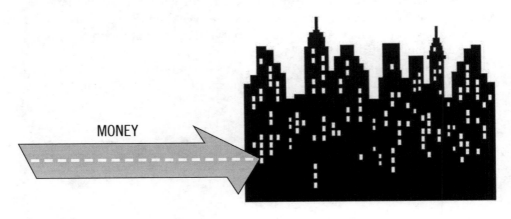

For many, prioritizing involves pursuing as much money as possible within a productive lifespan. Though it may seem like a far-off vision to you now because you are just launching your career or are making a major change in your professional direction, the single-minded pursuit of money yields just that: money. You arrive in *Success City* and find it lavishly furnished with the finest homes, cars, clothes, and all the accouterments of wealth. However, there are no people there; you are there alone because personal relationships cannot withstand the kind of perpetual exclusion created by the demands of money-oriented life pursuit.

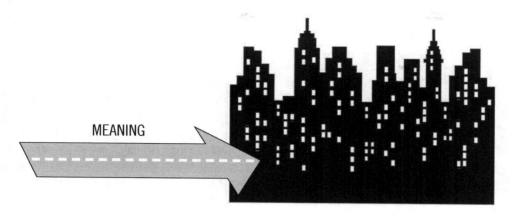

MEANING

On the other side of the priority road is the path of meaning. This pursuit gives great satisfaction and sense of purpose to those who embrace it. Many people on this path relate that they feel a sense of purpose and fulfillment in what they do and the contribution they make. When these people arrive at *Success City*, it is teeming with people, but the cars are often broken, the houses have little furniture, and the people work until they are quite old because they need the money to live.

Before this begins to sound like a discussion on the evils of money or the noble, but financially anemic, life of service, take just a moment to consider the following proposition as you think about setting priorities in your own life.

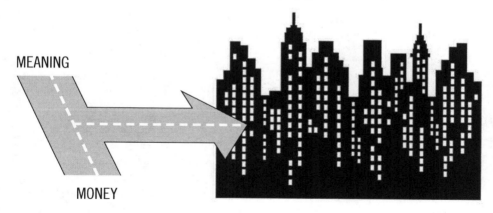

MEANING

MONEY

Making a decent living at something that brings you joy and purpose is not an immoral or self-absorbed pursuit at all. People who are addicted to work have convinced themselves that success is about money, but they have never quite figured out how much money it will take to define that success. So, they step onto the work-more–be-more-successful wheel that rolls right past their relationships.

On the other hand, those who enjoy pursuits that make meaningful contributions too often find they can barely eke out a living. In the case of many service careers, such as social work, teaching, and health care, the burnout rate is tremendous, creating hordes of walking wounded. Individuals may stay year after year in careers that drain them, or they may abandon their original pursuit from sheer exhaustion. These people may end as casualties of the endless need in our society.

As a person draws to the close of her life, the quality of that life is what is remembered. Several elements go into an assessment of the quality of life. Ideally, you find a job that pays you comfortably for doing only what you enjoy and are good at (some people's definition of success). More realistically, though, you come to that position in life after some careful investigation of the career world and some calculated resume building. But the person pursuing success defined by money never quite gets enough. To define and set priorities for your own successful life, you may want to consider the following perspectives:

- The 40–60 years that you have to actively pursue employment leaves time for at least two 20-year careers.
- Honest introspection to differentiate what you *need* to be happy from what you *want* dramatically affects how you define success.
- The job you need to be both successful and happy may have to be created by you or discovered at some later date.
- Understanding and pursuing balance in all elements of your personal and professional life brings joy; a life out of balance often fails in every quarter.

Without setting your physical, emotional, and relational well-being priorities, you can easily find yourself feeling isolated, frustrated, and burned out. Priorities that include both personal and career growth will lead you to the goal of a satisfying and rewarding career position.

Clint and his wife-to-be felt strongly about developing a source for spiritual inspiration in the form of Christian music and messages. Their careers in the technology industry provided a comfortable lifestyle, but not enough money to start a radio station or buy time on a cable TV channel for that purpose. Now, however, the Internet has made it possible for them to achieve their goal through a religious Web site.

Goals

It does not matter whether you are leaving college at the end of 16 or 17 straight years of education, changing your profession after a career dead end, or entering the workforce after having been away from work and school for many years. The challenge is the same for all: set goals that reflect who you are and where you want to go with your life.

- The goals must involve both you and those close to you.
- The goals must have flexibility built into them to allow for unanticipated opportunities.
- The actions required to reach the goals must offer some satisfaction in themselves.
- Goal statements should include benchmarks to note your achievements along the way.

Look at the goals for a small town. The goals grew out of the dream city planners had for a quality life for the citizens.

"The community is safe and feels safe." (vision—dream)

Action items (goals) to make this happen:

- Increased police presence in the neighborhoods
- New strategies to improve the business district
- Improved policies for extended-stay hotels
- Improved commercial environment (including lighting)

"The image of the community is positive." (vision—dream)

Action items (goals)

- Boundaries are defined and attractive
- Landscaped medians, rights-of-way, and sidewalks are well maintained
- Litter is removed consistently

Each goal should have action as its guideline, but include an element of flexibility. Each new skill you acquire and each change you make in yourself or your situation alters your options. A goal you have at one stage in your life, such as maturity or skill development, may be too limited later on. When you achieve growth, you are at a new level and new possibilities are within your reach. A good parallel to this is mountain climbing; each new height you reach gives you a new vista that was unavailable to you from the lower levels.

In a rapidly changing world, you cannot know your options even just five years down the road because new careers and lifestyle choices are emerging constantly. Goals that are evolving and that reflect changing aspirations are not set in concrete; rather, they are malleable to allow for freedom of choice and to reflect growth.

Whichever way you direct your life, the goals you develop should be balanced in two areas:

1. Self-nurturing—goals that relate to your personal and relational life.
2. Self-advocacy—goals that are appropriate for advancing your professional life.

The goal activities should offer some satisfaction or joy in themselves. Great golfers and great musicians know this; they derive pleasure out of the basic activity of their profession. The great golfer still enjoys hitting the ball; the great pianist will seize every opportunity to play, paid or not. Your goals should spring from knowing what is valuable to you and what gives you enjoyment. Remember, define goals as things you will do, not "wouldn't it be nice if . . ."

Finally, some major life goals are so far away that it is easy to run out of steam before you reach them. When you set *benchmarks* or milestones along the way—intermediate and short-term goals—then you have many opportunities to celebrate success. Goals should inspire, not be reminders of how much you have not yet done. When you recognize achievement at points along the way, then you can stay motivated and feel good as you progress; you do not have to wait until you reach the final goal to feel successful.

In an interview, a well-known actor said that he wished his mother had made him practice the piano when he was young. If she had, he would be able to play expertly today.

1. What is the weakness in his logic?
2. Whom does he hold responsible for his lack of success?
3. What do you think makes a person doggedly pursue excellence in her field, whether it is highly lucrative or not?

16.3

ACTIVITY

Write a goal statement that will help you verbalize the specifics of your dream. List two benchmarks you can use as success points along the way. (Be sure that the benchmarks are not longer than two years apart.)

Goal _____

1. _____
2. _____

Assessment

By thoughtfully looking at where you are now, in relation to where you want to be, you are making the first move toward improving the quality of your life and ensuring positive transitions. After you have begun the examination process, you will have a clearer picture of the areas of your life or behaviors that have to be changed. The assessment process helps you recognize the strengths you already have and uncover areas that need shoring up.

TRANSITION TIP   *Major George Kelly (retired)*

Getting out of the military after 20 years, which was my whole adult life up to that point, scared me, stressed me out. But five years before retirement, I started to plan. I did a self-evaluation of skills and qualifications that would translate into private sector terms. I engineered internal moves from weapons, where I had been trained originally, to computers. A move into a new job is stressful; a whole new career is even more so. Just look at the options that will take you where you want to go, then find out what it takes to get there. After that it's just a matter of picking up the skills and knowledge.

Don't be afraid to look at yourself honestly. Don't let the need to be perfect get in your way. Your weaknesses are temporary and can be worked on constructively if you address them realistically now with an eye toward your future.

Lee, a 35-year-old video production assistant, worked for a documentary filming company, but dreamed of actually producing these types of films. He went back to school to get the degree he needed. But as an adult with Attention Deficit Disorder (ADD), he had already lost two prior jobs because of his inability to organize and complete all of his work. When he assessed his situation, he realized that he had to work with professionals who could help him manage his ADD. He consulted a medical doctor and also joined a group of adults with ADD. There he met a producer who had a company that made educational films for children.

1. How do you think Lee's chances for reaching his dream have been affected by his straightforward assessment of his situation?

2. Why do you think he waited as long as he did (losing two jobs) to address the problem that was limiting him?

Periodically doing a check-up on your situation helps you keep your life on track: your WHOLE life, not just your personal and not just your professional life. Keeping a watchful eye on your relationships, looking for potential areas for growth, and monitoring the direction your career is headed are regular check-ups that let you catch and fix problem areas before they have a negative effect on your progress.

Improving relationships just makes everything else in your life go better. By applying the knowledge and skills gained from making successful transitions, you can envision the other side of any troubles or uncertainty. You can see the place where life works both for you and for the people close to you. By remembering to set relationship goals as well as professional goals, you not only improve your present situation, you can also begin to explore future possibilities with confidence.

Increased relationship stability will improve your home life (your self-nurturing support) and increase your professional networking abilities (your self-advocacy opportunities). An added bonus of continually improving your relationships is that you teach any children you may have how to develop good relationships. There is no better legacy to give them for their future happiness.

Once you have determined where you want to go and, based on your assessment of the situation, what is required to arrive there, you have to start gathering the resources you need.

Resources

Any person who is facing life changes has to construct the transition process with the right tools and skills. Hanging a storm door without an electric drill or a screwdriver is arduous and inordinately time-consuming. Knowing the best methods for positioning and hanging the door is also important.

Just as none of us are born with all of the skills we need to hang a storm door, none of us has come equipped with all of the resources we need to go though life in a perfect way. It is necessary for us to constantly discover what could help us along. What each person requires is a set of tools that can be stored and brought out when the need arises. It is like what a carpenter would do when he builds a house.

A tool is a resource that makes it easier to perform a job or manage a life. Obviously, the more tools, the easier it is to address difficult life events and construct effective transitions. Although everyone does not need the same tools, there are general categories.

Information Services

One tool everyone requires to ensure successful transitions is information. Many vehicles exist today that can help you find out what you need to know.

You are exposed to newspapers, books, magazines, computers, and experts in many fields. The Internet, CD-ROM information services, and databases with seemingly inexhaustible sources can be found in public and college libraries as well as in hundreds of thousands of homes across the country. Information is a tool that becomes part of every task you do in your pursuit of a successful life.

Skills and Knowledge

After you learn a new skill, you have to practice it on a daily basis as many times as you can. This includes relationship skills, such as conflict resolution, as well as career skills, such as keyboarding or customer service. Though any new skill you acquire may feel unnatural at first (old ways die hard), the good news is that after a while, the new skill will feel perfectly comfortable, and using it will make things go better for you.

An excellent example of incorporating new tools into your everyday life is vocabulary building. You are expected to have a command of the language of your profession and to express yourself in everyday communication. As you learn a new word, the more you practice by incorporating it into your daily speech, the more natural it feels. Learning new software, a foreign language, or new methods of managing conflict in your family is the same. Once you take the time to learn, these skills become habits that you call up anytime they are needed.

People

You cannot possibly know now all that will be required of you as you move through your career and relationship transitions. Keeping an eye out for others who can help you is always a good practice. Some help you with information, others with support.

Coach

A source of information and career skills is the professional "coach." Coaches are experts in a certain area who share their specialized knowledge with clients. Some do this as a profession; some coaches, though, are just good at teaching their particular skill informally to others and enjoy helping. They may serve as resources for workplace skills, or in the case of a therapist, for relationship skills. If you are interested in hiring a coach, look for a professional who is an expert in the field and who has a good reputation. Networking groups, colleagues, and friends who work in similar jobs or industries can sometimes be called on at no charge for this type of help.

Mentor

If you are lucky and have a mentor or role model in your life or profession, you have someone in your corner who has a personal investment in showing you the path to success. Sometimes a manager or supervisor can become a mentor. However, this is not something that you should automatically expect. You should, instead, be grateful for anyone who chooses to invest their time and knowledge in you in such a way.

Moral Support

The case of Gene is an example of the role of moral support. Gene was the classic "geek" youngster—bright, not socially adept, physically small—who lived in a community that was very sports oriented. His older brother and sister were both athletes and went to college on athletic scholarships. His passion, however, was reading and later, writing, which he kept quiet about for the most part. One aunt always invited him to read his latest writing when he came to visit. "She was my most unabashed fan," he remembered. Her enthusiasm and focused attention carried him through some lonely times and frequent literary rejections. "I probably would have quit writing altogether if she hadn't kept encouraging me."

Dreams, goals, and plans. Even the highest resolve, focus, and dedication need shoring up from time to time. An invaluable resource is the person or group who will go forward with you and support you when you need it.

Media

High-quality audio and video programs can provide skill training and information comparable to that provided by a coach or class. Bookstores and record stores carry these; some can even be rented. Time in a car often becomes dead time; you can make this enriching time by adding to your knowledge with tapes.

You will reach your goals more easily with the right resources. Once you have the resources you need, you can begin to implement your plans.

Action

Once you have researched, improved, and developed your transition skills, you are ready to put the plan you are developing into action. Without action, even the best of plans are worth nothing. You now have to decide how and when to act. Remember, you are learning to be in charge of your future and your happiness. Your goals and plan will become your personal road map for high performance and allow you to approach new thresholds with confidence; confidence that you will make a successful transition to a new level of satisfaction in your life.

One thing that stops many people from acting on their goal-related plans is uncertainty about the effects of the choices they make. When you do not know what a specific outcome will be, you might hesitate. Business decision makers deal with this all the time, and like them, you can thoroughly investigate possible outcomes of the actions you have chosen to implement. Even then, though, you may not be able to allow for all eventualities.

Sometimes, you may just have to take the step, assuming you have designed the step with reasonable care. Besides, outcomes are not always predictable, even with the most seemingly routine actions. Rather than worry about the chance of a negative or undesirable outcome, approach your implementation steps with the idea that you will observe the result and adjust your next step based on what has occurred.

Building a life requires that you act on your plans and use your resources. The events in your life are the materials; the way that you acquire and use tools and skills is your part in crafting those materials into a satisfying life. Have you ever heard the saying, "Don't think, don't try, just do"? This does not mean to act rashly or without planning and care, but it does mean to begin putting into effect what you have developed from your goal and assessment activities.

You can start with the easiest tasks that support your goal, but anything that moves you in the direction you have chosen should be a priority.

Assessment—Again

Each time you implement your plans and apply new skills, take a moment to assess where you are and what effects you have created. Some actions will take you further than you ever expected; some will either not work at all or not have the desired effect. Stumbling is often part of walking or running. In addition, every time you walk through a different door, you are in a different place. Assessment, a check-up of results against goals, helps you keep your direction or change it if new conditions warrant.

Remember, at each step in this growth process, you alter your potential; you improve your ability to succeed in your own life transitions. The formula is complete. See Figure 16.1 for a visual representation of this concept.

FIGURE 16.1   The assessment cycle.

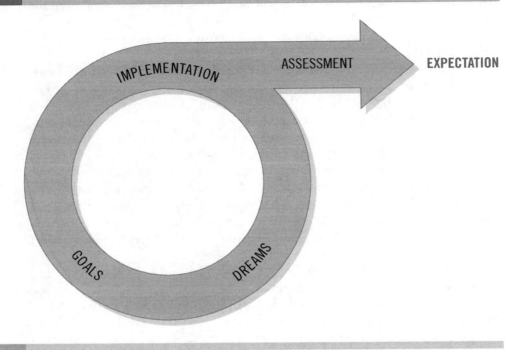

You've probably heard people say they are *born* to a certain destiny, while others *seek* their destiny. Right here, right now, it is your road, your life. If you like it, congratulations! You have found the key to lasting happiness. But if you don't, you can define your own potential by setting goals. Goals will help you recognize thresholds and manage transitions to new levels. You are where you are today because you wanted more control in the direction of your life or perhaps more freedom in the way you live it.

There are many paths to the same goal. When you have chosen a direction (not even necessarily an endpoint), events, circumstances, and people you meet every day begin to appear as thresholds to where you are going.

The simplicity of this approach to transitions makes it useful throughout your life. Turning loose your limitations allows you to expect a wondrous and satisfying life, the beginning of the process to achieving happiness. Regularly assessing where you are in relation to where you want to be is an important factor in maintaining a workable formula and achieving growth. Any movement forward or any adaptation to a major life event requires that you seek out the pertinent information and learn the new skills necessary for the transition to the other side of the event. Finally, as you enlarge and expand your repertoire of coping and life-managing skills, you find much more freedom of movement, both personally and professionally; movement leading to satisfying results: your future.

Making solid transitions as you move through your professional endeavors and your emotional and relational life ensures your safe arrival in *Success City*, a city you have designed and built.

TRANSITION SKILLS SUMMARY

Expectation

Dreams

Priorities

Goals

Assessment

Resources

Action

Assessment—again

GOAL SETTING

Self-nurturing: My goal statement for my personal and relational life is:

_____

_____

_____

_____

Self-advocacy: My goal statement for my professional/work life is:

_____

_____

_____

_____

COACH'S CORNER

The move from school to industry is one of the largest a person will make in early adulthood; in some ways it signifies the transition into adulthood. The following general suggestions to those embarking on this stage of life will be useful for the entirety of their career lives, as they will meet challenges all along the path.

- Communications skills should include an orientation to team and close work environments. Almost no one works in a vacuum.
- Remember to take care of yourself and be alert to symptoms of stress or burnout.
- Stability at home is the springboard for launching into any new career direction.
- Learn to solve problems of all types—an absolute necessity for the sometimes crazy world of industry.
- Do a thorough self-assessment: know what you are good at, but also what you might be interested in learning as a growth area.
- Work to situate yourself in a company's culture; be able to work with all kinds of people.
- Attitude can make or break you, attitude determines performance. Attitude is a choice; a positive attitude leads to success.
- A personal mission statement is an absolute necessity. What your intention is as you direct your life should be put on paper in a clear way.

TINA BERRY TAYLOR, L.C.S.W., CEAP, MSW, is an experienced trainer and employee assistance consultant.

CHAPTER 17

Organizing Time and Tasks

John's office is neat in the morning when he arrives, in the evening when he leaves, and even during the day while he is working. Sherry works, drives in a car pool, and is the team mother for the little league team. Both of these people appear organized and in control of their lives. They are also living examples to the rest of us who wish we could be that way.

Though some people are more structured and detailed than others, most of us agree we could improve in this area. The difficulty is that you, like everyone else, have "multiple priorities" in your life; that is, many important things to accomplish and rarely enough time to do them. Whether you are an executive who directs a multimillion-dollar company, an electrician who wires buildings, or an at-home mother who balances parenting with running a household, you know how necessary being organized is. Bringing structure and planning into your life is not to be valued just for its own sake. Managing your time and tasks affects your ability to lead a satisfying life. The benefits are many:

1. Efficient management of job tasks leaves more time, energy, and focus for outside activities and relationships.

2. Accomplishment is emotionally liberating and energizing.

3. Focusing effort prevents the feeling of being overwhelmed.

4. A more relaxed life results from being in control of demands on your time.

Career professionals face challenges that can be clearly defined in terms of the hours in the day.

Taken from: *Transition Management: A Practical Approach to Personal and Professional Development*, Fourth edition by Sandra L. McKee and Brenda L. Walters

FIGURE 17.1   Allocating the hours in a day.

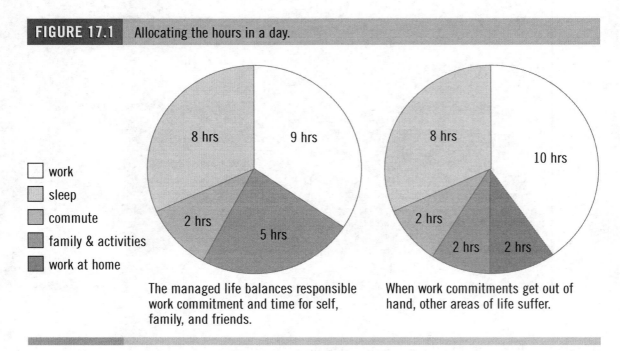

work

sleep

commute

family & activities

work at home

The managed life balances responsible work commitment and time for self, family, and friends.

When work commitments get out of hand, other areas of life suffer.

Granted, some people seem to be born to be orderly. A few are trained to be that way, as in the military. Some of us, though, never seem to quite get our lives under control—try as we might. But having a life where you can plan, get things done, and still find time for yourself and for those you care about *is* possible.

In Activity 17.1, you are asked to make a start on the road to organization by choosing those parts of your life you wish to handle better.

17.1   ACTIVITY

I wish I had more time for _____

    I believe that if I could just manage _____ better, my life would seem more in control.

This chapter is about how to manage your life's daily demands. It is not like those books that casually dismiss the problem by saying, "Don't sweat the small stuff." If your life is like that of most adults, you wish there was some "small stuff." It *all* seems like "big stuff." That is why it is difficult to manage. Understanding how you look at organization in general will help you see why some situations are more difficult for you to "get a handle on" than others. In addition, in this chapter you will learn the skills you need to approach life's time and task challenges in a confident and successful way.

Organization Challenges

People who seem like "born organizers" in some respects really are. Just by the way their brain works, some people think and operate naturally in a methodical, structured manner. These people are probably not reading this chapter, so don't worry about feeling intimidated by them anymore. You are going to learn to do the same thing with your life, and no one will ever know you weren't a "born organizer" yourself.

We will explore the difficulty most of us have in gaining a sense of control. There are many reasons for this difficulty besides differences in thinking style. They range from everyone's demands on us to our own inability to manage too many and diverse tasks. Other reasons stem from the value we place on organization, which translates into the amount of energy we are willing to expend to achieve an ordered or more manageable life.

Thinking Styles

The way thinking style enters into our ability to manage our time and tasks is best shown by the example of two brothers: Kyle, 15, and George, 12. Both have the task of cleaning their rooms, which are perfect examples of chaos and disarray. Kyle looks at the mess and sees the room as a gigantic, insurmountable mountain of disorder. Being completely overwhelmed by the immenseness of the task, he becomes agitated, tries picking up a few pieces, then begins to wander around aimlessly. Eventually, he says he cannot do it alone and begs for help.

George, on the other hand, surveys the mess (equally intimidating to the observer) and attacks parts of the task separately: toys, then clothes, then bed, then sweeping. He is done in half an hour. There are a few pieces that did not quite make it to the proper places, but on the whole, the task of making the room look better was accomplished.

On the adult level, we see this in another way. Josh, an electronics troubleshooter, tries the broken hardware, gets a feeling he knows what the problem is, and goes to it. If he is incorrect about his guess, he tries again. His partner, Randy, approaches hardware problem diagnosis differently. When he reports to a customer site, he questions users about the problem, how it occurred and when, goes through a series of diagnostic procedures, and isolates the problem. Both are successful service engineers with high customer satisfaction.

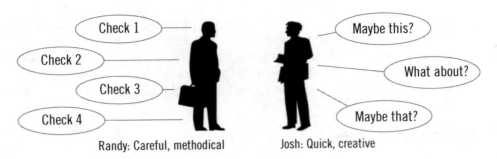

Randy: Careful, methodical   Josh: Quick, creative

Josh makes slightly more errors than Randy on the first try, but he corrects them quickly and is often finished with his calls for the day before Randy. Randy regularly takes longer than Josh, but seldom makes an error. When he does, he usually calls Josh in because the problem is generally some new or perplexing difficulty he doesn't have a procedure for uncovering.

Who has a more effective troubleshooting style? Randy appears to, but Josh likely uses a clear process that isn't apparent to the observer. Josh is a gifted, intuitive, gut-level diagnostician. But sometimes his first impulse is wrong. Randy is a methodical, perseverant, well-trained problem solver. Sometimes, though, the problem is outside the expected, and he can't discover the solution. The success of their business is that the combination of the two styles can handle anything that comes along.

You probably have ways you approach organizing or performing tasks that work quite well. Though successful in some situations, in others these methods don't work at all. By understanding your approach to organization, you will quickly see why some tasks overwhelm and paralyze you and others don't. As soon as you have a clear picture of your style, you can learn additional approaches to apply to tasks that challenge you.

17.2   ACTIVITY

Look at the example of Josh and Randy, and then at your approach to challenges. Identify your task-management style as "quick, creative thinking" or "careful, methodical thinking." Give an example to explain why you chose the answer you did. (Note: This understanding of your style will help you to communicate your style during a job interview.)

_____

_____

Be careful not to confuse a natural organizational style with the conclusions conveyed in the following: "I guess I'm just born to be messy. I know my mother was, so I guess I inherited it." There is not, to the knowledge of medical science, a you-will-be-disorganized gene. Your approach to organization may predispose you, though, to have difficulty with certain situations. Learning organizational skills will help you with those challenges you cannot solve easily.

Value Placed on Organization

How much someone values organization has a direct effect on how much effort the person devotes to achieving order. In your personal life, you may like to have a clean home and spend several hours each week to keep it that way. Your spouse or housemate may appreciate a clean house, but not enough to work to keep it that way. In Activity 17.3, rate the value you place on different areas of organization in your life.

ACTIVITY   17.3

Circle the number that most accurately describes the value you place on the following items:

1. Orderly physical space at home and work

    (Not at all)   1   2   3   4   5   (I work to keep things orderly)

2. Time scheduled in a careful way

    (Not at all)   1   2   3   4   5   (I schedule my day carefully)

3. Time versus physical organization

    (Physical space)   1   2   3   4   5   (Time)

What conclusions can you draw about your natural tendency in regard to organization?

_____

_____

_____

In your personal life you are free to be as organized or disorganized as you like. Perhaps throughout your education you managed just fine, made it to most of your classes and finished reports on time. Once you begin your job in the corporate world, the number of things you have to keep track of and complete increases dramatically. You are expected to be able to manage tasks, such as:

- be at meetings on time and prepared
- deliver projects and reports within deadlines
- apprise management of project status
- locate important information quickly

Fortunately for professionals, many organizational tools and aids are available.

Lack of Skills

When we are young, life is relatively simple. One reason is that when we are young, we don't have as many "things," in the way of personal property or responsibilities to keep track of or maintain. Car ownership, for example, brings with it car payments, insurance payments, oil changes, tire rotation, and washing. None of this exists for the young person. So, as young people, we rarely develop good organizational or planning skills. The most visible evidence of this difference lies with mail and phone.

When you were a child, you managed your school life and your social life with help from mom and dad and maybe a brother or sister. When you become an adult, you manage your own life and you must assist those with whom you interact. You counsel a friend, coach an employee, help your boss, haul the kids, meet a coworker for lunch, call your aging parent, or visit your sister.

Whew! How do you do it? Many of us feel like we end up not handling any of what we do well. Some of your success at managing your tasks depends on the skills you have learned. In Activity 17.4, you will report any skill training from your childhood or adult life that has helped you to handle multiple tasks.

17.4   **ACTIVITY**

Write down organizational techniques you were taught while growing up. For example, "My father taught me that paying bills as they come in helps to prevent a pile-up at due dates." "My brother kept a small cassette recorder in the car to record things he wanted to remind himself to do."

1. I remember: _____

2. I remember: _____

Now, write down an example of the way you have organized your responsibilities as an adult.

_____

_____

_____

If you are like most people, unless you have attended seminars, read books, or received specific instruction on methods for managing multiple tasks, you probably do not have a good set of skills to apply. But even the most skilled person cannot use that training until he learns to be assertive about the need to organize.

TRANSITION TIP   _Scott Davis, Business Development_

The first realization that hit me about time is that suddenly I didn't have summers off. Fun had to come in short weekends. Also, the importance of time management really hit when I realized the organization required in a flexible collegiate environment was very different from the requirement of the 60-hour work week that ran six days. The advice I would give the person just out of college is this: Now you are completely free to make all of your decisions and manage your own life. You are also accountable for all of those decisions, so you have to police your life yourself if you are going to make it.

Like any other challenge, time and task management is addressed at two levels: defining the challenge and developing skills to meet it. So far, you have begun by defining the challenges.

For the skills, we can draw from the experience of professionals who manage complex tasks and deadlines for a living. These people are called project managers, and they have some helpful approaches you can use in your daily life as well as on your job. They accomplish their goals by keeping three issues in focus regardless of the size or complexity of the job:

- setting priorities
- securing necessary resources
- completing tasks

You can move one step closer to successfully organizing the activities in your life by learning what these professionals know and use every day—methods for organizing time and tasks.

Setting Priorities

Figuring out the most important and productive ways to allot time is a challenge for most people. Everyone has limited time; most of us work hard. Yet, some people accomplish a lot, while others just get tired. How is it that with the same number of hours in a day some get more done than others? Successful organizers plan. They take the time to think about their tasks or goals to decide what is most important to finish. Then, they direct their time and energy there. They understand the notion of the critical path. The *critical path* is the set of steps you have to go through, in proper order, to accomplish your goal. For example, if the goal is to get to work on time, specific activities must be completed in order:

MORNING ROUTINE

1. Get up at 6 A.M.
2. Shower
3. Dress and make coffee
4. Eat breakfast
5. Feed dog
6. Set burglar alarm
7. Lock door

Parts of the process must occur in order, and you must complete all of the steps necessary to reach your goal satisfactorily, but some tasks can be done simultaneously. Chris wants to build a fence for the dog. He knows that he has to have his property surveyed, draw out the plan for spacing the posts, buy what he needs, and put the fence up.

He cannot buy materials until he has the survey because he has to measure to see how much he needs. He cannot put up the fence until he has all of the materials. If Chris does not prioritize the specific steps and allow time for each one in order, he will not reach his goal.

The critical path helps to set priorities. Prioritizing helps Chris plan the best use of his time in other ways. If he has two hours to wait for a plane or an hour to wait at the doctor's office, he can use this time to make up his list of materials or draw his fence plan, instead of sitting in the airport bar or reading a magazine at the doctor's office.

Remember, stress can occur in your life when you fail to do what you think you really should be doing. If you get distracted, your priority plan reminds you to keep focused. Completing each step toward your goal is easier when the steps are clearly defined and priorities are set for their completion. *If someone seeks to involve you in an activity that is not on your critical path, you have the right to decline.*

Setting Priorities at Work

Every employee should understand the priorities of the workplace. All too often, however, employees, especially new ones, fail on the job by spending time on tasks that are not priorities. Employers complain about this relatively common problem.

> Duane took a new job at the Blue Rock Farm. His supervisor directed him to the field where he would be performing his job, which was picking up rocks. To make a good impression his first day, Duane diligently went about his work. He picked up rocks: blue ones, yellow ones, green ones. He even dug up some silver and gold ones he saw barely protruding from the ground. At the end of the day he had filled an entire dump truck and drove it proudly into the yard for his supervisor's inspection.
>
> The supervisor walked around, looked at the load Duane had gathered so painstakingly, shook his head and said, "What is this?"
>
> Puzzled, but still enthusiastic, he explained, "I filled the entire truck like you said. I picked up pink rocks, green rocks, and I even dug up some of the silver and gold ones, see?"
>
> The supervisor looked right at Duane and said, "Son, what's the name of this farm?"
>
> Realization hit Duane, and his enthusiastic look disappeared.

Unlike school, where compassionate teachers give credit, and maybe even a passing grade, for "effort" or "trying hard," in business this is not true. Working late, coming in on weekends, taking work home; none of this matters if you do not advance company goals with your activity. Pushing on a sitting elephant all day would be considered inconsequential if your job was to move the elephant. This is why status reports are often set up with two headings: *Accomplishments* and *Goals.* No one cares what you did, just what you accomplished. And no one cares what you accomplished if it was not related to the goals of the company.

This is why if you are asked to stay late to help a fellow employee on a project, your best choice might very well be to decline. If the request does not relate to the activities for which you are held accountable, then the time might better be spent with your family. That is not to say that you never help coworkers. The truth is, however, that your salary and performance reviews are based on the goals set for *you*.

Ideally, you and your manager have a conversation about the role your job plays in the overall success of the organization. This conversation takes place both at the start of your new job and periodically over the first year with a new company. Unfortunately, this is more likely *not* to happen than to happen. Some organizations and some managers will prove to be excellent support for your success. However, a great many will not. Thus, the process of determining the best way to prioritize your time may very well be left to you. Following are some guidelines for ascertaining the path to accomplishment.

1. Read the financial or stockholder's report to get a clear picture of the company's vision, strengths, markets, and competition.

2. Secure from your manager a description of how your position fits into the company's goals. (You may have to ask many questions to get this information.)

3. Observe those who receive promotions or bonuses—see what kinds of projects they are working on.

4. Be aware of what activities you prefer to do and how those relate to your overall duties—are you spending all of your time "picking up blue rocks" or are you doing other things you enjoy more instead? (If you find that many of the things you enjoy are not part of the duties for which you are accountable, then it may be time to change jobs.)

Securing Necessary Resources

You have probably driven down the road behind an old pickup truck that is loaded with pine straw, bags of grass seed, small shrubs, and an assortment of shovels, rakes, and brooms. There may even be a lawn mower balanced tentatively on top of it all. This truck is an example of good resource planning. Lawn care businesses send out their workers in the morning loaded for the day's work. A trip back to the storage site to pick up supplies or tools is time consuming and unprofitable. Planning, based on the jobs of the day, prevents extra trips or unnecessary purchases.

Materials and Tools

At a technology research lab, the failure to have the necessary parts on hand can delay the development and delivery of a million-dollar product to a customer. In your own life, you have probably been frustrated more than once when the pen by the phone is out of ink or there is no paper to take a note on. This is a simple problem, but it illustrates that having the resources needed to perform a task is necessary to make your life flow smoothly.

Gathering the resources for any task requires that you think about what you need to achieve, what you want to do. In the example of Chris building a fence, he had purchased a booklet that suggested the types of fence pullers and other tools he would need. So, with about two hours' planning, Chris saved himself nearly a day's time because he wouldn't have to stop to get something he needed. He also avoided the irritation of needing something he did not have. As part of the planning, Chris also discovered that he was lacking another important resource—help. As you do your planning, don't forget to include the human resource factor—people to help you do what needs to be done.

People

People can make the difference in whether you can accomplish a task or not. A lack of child care can prevent you from having adequate time for work and home tasks or even certain recreational activities. Friends or hired labor can provide an extra set of hands and contribute to the timely completion of a job. Once you decide what help you need, then you can determine where that help will come from.

Remember that you might not be a "planner" by nature. If you are not, then you probably have quite a few tasks that frustrate you because you cannot seem to get them out of the way. Resource planning, like any other planning, takes time. This is why so many people don't plan. They get into the frenzy of "I have to get started." What they don't realize, though, is that people who don't plan frequently spend a great deal more time on their tasks than those who do plan—including planning time.

The most important people resource is you. The place to start assessing resources is yourself:

1. What do you already know about this project or challenge?
2. What skills do you have that you can apply directly?
3. What do you need to know that you do not know?
4. How can you fulfill that need? Learn? Ask or hire someone?
5. How much time can you allot to this task?

6. Is it better delegated to someone else because of the value of your time or the availability of skilled people?

If you use people resources, you should consider the following:

1. What are the skills and knowledge of those in your immediate sphere?
2. How committed are they already to other tasks and priorities?
3. How dependable are they? What is the quality of their work?
4. Is this a project they would be interested in helping with, learning about, working with you on?
5. How can their time be freed up for your project? Negotiate a barter of time, resources, or pay.
6. How much of your budget for this project can you devote to paying people?
7. Is the deadline important? (Note: budget and deadline are directly related in business. The longer something takes, the more it costs in terms of resources. For personal projects, if you are not in a hurry, this is not necessarily the case.)

Organization Support Tools

Organizing in your head may work with small projects or daily planning demands, but for anything complex or for lives with numerous activities and obligations, tools specifically designed for organization are almost a necessity. Following are some tools that you might find useful.

1. Computer software can record and remind you of tasks and appointments.
2. Records or data-management systems can automatically sort and organize information to make it easy for you to use.
3. Day planners or appointment books allow you to record important information and deadlines.
4. Personal digital assistants that fit into a pocket, purse, or briefcase allow you to record appointments, phone numbers, and so on, so you don't have to remember them.
5. Reminder services call or e-mail you to let you know that a loved one's birthday or other occasion is coming up.
6. In those cases where the luxury of an assistant is available, a person who sets a high value on and has considerable skill with organizing can be a lifesaver.

7. Project management environments have forms or software into which you enter the status of activities as well as deadlines. These programs can prompt you when something is due.

8. Color-coded folders placed in a tiered rack on your desk or in a file drawer make your organization system visible and easily accessible.

9. Meeting notes and phone messages kept in one spiral-bound or hard-bound notebook are there when you need them. (Yellow sticky notes can disappear precisely when you need the information on them. Get into the habit of putting written notes of any kind in a notebook.)

10. A large calendar that hangs on the wall in a conspicuous place can serve as a planning tool.

Bill has to prepare two proposals for clients of his company by Friday. His children have a baseball game on Thursday night, and he has promised to attend. Bill's goal is to accomplish both by the end of the week without sacrificing one or the other.

1. What are the activities required for Bill's tasks?

2. Can any be done simultaneously or are they all in a critical path?

3. What resources would you suggest Bill use to complete the tasks?

Completing Tasks

The final step in organizing is completing the tasks. This seems like a natural conclusion, but many things can interfere with your efforts. We will look at two common impediments and help you develop strategies to deal with them: time just gets away and there are too many things to do to finish any. How many days have you started the morning with great intentions? You may even have taken a day of leave from work just to "catch up." For both barriers to completing a task or reaching a goal, the solution is *awareness*.

Time Just Gets Away

Often when a distraction comes along—phone, office talker, someone with a problem—we find ourselves redirected from our goal activities. If we are not aware of the time we are spending on these distractions, we can end the day without completing anything. What's worse, we seldom remember exactly how we got off track. *Be aware of distractions and keep them temporary.*

Two hints will help you. *First, make sure phone calls meet your needs and not someone else's.* Our adolescence left us with a priority of always answering the phone because of the teenager's need to communicate. As an adult, you have to separate that urge from a real communication need that supports your goals. In other words, use a machine or let the phone ring during the times you are working on your necessary items. Sales people and chatty friends have a high need to communicate with you. This may not support your need to complete your priority tasks.

Second, throw away junk mail without opening it. The time it takes to wade through all of the worthless "stuff" could be spent meeting your own goals. Time is allotted to each of us in the same way each day. How you use that time sometimes makes the difference between accomplishment and frustration. By eliminating some activities, at least for the time you are pursuing a specific goal, you make yourself available for your priority items.

Each one of your goal steps takes time. Carefully assessing the time required to perform each step helps you plan more successfully. One of the biggest hurdles for anyone trying to plan activities based on time, though, is that in many cases you truly have no idea how long something will take. Especially on a new job, you have no prior experience with the tasks and thus no good estimate of the time needed. In this case, you can ask people who have done similar tasks. For future reference, it is a good idea to keep notes on how long activities actually take to perform.

17.5   ACTIVITY

Choose one goal you want to accomplish in the next two weeks. Develop the necessary steps to complete it and decide the order in which they must be done. Also, estimate the time needed to complete each one.

Goal: _____   Completion deadline: _____

Necessary steps	Time needed
Step 1: _____	_____
Step 2: _____	_____
Step 3: _____	_____
Step 4: _____	_____

(It is a good idea to return to this exercise after you have completed the tasks and compare estimated time to actual time.)

Now, you have drawn a clear picture of the tasks required to reach your goal because you have written down the goal, the steps, and the time required. You are able to develop a realistic plan for making those steps happen. (A time and task organization sheet is included at the end of this chapter to help you.)

Too Many Things to Do

If you are doing too many things, you are probably not doing any of them very well. Then, you get angry with yourself for not performing as well as you know you can. At work, your job may be too much for one person, in which case you might have to ask your boss for help.

Be careful with this though. You may be perceived as not being able to manage your time well. Be certain that you are truly overcommitted and that you can document multiple, overlapping tasks. Sometimes your manager will "lend" some of your time to a manager for another project. When you become overloaded, go to your managers and ask them to decide which tasks they feel your time is best spent completing. That way, you are not put into the position of being unable to meet deadlines.

In your home life, on the other hand, just the sheer number of people in a family multiplies house cleaning, bill paying, repairs, shopping, cooking, laundry, and errands, and these needs don't stop just because you work.

Saying "No"

Too often our lives become overloaded not by those tasks required to maintain ourselves at home and at work, but by those tasks "required" by others. Those tasks may appear to be "required," but in reality, they may not be. Are these pictures of your life? Look at the following examples.

"Stephanie, we need someone with your experience to manage the fund-raiser for the new fellowship hall."

"Mom, would you drive Zack and me to the ballgame and pick us up at Benny's at nine? Oh, and can you change my orthodontist's appointment to next week? A wire broke on my braces."

Mack is a newly-employed accountant with a cleaning services company. He is heading out the door at the end of the day in order to attend a professional meeting on behalf of his company. A coworker calls to him, "Mack, the Jackson account says their software has bugs in it, and they're not able to process their payment on Thursday. Can you help me with it?"

Other individuals felt entitled to ask that Stephanie, "Mom," and Mack help out. In each of these cases, these individuals could have said, "No, I'm sorry, I have another obligation." This response might have kept them from feeling over-loaded. Other people's priorities can become yours very quickly if you let them. Have you fallen into this pattern with those you live and work with?

17.6 ACTIVITY

1. If you did something recently that you didn't have time for, but did anyway, what happened?

   _____

   _____

2. How did it affect your ability to do what you needed to do?

   _____

   _____

3. What might have happened if you had said "no"? Describe the positive and negative impacts on you and on the other person.

   Effects on you: _____

   _____

   Effects on the other person: _____

   _____

Your survival depends on taking action to get yourself off the merry-go-round of a hectic life. In case you haven't noticed, the horses on the merry-go-round are wood; you are not. *The best reason for managing your multiple responsibilities better is your own well-being.*

Your family can do their own laundry, coworkers can survive without your help on every task, and your friends will understand if you can't meet them for every gathering. Stop doing everything and train others around you to support what you do. Find a baby sitter who can help the kids with baseball or home-work. Locate a temporary agency that can supply short-term help for your work. Look at your responsibilities and find ways to delegate some things.

The workplace and the home are, of necessity, team environments. Use the team. Analyze the tasks, the steps, and the resources, then decide how you will complete the undertaking.

Eliminating "Dead Air"

A big productivity loss can occur because of "10-minute dead air." This is wasted time. The minutes just before an appointment or an important phone call or the time spent waiting for someone become dead air, a term used in broadcasting to describe those moments of silence that occur due to a technical failure or operator error.

ACTIVITY   **17.7**

Review your activity plan for a major project you have coming up. After you have written down all of the major tasks and their time requirements, describe at least four activities that can be done in 10 minutes.

Example: _"I need to get involved in a networking group to advance my career potential."_

10-minute activities:

1. _Look in phone book or on the Internet for networking organizations._
2. _Determine two or three that seem most likely to target._
3. _Review notes from conversation with leader of networking group._
4. _Send e-mails to a networking organization requesting information._

Goal: _____

_____

10-minute activities:

1. _____
2. _____
3. _____
4. _____

Eliminating Time Wasters

To complete your goals, you must be aware of time wasters. Following is a list of time wasters that you might encounter when you try to accomplish goals:

- Focusing on minute tasks instead of larger, goal activities.
- Hurrying, which causes mistakes that can sabotage success.
- Becoming distracted or paralyzed by worry.
- Not taking time to read instructions, then having to start over.
- Spending time trying to "do it yourself" when assistance is really necessary.
- Not planning, which creates delays (not having tools needed).

An example of a time waster that may be difficult to deal with is the friend who asks for your time. "Bill often sees me outside when I am doing a landscaping or building project and asks me to help him with something he wants to do right then." A good response that is respectful of everyone's goals might be, "Sure, Bill, but right now I'm going to finish this deck. Why don't we plan to look at your project tomorrow. I'll be finished by then."

Building the well-managed life is not easy, but the necessity and the rewards are undeniable. Changing your old habits of being everyone's best resource or of plunging into work without planning requires discipline at first. But, like other skills you are learning, time and task management can be learned. The reward is a happier and more relaxed *you*.

TRANSITION SKILLS SUMMARY

Address organization challenges

Set a value on effectively managing time and tasks

Define specific time and task priorities

Secure resources

Complete tasks

GOAL SETTING

My self-nurturing time and task organization goals are:

_____

_____

_____

My self-advocacy time and task organization goals are:

_____

_____

_____

C O A C H 'S   C O R N E R

The operative word is clutter; clutter that builds up more quickly than most people can deal with it. But clutter is just delayed decision making—too much stuff due to an ineffective decision-making system. Think instead that every piece of paper that comes to you must be put into a specific category. This is the basis of the _Clutter-FREE™_ system.

File

Refer or delegate

Eliminate or toss

Execute or take action

Surviving on the job, especially a new job, requires that you focus on organization from the first day. Your setup is the key to heading off clutter problems before they become so huge they are intimidating. Start with four trays on your desk, credenza, or cabinet. Label them "in," "out," "file," and "read." Every piece of paper goes into one of these trays and is acted on accordingly. E-mail can be handled the same way:

F—create folder

R—refer or forward

E—eliminate by deleting

E—execute by reading, replying or acting

There is no reason to store endless streams of e-mails in your computer's inbox. Because your system administrator will notify you that you are overloading the network, you will have to deal with your e-mails eventually. (Ms. Wilkowski's company offers software, "Taming the Paper Tiger," that allows you to catalog data through keywords and cross-reference words. This allows you to "find anything in five seconds or less.")

BETSY WILKOWSKI is a professional organizer and founder of The Organized Executive, Inc. (www.organizeyouroffice.com).

Time and Task Organization Sheet

Goal to be completed: _____   Deadline: _____

Necessary steps   Time needed

1. _____   _____

2. _____   _____

3. _____   _____

4. _____   _____

5. _____   _____

6. _____   _____

Resources needed:

    Supplies: _____

    Tools/equipment: _____

    Human resources: _____

    Additional help or expertise needed. Hire? Friend or favor? Delegate?

    _____

    _____

Potential time wasters:

_____

_____

Strategies for time wasters:

_____

_____

Timeline:

    By / / _____ should be completed

    By / / _____ should be completed

    By / / _____ should be completed

CHAPTER 18

Confronting Conflict

onflict is a part of everyone's life. Yet, few of us approach conflict with enthusiasm. Part of the discomfort is that growing up, we seldom get the opportunity to learn positive conflict resolution. We all remember seeing conflicts; these are natural in every family. Probably, though, you do not remember seeing conflicts resolved. In this chapter, you will learn where conflicts come from and how to recognize them at their source. You will also come to understand your own and others' reactions to conflict. Finally, you will learn a positive approach to truly resolving the difficulties in your life that result from conflict.

Once you become competent in conflict resolution, you will:

- be able to create and maintain harmony
- be able to sustain relationships over time
- lower your stress level in interpersonal interactions
- gain confidence in your own ability to create positive outcomes from difficult situations

Taken from: *Transition Management: A Practical Approach to Personal and Professional Development*, Fourth edition by Sandra L. McKee and Brenda L. Walters

Conflicting Needs as a Source of Interpersonal Conflict

Conflicting needs are a fundamental source of discord in relating to others. Any time my need is different from yours, we have a conflict to some degree. How we treat that conflict is subject to our learned approach to conflict, degree of need, kind of relationship, strength of emotion, and level of self-esteem. Thus, if the conflict of need is in an area where you do not have a strong emotional involvement, you may be calm and logical in your handling of the situation. If the other person involved is someone you like and respect, then you will likely be highly motivated to seek a positive solution that is acceptable to both.

On the other hand, if your feelings are hurt or if you feel that the other person's need is overbearing and unfair, then you may react with anger. Conflicts can be quite volatile under these circumstances, but they do not have to be. The following situation illustrates a simple need conflict.

Phillip is a furniture designer and works much of the time at home. Sometimes, he is up very late, especially when he has a deadline to meet, because he likes to take a break when his sons come home from school. Jorge, Phillip's neighbor, is a programmer and works the 11 to 7 shift so he can keep his young daughter while his wife works. At four in the afternoon, Phillip takes his break to be with his sons. Many of the neighborhood boys visit because Phillip has built a skating ramp in the driveway, and Phillip helps them to practice their tricks. Jorge goes to bed about 4 P.M. when his wife comes home. The sound of the skates on the ramp keeps Jorge from sleeping.

There is a need conflict. Jorge knows he sometimes has a bad temper and that if he speaks to Phillip, there is the potential for an ugly argument. So, knowing this, Jorge might act in any of several ways depending on his learned approach to conflict:

- He may not say anything in order to avoid creating bad feelings.
- He might yell and threaten Phillip, or make noise early to waken him.
- He could become depressed over his inability to control the situation.

18.1   ACTIVITY

In this situation, which of Jorge's possible reactions might most closely resemble your own approach to conflict?

Your approach is:

_____

_____

An example of this might be:

_____

_____

Conflicting Goals as a Source of Organizational Conflict

You will find the same kinds of interpersonal conflicts in the work environment as you do outside: people feeling threatened and acting out some angry behavior, people becoming frustrated and venting. But, you also will see a larger type of conflict: goal conflict. In these cases, the conflict is not with needs, but a goal-directed activity. Issues of "ownership" and territory can be present here as well.

The new employee cannot immediately know where these festering conflicts might lie and can inadvertently be pulled into them. In the movie *Office Space*, many typical organizational conflicts, as well as some typical responses, are humorously illustrated. After reading further, you might enjoy identifying the various approaches to organizational conflict shown in that movie.

When you find yourself in a turf battle or the object of a power-display conflict, it can be very disconcerting. But when you understand the dynamics of goal conflict in companies, you will see that they are very similar to interpersonal conflicts that occur in daily life. The stakes in business are high because, in many cases, achieving a goal means saving one's job. If one manager's goal conflicts with another manager's, then the conflict could reach into other departments.

A simple but pointed example is the strategic plan for product development. Companies move forward, grow, and stay profitable by making good choices about what products they bring to market and what products they retire. Jeff is involved with developing battery-charging technology for digital cameras. Tony's division has many hours and a considerable budget invested in charging controllers for cell phones. The board has met and decided that the company is not well served by trying to do both. One of the development efforts is to be discontinued, possibly resulting in the layoff of engineers and salespeople connected with the product. Neither Jeff nor Tony is likely to be laid off, and each will be allowed patent co-ownership on whatever is developed and ultimately marketed by the company. However, each manager hired the engineers reporting to him and each feels a great deal of loyalty to them.

1. What are the issues in conflict here?

2. What will happen to the company if this is not resolved quickly?

3. Why would Tony and Jeff be concerned about the conflict?

4. Remembering that profitability is an absolute necessity to keeping a company alive, what might a good resolution be to this conflict?

The individual employee performance review can also be a source of conflict when the employee and the manager have different perceptions of the performance. Conflict around you, as well as conflict in which you are involved, can cause inordinate stress. You will feel much less threatened by organizational conflict scenarios, though, when you understand reactions to conflict and effective methods of dealing with conflict.

Common Approaches to Conflict

As noted previously, people view the potentially disruptive situation of conflict differently. In the following sections, you will see individual reactions in interpersonal relationships and reactions to conflict in organizational settings.

Conflict in Interpersonal Relationships

Evasion

Some people evade altogether situations that might lead to conflict. A wife finds out her husband is cheating and keeps up appearances, pretending everything is okay. Employees keep bad news away from the boss to avoid a scene. Customers sometimes keep defective products, so they do not have to assert themselves to a customer service person. This pattern of evasion is learned very early in our lives and supported over time.

Those who grow up in troubled families learn to tread lightly around many issues to prevent a flare-up of anger in the household and the effects of that anger on others. These individuals feel that by evading conflict, they can prevent problems from erupting. Thus, they never learn how to address issues and see a conflict through to a positive resolution.

These early patterns set up an unconscious mechanism that causes a withdrawal from conflict of any kind. In adult life, then, conflict avoidance becomes a pattern that we are not even aware of. This evasion reaction becomes ingrained in us and causes us to resist, often at great cost, any entry into a disagreement or conflict.

Some people go to such great lengths to avoid these situations that they make themselves physically sick. Todd was taught all his life never to argue with authority, to just "take it." Eventually, after years of unresolved conflicts at his job, he began having stomach pains like those associated with ulcers. He sought out counseling at the suggestion of his medical doctor. His case is not an uncommon one.

At first, he was reluctant to talk about the problems causing his stress. "I don't know what you can do for me. I've just got some stuff that I have to work out." The discussions that followed did bring out some rather serious conflicts Todd was having at his job. When asked if he had discussed any of these with his manager, he responded, "When I was growing up, it was always, 'Keep your mouth shut and do what you're told.'" Consequently, Todd held inside the anger from every conflict he avoided. His learned conflict avoidance eventually showed up in the form of a potentially serious health problem.

ACTIVITY 18.2

Take a moment to recall the kinds of conflict in your upbringing. What do you remember about the way it was handled and how it made you feel?

_____

_____

As you work through the next two sections, try to determine the conflict style you have developed as a result of your past experience.

An evasion approach may cause us a great deal of emotional pain. *By avoiding conflict, we avoid the depth of close relationship.* As long as people in the world think differently, there will be variations and conflict to some degree. Part of the richness of a relationship is learning about the opposite views others may hold. We broaden our own thinking by exposing ourselves to alternative views.

Conflict is a method of enhancing this process. Conflict is a fact of life. It is as natural as breathing, loving, or eating. Once we understand that *conflict is an important part of emotional and intellectual growth*, we then relieve ourselves of the dread we feel when we approach and deal with it. All of the energy that used to be spent worrying about or evading conflict situations can instead be directed toward positive resolutions.

Anger

Another way of responding to conflict is anger. Our bodies respond to anger the same way they do to a life-threatening situation. Adrenaline causes the heart to frantically pump blood to the muscles. The stomach churns. All of that energy has to go somewhere, and sometimes it translates into angry blowups. This issue of the perceived threat is very individual, however.

If a man feels that his family is threatened by an undesirable tenant moving into the apartment complex, he might storm angrily into the rental manager's office. In this case, fear is translated into an angry behavior. If an engineer begins to suspect that the product he has designed will not be chosen for production, he might perceive that his job security is in danger. In this situation, there is an issue of control—not being able to control the outcome of the product assessment—and fear of the loss of employment. Anger may be the way he behaves in such a situation.

The energy resulting from an anger response allows us to defend ourselves in a threatening, hand-to-hand situation. Thus, it has a basis in the instinctual survival reaction. In the office or at home, however, the urge to respond to a conflict with a loud show of anger or with violence is unacceptable. (In those situations, there is much more to lose than the conflict.)

Another of the sources of anger is emotional hurt. When self-esteem is damaged, our mind translates that into an attack at some level and responds—sometimes with hostility. If someone criticizes your clothes, you might feel indignant and want to answer the criticism smartly with anger. You can also get angry from the hurt of embarrassment, as when you are the butt of a practical joke. Any of these situations can lead to a highly charged conflict that will be difficult to resolve because of the emotions involved.

You will be asked in Activity 18.3 to look at your own or others' responses to hurt or threat. In addition to learned behaviors, some personality elements enter into your reaction as well as learned behaviors. When hurt emotionally, some people respond in an aggressive or angry way, while others may shut down and become sad, which is a passive response. We all do both of these on occasion, but will generally show a pattern of response toward one or the other. By careful self-observation you can very likely determine your typical response pattern when hurt. When you understand your habitual pattern, then you can work to develop a more beneficial, strategic approach.

ACTIVITY   18.3

Write down a conflict situation that you can recall where anger was the response. Try not to describe the angry behavior, but identify the source of the anger for yourself or for the other person. Label the type of anger as emotional pain (or threat), physical pain (or threat), or lack of control.

Conflict situation:

_____

_____

Source of anger:

_____

_____

How could you tell what the source was?

_____

_____

What you may notice is that your anger comes out of the circumstances. If anger is your conflict style, then you are indeed experiencing a lot of stress because of the way you are approaching conflict in your life.

Sadness

Another possible reaction to conflict is sadness, or in its chronic or more intense form, depression. Some people just shut down and feel powerless in the face of a threat or pain. Instead of meeting the conflict head on and resolving it, they retreat within themselves and consistently give in when a conflict occurs. This continual denial of their own needs in the face of others' needs eventually mounts up. They begin to feel an unexplainable sadness, and may even suffer from serious depression.

Some of this sadness comes from being powerless to act as they feel they should. When a verbally abusive husband consistently screams at his wife, often the male child withdraws and becomes depressed. He feels he should protect his mother and cannot. A verbally abusive manager can create the same reaction if you feel you cannot respond. In a job situation, you might become sad when you have a conflict with a coworker or friend and you do not resolve it positively.

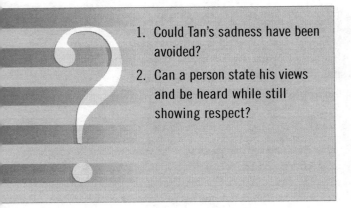

1. Could Tan's sadness have been avoided?
2. Can a person state his views and be heard while still showing respect?

Tan disagreed strongly with his father's decision to expand the family business. He felt that it would cause competition between his brothers. In addition, it would separate the family geographically because the new locations were outside the city. Having been taught that it was disrespectful to argue with the head of the family, Tan remained quiet, but became less and less enthusiastic in the discussions about the expansion and withdrew to his room each night immediately after the evening meal.

Conflict Reactions in Organizational Settings

A critical look beneath the surface of conflicts in companies reveals the same types of reactions, but the ways they are acted out in business situations may appear differently.

Territoriality

This behavior grows out of a perceived threat to an individual or a department. Generally, it is acted out by refusals to do tasks outside prescribed duties: "That's not my job." Or, it may appear as information withholding: "No, those are my accounts, you stick with your own." The latter is unfortunately common in sales environments where commissions and bonuses are awarded on the basis of individual revenue generation. Setting people in competition with each other unfortunately often fosters detrimental conflict.

Power Plays

In organizations, the coordination of effort among many people is required to achieve goals and meet objectives. Thus, when a goal conflict occurs, people tend to gather allies around them by exercising what power they have over those people. Conflict brings out the need to use power to force a win in such situations.

Sabotage and Backbiting

When conflict is not met head-on, that does not mean it has disappeared. Often, it bubbles up in more subtle ways: people conveniently forget deadlines on projects important to others, or carefully place reports of oversights or mistakes that could hurt someone's credibility or reputation. Interestingly enough, absenteeism is often attributed to unresolved conflicts in the workplace. The attitude is, "I'll show him; I just won't show up today. That'll mess his schedule up good."

Loss of Morale, Negativity

This is often the result of the conflict that occurs when expectations are not met. Employees have certain expectations of their jobs, such as fair pay, respect, opportunity for professional fulfillment, and advancement. When the employee feels as if the company (or the manager) has not met these expectations, then there is a conflict between the expectations and the reality. If this type of conflict is not confronted in some constructive way, productivity drops and the work environment becomes unpleasant.

Retreat, Rebellion

Conflicts between management choices and employee well-being that are large and far-reaching can be resolved with open communication and a genuine desire to arrive at a mutually workable solution. An example of this type of situation is when management chooses a direction for the company that will result in layoffs or a change in location. If employees feel that broaching or challenging the issue is fruitless, or if they feel that the choice was self-serving by management, widespread departures by good employees can occur. In some cases, this type of conflict leads to covert alliances within the company that result in the deposing of one or more upper managers.

None of the responses mentioned to this point are constructive ways to handle a conflict. And, if you observe the patterns, all of these reactions assume that the conflict could not have a positive outcome for all concerned. If you believe that conflicts necessarily go badly and that you have no control over the outcome of conflict, then you may readily adopt one of those approaches.

Handle Conflict Constructively

Conflict resolution is for the person or company that genuinely cares about both self and others, and is motivated to resolve, rather than temporarily stifle, conflict. This requires a certain amount of maturity. Experience teaches that unresolved conflicts come back over and over. There are several very effective techniques for conflict resolution.

The best way to approach conflict is to do it from your own sense of inner strength, and with a positive expectation about the outcome. When you are self-assured and positive, you are less likely to react to the conflict situation in one of the ineffective ways described previously.

Handle Emotions

When you have a sense of strength about yourself, you can back off from a situation that could be volatile. By taking one step back, you initially give yourself an opportunity to detach somewhat from the intensity of the conflict. Though there are no concrete rules of interpersonal conflict, there are guidelines for communicating that can help the whole process go smoothly.

When discussing conflict, focus on the situation as the topic to be resolved. Using the "I feel" statement is key here. You might say, "I feel . . . (insert emotion) . . . when you . . . (insert the problem or issue)." This way of communicating ensures a discussion related to the issues, rather than an individual, emotional response to the character of the person.

It is easy to get lost in emotion in a conflict to the extent that emotion becomes your entire focus. Feelings, however, are not the issue. Behavior is the issue. By using "I feel . . . " statements, you begin to separate the emotions from the issues. When there is intense emotion, it might be appropriate to ask yourself, "Why am I this upset about this situation?" or "Why might this other person be upset about the situation?"

Sometimes we bring old baggage from previous, unresolved conflicts to the discussion. This baggage could be in the form of anger or hurt left over from an earlier, and maybe unrelated, situation. If this is the case, then it is even more important to separate this excess emotion from the issues at hand. Focus on the issues rather than the person. *Acknowledge the feelings, but recognize that resolution of the behavior issues will solve the conflict situation.*

The more your emotions become hooked into the scene, the less likely you are to be able to think clearly. You will also be less likely to come up with solutions that could be suitable to both parties. *So, the first step is to back off and get a handle on your own emotions.* (An effective way to do this is to ask yourself what emotions you are experiencing at the time.)

Interestingly enough, we cannot seem to be logical and emotional at the same time. Thus, if you can evoke reason and observation as a response in yourself, you will see the emotional fallout diminish.

18.4   ACTIVITY

Over the next two days take note of the times you feel emotional in a conflict. Say to yourself, "I recognize I am angry (or hurt, or embarrassed), and I need to look past my reaction to see the real problem in this conflict."

Conflict situation:

I recognize that I am _____

I think _____ might be one of the problems.

Did you notice any difference in the intensity of your feeling after you identified it? Did your ability to separate the emotions from the issues help you to think more clearly?

Listen to Details

The second step is to listen with great attention to detail. After you have taken your emotional step back, try to listen very carefully to what the other person is saying, so carefully that you can repeat exactly what that person has said without missing a word. This kind of attention allows you to enter into the other person's world. When you do this, you learn something vitally important about the other person's inner workings and needs. You may even choose to clarify what is being said: "I don't understand exactly what makes you feel so angry about this situation. Can you explain it in a different way?"

The next time you find yourself in a conflict situation, listen carefully to what is being said. Look for fact (issue) statements and feeling (emotion) statements.

Look at the following dialog and analyze it for conflict elements.

LaShonda and Venson worked together on several overlapping projects. Venson designed the wording and the strategy for presentations to be given by the marketing department. LaShonda developed the art and set it all up on the presentation software.

"LaShonda," Venson said, "why don't you have that presentation ready? Mark needs it in two hours, and he wanted to run through it first. You know it doesn't look good when things come out of our department late."

"Venson, that stuff you gave me yesterday took me most of the night to do."

"Why? I gave you the outline and the spin we wanted to put on the proposal."

"Yeah, but you didn't get it to me until 3. I hate it when you do that dump and run thing."

"What's your problem? That's your job. Did you miss a night out partying?"

"I resent the implication in that. I am a professional and I do good work."

"Yeah, but who cares, if you can't meet timetables?"

1. What are the feeling statements in Venson and LaShonda's exchange?
2. What are the fact statements?
3. What is the real conflict here?

So many of us are poor listeners. We become intent on stating our case or voicing how unhappy we are with someone else. Then we fail to really tune into what the other person is saying. When the issues are broached, listening ensures that the situation is clearly defined for both parties.

State Your Needs

Now, you can make your needs known. Keep in mind here that a person with whom you have an ongoing relationship, especially a personal one, should listen and respond appropriately to this statement of need. Most of the time, however, we are more interested in speaking our case than in listening actively to the other person's case. Assert your needs in a straightforward and nonemotional way. This conveys that your view of the situation is as valid as the other person's.

If Sharon feels that her car was not repaired properly, her first response might be to avoid a confrontation and pay her bill anyway. Instead, she could be assertive and ask the technician to explain what service was done to her car and why it was done. She is expressing her need to understand where her money is going and how her car has been repaired.

Sometimes this is the point where you begin to clarify why there is a conflict to begin with. One author, Pete Bradshaw (1985), breaks down our needs into four areas:

1. Power, control, and influence
2. Achievement, accomplishment, and mastery
3. Behavior consistent with beliefs and values
4. Security in being cared for and liked

He explains that a needy condition in any or several of these areas of a person's life makes a conflict in that area more disturbing and the response, thus, more zealous. For example, if a person feels out of control in her life, a conflict in that area creates a control issue that will not be resolved until that issue has been addressed. In the earlier example, LaShonda needed to feel that her efforts and skill were noted, and she probably would remain agitated about the situation until that part of the conflict was resolved. Her coworker, on the other hand, needed to behave consistently with his belief that work should be delivered to clients on time.

Rarely in conversation, especially in the workplace, do we receive a good reaction if we say, "In this conflict, I need to feel cared for and valued." But if we are aware of our needs and can voice them in a way others can understand them, we are more likely to get at what is important to resolve the conflict. If Harry and Estelle want to meet for lunch, and Harry suggests an Indian restaurant, Estelle, who really doesn't like Indian food, has several options:

1. Go to the restaurant because Harry wants to and sit with nothing to eat.
2. Tell Harry she doesn't want to have lunch with him.
3. Tell Harry she really doesn't like that type of food.

Option 3 is a voicing of her need or concern. Estelle needed to meet Harry somewhere she could enjoy having lunch too. When she did this, however, Harry attacked her taste, saying she probably did not know if she liked the food or not. He did not respect her need or try to find a solution that might work for both of them. He could have, instead, responded with a need of his own. "There isn't an Indian restaurant near me, so I look forward to eating there when I come to town."

With both of their needs voiced, and a respect for those needs, they might have resolved the situation constructively. Instead, Estelle chose not to meet Harry for lunch.

When someone attempts to influence you, it can be at the expense of your own needs or limits. If you meet the other person's needs without addressing your own, there is still conflict, but it stays inside you. For a conflict to be completely resolved, your needs, as well as the other person's, must be affirmed.

ACTIVITY 18.5

Recall a conflict where you felt you gave in or ended up agreeing to a solution that really was not good for you. Write an assertive statement of needs that you might have used.

Conflict situation:

_____

_____

Assertive needs statement:

_____

_____

Sometimes, we are surprised that other people's needs are different from our own. We get so stuck in our own brand of thinking that we forget that many other views can exist on any given subject. So, when differences arise, it becomes necessary for each person to begin the negotiation process.

Discern and Acknowledge Others' Needs

In a successful negotiation, both parties state their needs and the value they place on those needs. Thus, each negotiator understands the other person's viewpoint and the reasons the other person feels so strongly about that viewpoint. It serves your own needs to understand the other person's position because then a resolution is equally supported by both parties. Recognize the other person's right to have opposing needs. One difficulty is that not everyone is good at expressing needs. So, sometimes you may have to guess what the person's needs really are.

You can bet that voiced or not, each person in a conflict has an idea of what a satisfactory resolution for him is. It may not be the resolution that you end up with, but until you understand the need or expectation of the other person, the conflict will continue. This is a common difficulty in conflict resolution. It is especially helpful when you can teach others around you how to verbalize needs and goals. Look at the next two exchanges. The first is a very simple example of what happens when needs are not communicated so they can be addressed.

Mom: "Hello, sweetie."

Baby: "Waaaaaaaah."

Mom: "You must be wet."

Baby: "Waaaaaaaaaaaaaaaaaah."

Mom: "Are you hungry?"

Baby: (louder now and with a red face) "WAAAAAAaaaaaah."

Mom: (becoming agitated) "What do you want?"

Baby: (turning purple and wailing loudly) "WAAAAAAAAAAAAAAH."

Before you roll your eyes at what may seem like an outrageous example, think of this: As adults we sometimes are not too far removed from the baby who cries when she is not taken care of. When this happens, the conflict turns into more of an argument and often becomes much louder. When someone with whom we are in conflict does not listen or respond appropriately, we tend to resort to stronger language. By recognizing the necessity to communicate needs, we can better manage the language of conflict.

Customer: "I bought this suit at one of your stores and it's trash."

Representative: "When did you purchase it and from which of our stores?"

Customer: "Look, you, I said this thing is junk. Why don't you just do your job, or can't you do that?"

Representative: "Sir, I understand this is an unpleasant problem, and we need to deal with it right away. I'm sure you purchased the suit for something important."

Customer: "You're d_____ right. I've got an interview in the morning and I need the suit!"

Representative: "We'll take care of this. If you'll tell me where and when you bought it, I'll authorize the store closest to you now to make one available for tomorrow's interview. You can leave the suit you are having a problem with, and the manager will work out a repair or replacement afterwards. But this will get you set for that interview right away."

Customer: "Well, uh, okay. That will work. It's my second interview and I have to look just right."

Representative: "Yes, I'm sure you'll do well, and thank you for choosing our company. Just bring your receipt or the tags with the suit. What store was that?"

Of course, part of the need was to have an intact and unflawed suit. That is what the customer voiced. The *real* need, however, was to be well dressed for the interview. Until that need was addressed, the situation was going to escalate.

Persist in Solving a Mutual Problem

Good conflict resolution requires time and persistence. There are quick solutions to most problems, and they are arrived at fairly easily. However, these solutions are rarely the best for either party and are seldom supported for any period of time. They are often only temporary bandages on a situation that requires major care. Sometimes, you just have to ask the question, "What will it take for you to be satisfied in this situation?" Surprisingly, the answer is often simpler than you think.

Sasha and her husband, Michael, have just had their tenth discussion, or argument, about a particularly sore spot in their marriage. Michael wants to have a baby and at this time Sasha does not. Michael has stormed out of the house, and Sasha has locked herself in the bathroom. Sasha has a career position on a senior management track at her company. Women who have children never seem to go anywhere in her company. There doesn't seem to be actual discrimination. It's more that those women don't stay late or come in on weekends like others on the management team do.

1. What emotion(s) do you think Michael is feeling?

2. What might Sasha be thinking?

3. What are the issues in this conflict?

4. What are Sasha's needs? Michael's needs?

5. What might be a mutually acceptable solution to this problem?

Michael came from a very happy family with three children and feels that a big reason he and Sasha got married was to eventually have a family.

The conflict between Michael and Sasha is not going to be resolved with any quick fix. Michael and Sasha, however, have a commitment to each other in the form of marriage, and with that comes a promise to work through issues such as these. Giving up on conflicts with family or with your work is not the way to keep your life moving forward.

A transition is by nature and definition a renegotiation for new conditions. Each conflict is an opportunity to move to a new level of understanding and interacting. When a marriage hits a wall and both parties say that they are not going to relate in the same way they have in the past, two things can happen. The people part company or they creatively look at their relationship and negotiate a new contract that is satisfying to both of them. In other words, they discard the *way* they relate, not the *desire* to continue to relate to each other. Couples who stay together and work through this renegotiation process describe a more intimate and mutually satisfying result.

Organizations work in much the same way. A little conflict forces employees and even departments into a problem-solving mode. The creativity and teamwork required to resolve complex business conflicts enrich the organization.

Your goal in conflict resolution is not to make the conflict go away, but to resolve the issues that created the conflict. As long as the issue is still a problem for the other person, it will continue to come up over and over and be a problem for you. Therefore, a mutual solution is the only workable option. As you can see, all parties must agree to persist to a resolution because anyone who gives in or walks away from the situation will not support the resolution. The conflict that is not fully resolved will reappear.

18.6   ACTIVITY

Select a conflict that is troublesome to you now. Describe the ideal solution for you.

Conflict description:

_____

_____

Ideal solution:

_____

_____

Now, describe what problems may develop or grow if this conflict is not resolved.

Problems for you:

_____

_____

Problems for the other person(s):

_____

_____

Come up with three possible solutions, at least one of which must be desirable to the other person.

1. _____

2. _____

3. _____

Give a good reason why you and the other person should persist to solve this mutual problem.

_____

_____

Resolution:

_____

_____

Negotiate

Some conflicts in business are so complex and far reaching that professional negotiators are brought in to help the parties involved work through to a satisfactory result. The following guidelines for negotiating may be applicable to other conflict situations as well.

1. Confirm from the start that the conflict outcome is negotiable and that all affected parties have input in some way.

2. Ensure that the person (or people) you are negotiating with have the authority to commit to the solution agreed on.

3. Ask questions to learn what the other party wants and needs and why she feels what she seeks is a reasonable request. (Whether you think it is reasonable or not is irrelevant at this stage. You must gain an understanding of why *she* thinks she is entitled to what is being sought.)

4. Seek to ascertain the emotional value of each issue under discussion. Beginning with less emotionally charged issues may lay the groundwork for later agreements on tougher topics.

5. Remove time as a parameter in the process. If you allow as much time as necessary, the other side may become pressed for a resolution to meet a timetable of its own. If a timely resolution is a necessity, secure an agreement from the other party for a "time's up" point.

6. Couch the wording of proposed resolutions in terms of the mutual benefits from each course of action. No one will agree to something that is not beneficial, but your creativity and understanding of the situation might be required to clarify the benefits.

7. Write down immediately all points of agreement, no matter how small or insignificant they may seem. As you proceed, you will need to remind each other of any common ground.

8. When an agreement is reached, attempt to elicit the plans the other party intends to put into effect to support the solution. Be prepared to do the same for your commitments.

9. Congratulate the other party on the intelligence and integrity shown by the resolution. It takes a lot to get to the point of agreement in the case of volatile or complex conflicts. Recognition of the effort and creativity required by all parties is a respectful way to leave the situation.

Conflict resolution is a healthy way of solving problems when our needs or goals differ. There will always be alternative ways of looking at any issue, and alternative values placed on these issues. *Conflict is not detrimental unless we let it cripple our relationships and damage our sense of self.* Businesses know that a little conflict is healthy to stimulate creativity, ensure good critical thinking on important issues, and prevent stagnation. A healthy session where important issues are brought forward in a caring and resolution committed way can keep any relationship moving to ever higher levels of adaptation and intimacy. *Transitions are necessary because new conditions conflict with old conditions.* Following good conflict management guidelines can ensure positive results, including increased satisfaction with new levels of your life.

TRANSITION SKILLS SUMMARY

Recognize symptoms of conflicts not addressed

Back off and handle your own emotions

Listen with great attention to detail

Assert your own needs

Acknowledge the other person's needs

Focus on the issues rather than the person

Persist in resolving a mutual problem

GOAL SETTING

My self-nurturing goal for managing conflicts in new ways in my personal life is:

_____

_____

_____

My self-advocacy goal for managing conflict in new ways in my professional life is:

_____

_____

_____

COACH'S CORNER

Mediation is usually ordered by a judge in cases where lengthy hashing out of issues would take up inordinate amounts of court time. Usually in divorce or property disputes where resolution is difficult, the parties involved agree to use a court-recommended mediator to help them reach an agreement. In situations with attorneys in a court, each attorney sees a "win" only if his client gets what the client wants. In mediation, the goal

(continued)

is an agreement—not necessarily one or the other getting what she wants. Successful mediation requires the surfacing of two major points:

1. Each party has to separate what is wanted from what is truly needed.
2. The mediator must establish what each party fears losing because that issue will likely be nonnegotiable. Deference to that issue may, however, be used to barter for a concession on another point later.

Sometimes in a company a conflict stops forward movement or production. Mediation in these situations must consider time as one of the issues. Sometimes, both parties have to acknowledge the bad effects they will share if the resolution process takes too long.

DONALD "SKIP" HALL, court-licensed mediator; e-mail: halls@yca.net.

Whatever subject it is that makes your heart beat faster, keeps you in discussion until 4:30 in the morning, or makes you wake up with a sense of urgency about the topic—that's where you are guaranteed to be successful.

Robert Vilardi,
student

ASSESSING LEARNING NEEDS AND COURSE REQUIREMENTS

Being an adult means taking responsibility for yourself and others; understanding the consequences of your behavior; and learning to act with authority at home, at work, and in the community. At first glance, it may seem that these qualities contradict the idea of being a student: someone who listens, follows directions, and meets other people's requirements. Being a student, however, is not a passive role. As an adult student, you are responsible for creating a plan for learning, seeking help if you need it, and engaging actively in the process of gaining intellectual authority.

Part of that process involves reflecting upon your own learning style, examining your strengths and weaknesses as a learner, and responding to your needs when you create your plan for learning.

In this chapter, you will learn how to:

- understand different learning styles
- evaluate your own learning style
- become aware of your needs as a learner
- choose classes where you can learn most effectively

Taken from: *New Beginnings: A Reference Guide for Adult Learners*, by Linda Simon

287

TYPES OF LEARNERS

In recent years, educators have conducted research on the ways students learn and the strategies that work best for different kinds of learners. Not everyone responds in the same way to reading, listening, studying, and memorizing. Knowing your own learning style can help you devise useful strategies for your own success. In the paragraphs that follow, see if you can identify yourself in one of the three students described.

Visual Learner

Even as a child, Lenny was the kind of student who kept orderly notes and could easily memorize lists of spelling words, definitions, or math formulas. He preferred courses where he could be graded on the basis of short-answer or multiple-choice tests; he felt anxiety, however, about essay questions or term papers. As a reader, Lenny prefers historical narratives that introduce him to people, places, and events that he does not know. He enjoys accumulating knowledge. He likes to do crossword puzzles, but jigsaw puzzles are no fun at all. Lenny:

- is logical and analytical
- is methodical
- concentrates easily
- pays attention to detail
- works well alone

Kinesthetic Learner

Terry calls herself a hands-on person. Her hobby is models—planes, trains, and cars—but she never bothers to read the instruction manual. Instead, she figures out the function of a part by handling it and trying to connect it to other parts. She prides herself on her sense of space and structure. She's the person in her family who gets called on when someone buys a disassembled bicycle or lawn mower. Terry:

- is imaginative and inventive
- is intuitive
- learns through doing
- perceives patterns easily

Auditory Learner

Ted is often the student who talks first in class and eagerly volunteers to give presentations. He is friendly, and if you met him, he'd know your life story in an hour. If he were to tell you, "I know just what you mean," you'd believe him. Once, when he worked as a campaign volunteer for a local candidate, he was given the task of producing an informational flyer about the

Visually-Kinestetic

EVALUATING YOUR LEARNING STYLE

19

Circle the letter of the response that most accurately describes you, then see the scoring section that follows to determine your predominant learning style.

1. When I study, I:
   a. can concentrate easily.
   b. get easily distracted.
   c. work best with a study buddy.

2. I prefer an instructor who:
   a. lectures in an organized way.
   b. gives students diagrams or charts to explain material.
   c. allows for plenty of class discussion.

3. If I take an exam, I prefer it to be:
   a. a short-answer or multiple-choice exam.
   b. an essay exam that asks me to draw my own conclusions.
   c. an open-ended essay exam.

4. In taking class notes, I prefer to:
   a. organize the notes as an outline.
   b. organize the notes as maps or pictures.
   c. tape-record lectures.

5. To memorize material, I:
   a. read it over and over.
   b. write it over and over.
   c. say it to someone over and over.

SCORING

If you answered (a) to these questions, your predominant learning style is visual; if you answered (b), your predominant learning style is kinesthetic; if you answered (c), your predominant learning style is auditory.

To further assess your learning style, respond to the following two questions:

1. List a few of your favorite courses from high school or college.

   Math, forensics/speech, English, drama

2. Identify the courses (such as science laboratories, theater, or physical education) as lecture, discussion, or participation classes. Identify the kinds of tests or assessment you had in each course. Describe the teaching style of your instructor. What conclusions can you draw about your learning style based on your responses?

   _____

   _____

   _____

candidate's positions. Although he worked hard on the flyer, another volunteer had to complete it because Ted had difficulty organizing the candidate's ideas clearly. Yet when Ted went out to distribute the flyers, he could easily convey those ideas and explain to people how the ideas applied to their own lives. Ted:

- can understand problems and ideas in context
- learns best through conversations
- is interested in other people
- is persuasive
- presents his views easily

Tips for Capitalizing on Your Learning Style

If you are a **visual learner:**

- Underline or highlight main ideas in texts.
- Use flash cards for memorizing terms or facts.
- Create charts or graphs to order information.
- Associate pictures with concepts or facts.
- Choose lecture classes with well-organized instructors.
- Make sure to collect all handouts and study guides.

If you are a **kinesthetic learner:**

- Engage in note-taking while listening to class lectures.
- Translate concepts into maps, diagrams, or action pictures.
- Reword concepts or ideas as action stories.
- Act out ideas.
- Choose workshops whenever possible.
- Look for instructors who provide diagrams and illustrations.

If you are an **auditory learner:**

- Tape-record lectures or class discussions (ask your instructor for permission to do this).
- Read aloud to yourself or a partner when doing reading assignments.
- Study by verbal drilling.
- Choose courses that involve class discussion.
- Take advantage of your instructor's office hours to ask questions or clarify information.

Understanding your learning style can help you make informed choices about classes, instructors, and study strategies. Remember, though, that your own motivation is significant to your success. Although one learning style may predominate for you, you still can be successful in many different courses and class settings with many different kinds of instructors.

UNDERSTANDING CLASSROOM FORMATS

Choosing a particular class depends on your academic goals, the requirements for your degree, and the requirements for your major or particular program. Sometimes, you may choose one class rather than another because the class format fits well with your learning style. There are basically three kinds of classroom settings.

Lecture

In a lecture class, the instructor talks; the students listen, take notes, and usually have an opportunity to ask questions at the end of the instructor's presentation. Lecture classes may range from 20 or 30 students to a few hundred. In a lecture class, students generally are assessed by short-answer or multiple-choice examinations (or, rarely, essay examinations). In a lecture class, you usually are expected to complete reading assignments before class meetings, but you may not receive feedback at each class to help you assess your understanding of the material.

Seminar

A seminar is typically limited to fewer than 20 students. The focus of class time is discussion. Students, then, need to be prepared for each class by keeping up with readings and assignments. Students may be assessed by examinations, by writing a paper, or by completing a project. Because a seminar class is relatively small, there is often significant interaction among the students.

Workshop

Like a seminar, a workshop is a small class focused on both discussion and other classroom activities. Activities include: editing (in a writing workshop); small-group discussions (where students work on problem solving with a partner or a few other students); projects (such as creating a document, report, presentation, or demonstration); and interviewing. A laboratory course in the sciences is, essentially, a workshop course because it provides hands-on learning opportunities.

To assess your own class preferences, complete the worksheet that follows.

ASSESSING YOUR PREFERRED CLASS FORMAT

Write *True* beside the statements that apply to you:

_____ 1. I prefer a large lecture class where I can gather information before I am asked to respond to it.

_____ 2. I prefer a small seminar where I can ask questions as they occur to me and where I can share my ideas with other people.

_____ 3. I am comfortable talking in class.

_____ 4. I like to feel that I have a lot of background before I venture an opinion.

_____ 5. I hate to write.

_____ 6. I read very slowly.

_____ 7. I am afraid everyone else is smarter than I am.

Scoring: If you answered *True* for questions 1, 4, and 7, you may want to begin with large lecture classes, where class participation is not required and where you interact with instructors only through examinations, through writing assignments, or in private conferences either after class or during the instructor's office hours.

If you answered *True* for questions 2 and 3, you welcome interacting with classmates and instructors and want to share the sense of community created in small classes.

If you answered *True* for question 5, you may want to select, among your first courses, a preparatory writing class to help you learn the skills of college writing that you will need throughout your career as a student.

If you answered *True* for question 6, you should monitor the reading requirements for your first courses and, at the same time, inquire about study skills classes in reading that may be offered by your college. Chapter 5 will teach you some useful strategies for note-taking; Chapter 6 will cover reading strategies.

RECOGNIZING DIFFERENT AREAS OF STUDY

What's the difference between American Studies and American History? Between Sociology and Anthropology? In the list that follows you'll find common terms used to describe the various disciplines offered by most colleges.

ASSESSING NEEDS 19

African American Studies. This interdisciplinary field focuses on the experience of African Americans throughout the American's history. Courses may focus on history, literature, the arts, politics, sociology, and psychology.

American Studies. This interdisciplinary field focuses on the life and culture of the United States. The courses may examine gender, class, ethnicity, literature, history, and the arts.

Anthropology. This field of the social sciences examines human groups and social behavior. Anthropology includes archaeology, which is the study of past cultures and human cultural evolution.

Art. Studio Art gives students an opportunity to engage directly in painting, sculpture, graphic design, or photography. Art History examines the work of artists throughout time and across cultures.

Asian Studies. This interdisciplinary field focuses on the life and culture of China, Japan, India, and other Asian countries.

Biology. One of the life sciences, Biology offers students a chance to explore such topics as plant biology, human biology, genetics, ecology, and physiology through lecture and laboratory courses.

Business. Designed to prepare students to enter the business field, these courses include management, accounting, taxation, organizational structure, finance, and business law.

Chemistry. This field explores the molecular and atomic bases of matter, generally in laboratory courses.

Classics. This field examines the literature, history, philosophy, religion, art, and archaeology of ancient Greece and Rome.

Communications. These courses feature print and nonprint journalism and the role of media in society.

Computer Science. These courses offer the logical, mathematical, and scientific foundations of computing.

Economics. More theoretical than courses offered through the Business department, Economics gives students a background in money and banking, the production and distribution of goods and services, and economic theory.

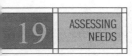

Education. Learning theory, history of education, and social implications of education, along with courses that lead to teacher certification, are among the areas covered by Education departments.

English. Departments of English offer courses on English and American language and literature, creative writing (fiction, poetry, and nonfiction), and expository writing or composition.

Environmental Studies. This is an interdisciplinary field that combines studies in the natural sciences, humanities, and social sciences, focusing on the life cycles of the natural world, the interaction between humans and nature, and the ethics of ecological decisions.

Foreign Languages. Colleges differ in their grouping of foreign languages. Sometimes a single department oversees all course offerings; sometimes language courses are separated into Romance Languages, East Asian Languages, Slavic Languages, etc.

Geology. Also known as Earth Science, Geology includes laboratory and classroom courses in oceanography, mineralogy, and environmental science.

Government. Also known as Political Science, the field of Government offers courses in American and international politics, philosophy, history, and law.

History. American History and International History often include courses in the history of groups, such as women, African Americans, and immigrants of various ethnic backgrounds.

Mathematics. This field includes statistics, geometry, calculus, algebra, and introductory courses for nonmajors.

Music. Courses offered by Music departments cover music appreciation, history, theory and composition, and performance.

Philosophy. Topics of study include ethics, religion, aesthetics, logic, critical reasoning, and the history of philosophy.

Physical Education. Activity courses give students a chance to engage in sports, exercise, or performance; theory courses introduce students to the physiology of exercise, sport history and philosophy, and nutrition.

Physics. Topics of these courses include gravity, electricity, magnetism, light, and atomic energy.

Psychology. The science of the mind and personality offers courses in theories of personality development, abnormal psychology, ways of learning, perception, and emotion.

Religion. Sometimes included in Philosophy departments, these courses explore the fundamentals of world religions through their various texts, art, and traditions.

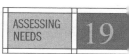

ASSESSING NEEDS 19

Sociology. This social science examines the ways human groups—such as the family or the community—organize, function, and change.

Theater. Courses include acting, directing, voice, set design, playwriting, production, history, and criticism.

Women's Studies. This interdisciplinary field draws upon literature, sociology, psychology, history, and the arts to examine the changing role of women in society.

CHOOSING YOUR CLASSES

Open up any college catalogue and you're likely to feel overwhelmed by the possibilities. A course called *Business Ethics* might help you on your job; a course called *The Arts: Opera* might open up a whole new aesthetic experience. Should you take a course entitled *Organizational Behavior* or *Organizational Change?* What's the difference between the two? What difference can the course make in your new career as a student?

Deciphering Course Descriptions

A catalogue course description is a brief summary designed to help you decide whether you want to register for the course. It is the first step in the decision-making process. As you gain some experience in reading course descriptions, you'll be able to decode them to answer the following questions:

1. Is this a *survey* course?

2. What *prerequisites* or *co-requisites* are necessary? That is, what courses do I need to take before, or at the same time as, I take this course?

3. Is this a *lecture* course, a *seminar*, or a *workshop?*

4. How much writing does this course require? The course description may indicate the writing requirements. Otherwise, visit the department and check the syllabus that the teacher may have on file.

5. Does this course require out-of-class activities or meetings?

6. How does this course fit into my long-range plans as a student?

7. Is this course required or recommended for my major?

8. Is this course one of my electives?

You'll see in your college catalogue that some courses have a description beyond the content of the course. The following will help you understand some of the terms commonly used in describing courses.

Survey. A survey course offers an overview of a large body of material. Typically, students will come out of the course knowing key figures, key terms, and key issues for the course topic. A survey course often serves as an introduction to more focused courses.

The following example is from a college catalogue (New York University):

Literary Romanticism

The genesis and evolution of Romanticism are traced through its literary forms. The course integrates the prose and poetry of Blake, William Wordsworth, Dorothy Wordsworth, Wollstonecraft, Godwin, Percy Bysshe Shelley, Hazlitt, Lamb, Scott, Marx, Carlyle, Lawrence, Goethe, Heine, Schiller, Lessing, Hegel, Sand, Hugo, Stendhal, and Nerval.

The long list of authors covered in this course is your clue that this is a survey course, looking at key British, French, and German writers—novelists,

Identifying Your Course Requirements

Knowing the requirements of your program is an important first step in deciding which courses you will take and in what sequence you will take them. You may want to answer these questions with the help of an advisor or counselor at your school.

1. What courses are requirements for all students at your college?
2. What courses are requirements for all students in your particular degree program?
3. What courses are requirements for all students in your major or concentration of study?
4. What courses are prerequisites for advanced courses in your field?
5. What courses are recommended by your advisor because those courses give good preparation to meet your goals?
6. What courses do you want to take as electives because they fulfill a special interest of yours?

poets, and essayists—during the literary period known as Romanticism. Students will read samples from each of these authors to become familiar with their style and subject matter.

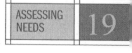

Prerequisite. A survey course is often required to give students a basis for more focused courses. For example, the course *Literary Romanticism* would serve students who want to study nineteenth-century French literature, Wordsworth and his circle, or women and Romanticism.

Even courses that are called *introductions* often have prerequisites. For example (New York University):

Introduction to Investments

Prerequisites: Math I; Principles of Accounting. An introduction to the various types of investments employed by individuals and institutions. The purposes, advantages, and disadvantages of each are discussed. Topics include objectives and methods of investing, short- and long-term planning, forecasting and timing, and kinds of investments (including stock options and mutual funds).

The prerequisites for this course tell you that without a background in basic mathematics, and without the information you would learn from an introductory course in accounting, you will be at a disadvantage in the course. You will not be learning the mathematics and accounting skills you need during this investments course.

Suppose, however, you have been working professionally in billing and accounting. If you think you have the necessary prerequisites because of your life experience, you should contact the instructor to help you assess your background.

Evaluating a Course Syllabus

A course syllabus may be available from the advising office of your college or directly from the instructor. A syllabus is a course plan, including general course requirements, required books, schedule of class discussions, homework and writing assignments, and dates for exams.

Here are some questions to consider as you look at a syllabus.

Questions to Ask About a Course

1. How heavy is the reading load?
2. When are papers due?
3. Am I expected to write papers during school holidays?
4. How will I be evaluated?
5. Are there out-of-class obligations?
6. Does the course seem well organized?

1. *How heavy is the reading load?* A novel a week may be too heavy a load for a slow reader or for a student working long hours. How much quiet reading time will you have to devote to the class? How quickly do you read? With these two figures in mind, you should be able to evaluate the reading load for the course you are considering.

YOUR COLLEGE CAREER PLAN

How close will you be to achieving your goals after five years? Fill in this worksheet with courses that you are taking or that you plan to take this year and in the following four years.

	FALL	SPRING	SUMMER
This year	_____	_____	_____
	_____	_____	_____
	_____	_____	_____
	_____	_____	_____
Year 2	_____	_____	_____
	_____	_____	_____
	_____	_____	_____
	_____	_____	_____
Year 3	_____	_____	_____
	_____	_____	_____
	_____	_____	_____
	_____	_____	_____
Year 4	_____	_____	_____
	_____	_____	_____
	_____	_____	_____
	_____	_____	_____
Year 5	_____	_____	_____
	_____	_____	_____
	_____	_____	_____
	_____	_____	_____

_____ Total credits needed for degree or completion of program

_____ Total credits expected to accrue in five years

_____ Credits needed after five years

_____ Expected graduation date

2. *When are papers due?* Compare the due dates with your own work and family obligations. Will you be able to complete the course requirements on time?

3. *Are you expected to write papers during school holidays?* If Thanksgiving means preparing a dinner for 12, you may not have time to produce the paper you need to hand in the following Monday. If Christmas vacation means family and child-care obligations or an increased workload at your job, you may not have time for library research. When are the papers due? When is the final exam? Do those dates give you time to work and study?

4. *How will you be evaluated?* Some courses ask students only for papers. Other courses have a midterm and final exam. Still others ask for class presentations, alone or as part of a group. The syllabus should indicate how you will earn your grade; you can decide if the requirements meet your own learning style.

5. *Are there out-of-class obligations?* Some courses require that you meet with classmates, attend film showings or other events, participate in class trips, or even attend additional lectures. Does the schedule fit in with your free time?

6. *Does the course seem well organized?* The syllabus is the instructor's week-by-week plan of instruction. You should be able to see what topics will be covered in each class, decide whether the topics seem to be ordered logically, and assess whether enough time will be spent on topics that interest you.

ONLINE LEARNING

More and more, adults are enrolling in distance learning programs, where they do not have to travel to a campus or walk into a classroom. Their courses take place online in a virtual community of learners. If you enroll in an online class, you need to have access to a computer, know basic computer and Internet skills, and be self-disciplined. Here are some questions to ask yourself if you're considering taking online courses:

- **Are you comfortable communicating through writing?** In an online course, you'll communicate with your instructor and other students by writing responses related to the coursework. You need to be able to write clearly and coherently to be a successful online student.

- **Are you self-motivated?** Most online courses are asynchronous—that is, students log on to the course site and complete assignments on their own time. You may do coursework at midnight or in the middle of the day as long as you can complete assignments when they are due.

- **Do you have the time?** Logging on to chat rooms or discussion groups is only part of an online course. Your instructor will provide you with a course schedule and assignments, some of which may require hours of reading or research. Make sure you have from 4 to 15 hours a week to

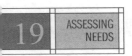

complete your work; your instructor may be able to help you estimate the time required for a particular course.

- **Would you prefer a physical community?** Some students enjoy classroom learning because it puts them in contact with other people who share their interests. Online learning sometimes feels a bit lonely to them. Before you choose an online class, ask yourself if you'd rather be sitting next to a real person in a real classroom.

In an online course, your instructor and classmates may communicate with one another through chat rooms or discussion boards. A *chat room* is an interactive site where participants send messages to one another in real time. In an online course, students often respond to an instructor's questions, to students' work, or to class readings by sending contributions to a chat room. Another form of real-time communication is instant messaging.

A *discussion board* is like a bulletin board at a community center or in the workplace, where people post announcements, responses, or items of interest to the community. In an online course, those items of interest will focus on coursework or readings, and students send messages through e-mail for posting on the board. Sometimes, students and the instructor communicate directly through e-mail, without making their contributions available to all on a discussion board.

Finding an Online Provider

Online learning has become a popular form of education. Sometimes, you can find courses offered by local colleges or universities. Even if you take courses online, these institutions may be able to provide you with library resources, advisors, study skills centers, and career offices. If you do not have a local school, or if the courses you want to take are not offered there, Peterson's *Guide to Distance Learning Programs*, updated yearly in print and online, lists accredited learning institutions, their costs, and their programs.

Accredited means that a national or regional certification agency has looked carefully at the course offerings, the faculty, the syllabi, and the educational mission of the program and has approved it. For students who would like to transfer credit toward a degree, to take courses to enhance their career, or to embark on a new career path, it's important that you enroll in an accredited program. Some professions maintain lists of programs that offer accredited courses specifically in that profession.

What You Can Expect from an Online Course

Your instructor will provide a syllabus or course outline, giving a schedule of course topics and sometimes including reading and writing assignments. Some instructors prefer to give assignments as the course progresses. The syllabus should give you information about the basis for your grade: How will your instructor evaluate your learning?

Your instructor will provide a list of readings and source material that may require you to visit Web sites or find material on the Internet. You will also receive instructions about how to communicate with the instructor and your classmates.

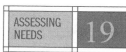

You should expect to log on to the course site several times weekly, to keep up with postings on discussion boards or in chat rooms, and to be a responsible and active participant in the class.

Successful Learning Online

- Make a schedule and keep to it. Keep up with readings and writing assignments, and devote enough time to the class so that you can contribute substantially to online discussions.

- Think before you press "send." Remember: Your readers are members of your class, real people with real feelings. It's easy to respond quickly, especially when you have strong feelings about a question or topic. It's more responsible to think about your ideas and make sure you express them thoughtfully and politely.

- Communicate clearly and correctly. Proofread all of your contributions. Some students recommend reading messages aloud to yourself before sending them to the class.

- Support your ideas with evidence. Make substantive contributions, rather than merely agreeing with others or repeating a comment that someone else made.

- Make your responses concise. If you make notes before responding, you'll find that it's easier to focus than if you simply "think out loud." Conciseness helps your readers to focus on your main ideas.

- Avoid emoticons and acronyms. E-mailing and instant messaging have developed a special vocabulary. :-), for example, means a smile or happiness; BTW means "by the way." But these images and letters may not be familiar to your classmates or instructor. FWIW (for what it's worth), it's better to use conventional vocabulary when contributing to class discussions—BYKT (but you knew that).

ADDITIONAL RESOURCES

The Distance Learner's Guide, 2nd ed. Upper Saddle River, New Jersey: Prentice Hall, 2005.

Peterson's Guide to Distance Learning Programs. www.petersons.com/distancelearning/.

CHAPTER 20

Launching Your Career

The big step, a new job: a first career position just out of school, a change to a new and better job, a return to work after years of child rearing, or a recovery from a layoff or being fired. Each of these presents its own challenges, but all require some standard, expected protocols to lead to success.

Employee selection is sometimes a very difficult process for companies. This is partly because of a shortage of skilled people from which to choose in certain industries. Even with this great need, for serious consideration you are expected to:

- locate job leads and potential openings, more or less on your own
- supply certain documents, such as resumes, applications, and letters, in prescribed formats
- showcase your abilities and demonstrate your potential in an interview

The Job Fit Challenge

Every company with a job opening wants to hire not just someone who could do the job, but someone who would be more: an asset to the company in many different areas. The company is looking for someone who will help them

Taken from: *Transition Management: A Practical Approach to Personal and Professional Development*, Fourth edition by Sandra L. McKee and Brenda L. Walters

make money or help them cut expenses. That is the bottom line of what an asset really is. They also, however, look for a *fit*. With a temporary or contract worker, they pick someone to fill a short-term, specific skill need, based mostly on a list of competencies. However, for full-time employees, the standards are different and the process, more involved.

In addition to technical skills (this term applies to any specialized skill within a particular industry), a prospective employee must also be able to:

- work as easily alone as in teams
- manage time and tasks for meeting deadlines
- demonstrate a good work ethic
- add to the synergy that occurs in groups that work well together

The person in charge of hiring, however, must determine all of this from a resume, one to two interviews (maybe only three or four hours total), and a few references.

A mistake in hiring costs a company a great deal. In a company that offers just a basic benefits package, an employee's cost is considered to be one to two and a half times that employee's salary per year. In addition, anyone new has to learn the processes, procedures, and strategic priorities of the company as well as sources to secure information and services. This takes time, time that is not at maximum efficiency. If an employee fails within a year, that up-to-speed cost was wasted, and the company must bring in someone new, who will take several months to reach reasonable productivity. Many companies figure the average cost of hiring a new employee at $8,000 to $15,000.

This figure is necessarily higher at higher levels of the company and in cases of scarce expertise where an international search may be involved. Though professional search firms (sometimes called *headhunters* or *recruiters*) charge a fee to take on this responsibility, many companies feel that the fee is still less than the cost of the time spent by their own employees on the hiring activity rather than on their own jobs.

In short, employers need you, perhaps even desperately, and truly want you to be just what they are looking for. Your job is to make that decision easier for them, to show them that you can do what they need and that they can trust you to act in the best interests of the company. That includes getting along with your coworkers and showing initiative as well as good judgment. The previous chapters have oriented you to many of the expectations a company will have along these lines, and a review of the highlights of that material may help prepare you to present yourself in the best possible way. A candidate who can demonstrate *savvy*, an understanding of the challenges and inner workings of a position, as well as the general demands of the workplace, is likely to receive an offer quickly.

When you finally do find that perfect *fit*, the job and company that suits your professional style and values your expertise, the transition becomes one to:

- an opportunity to do something you enjoy in an environment that fosters that enjoyment

- a place where you can be productive and make a visible contribution to something larger than yourself

- a source of stimulation and support in the form of colleagues and experts

- an environment in which to apply your creativity to complex problems and grow in your knowledge and experience

- a notable step toward achieving your ultimate professional and personal goals

The Search

Several expressions describe the search process. One expression, "license to hunt," suggests that with certain credentials, you will find prospects available to you that might not be available to others without those credentials. For example, some jobs require a bachelor's or associate's degree as an absolute cutoff for consideration. Others may expect certain professional certifications or licenses to be held by their serious candidates, such as Certified Network Administrator or licensed physical therapist. In any case, some aspects of your background, experience, credentialing, or special talents will allow you into different ranges of jobs.

Where one company might be predisposed to hire people from certain colleges, others may offer a preference to minorities or to handicapped individuals. Though there are still subtle, but detectable, cases of conscious bias—either for or against certain individuals or groups—most large companies these days work very hard to preserve fair hiring practices, both in policy and action.

Many of the best jobs never show up in ads or on recruiters' desks; they are only discovered through word of mouth. Notes Blair Boyer, career counselor, "Most estimates I have seen indicate that the hidden job market (those that don't show up in ads) comprises approximately 85 percent of available positions." In special cases, a person who can give you an "in" to a company may offer freer access to potential positions than you might have found without it.

Your own search strategy should identify and target jobs that will be potential assets in your journey toward your life goals. Several different approaches to the job search are described below, but these are primarily approaches to finding suitable job openings or opportunities. Later in the chapter, guidelines for evaluating a job to determine whether it would be a good fit are discussed. The most common sources of job leads are:

- college career placement offices
- alumni
- ads in the newspaper
- ads in industry periodicals
- Internet postings
- career counselors or recruiters
- prospecting—networking, unsolicited approaches, company Web sites

Though each of these sources has led to many successful career fits, a combination of several usually ends up being the most effective.

College Placement Offices

Of course, the individual anticipating graduation from any educational program should consult the career services department of the college or institute, but a surprising number do not. Companies recruit from colleges; thus, the contacts your career services counselors have are some you cannot obtain other places. Career fairs hosted by your school or by a professional organization at your school may result in immediate offers. In addition, if there is a particular company you are interested in, a call from the placement representative of your school might be received more graciously than your own effort.

Many schools at the postsecondary level also offer career testing that allows you to discover the best places to direct your skill and operational style—job types you may not have thought about. When companies do large layoffs, many of them offer these same types of services, called *outplacement assistance*. Leads, testing, counseling and, sometimes, mock interviews for practice, as well as resume and clerical support, are all available at college placement offices. You can consult career offices other than your own college, particularly if you are trying to relocate. Many offer services to the public or to graduates from other colleges (e.g., colleges that are members of NACE often have reciprocal agreements to assist students from other NACE colleges).

Alumni

There is no better person on the inside of a company you might want to pursue than a graduate of your school. If the company likes the graduate's performance, they may favor applicants from the same school. If you do not know any alumni, the alumni office may have directories to consult, or career services coordinators can contact others they have placed. Active involvement in alumni groups and functions may continue to provide you contacts beyond your first job as well.

An extension of the alumni contact is the professional or service organization. Many of these have college or other educational branches. If you have participated in one of them, then you will be most welcome to move into the full-blown organization once you have left school. Because many of these organizations are national, such as IEEE or Alpha Phi Omega, members could be of assistance in helping you find your way into companies in cities across the country.

Ads in Newspapers

Many of these ads are looking for people with specified experience. However, ads can also give you a contact name or address for a future search effort. Ads give you some perspective on where the most job openings are, which companies are hiring, and the qualifications for particular positions. The latter information will help you clarify your goal-related activities. Companies that have strong training programs may look for applicants through newspaper ads. In addition, ads requesting two to three years of experience might be worth a follow up. Often someone may be promoted internally, making an entry-level position available.

In general, though, ads are not a good source for an entry-level position, except in areas where skilled professionals are scarce.

Ads in Industry Periodicals

Sadly, many graduates, even in specialized fields, are not familiar with the journals and periodicals of their chosen industry. Libraries have many of these, but the very best for their job-lead potential are likely to be those highly specialized insider publications (or Web sites) that only people in the industry subscribe to. These have the industry gossip: who's being bought, who's just gotten a big contract, who's partnering with whom on a new product or service, what trends the industry sees coming, all information pertinent to your job search.

Some have ads for job openings as well. Just be certain you have a recent version; check the date. If you do not know anyone who could give you one of these publications, you might check the library or pick up copies at trade shows.

Philip had an interview that was set up by his college placement office with a company in his field. The position was not his first choice, but he had agreed to go for the prac-

1. Why do you think Philip received the job offer?
2. What information besides job ads might Philip have found useful in the magazine?
3. Would ads for jobs be the only ads that might be helpful for generating leads?

tice. While he was waiting for his interview (he was put off for over an hour), he looked through the magazines on the table in front of him. None of the titles were familiar to him, but they seemed to be talking about products and issues in the industry. After reading for some minutes, he ran across an article on the company he was visiting. During the interview, he referred to information about the company that he had gathered while reading. When he left, he asked the receptionist if he could take an issue that was a few months old with him. Two days later, the company he interviewed with called him with a job offer. He turned it down because he was actively pursuing a company he had read about in an ad from the magazine for a job that was exactly what he was seeking.

Internet Postings

Certain Internet sites allow you to broadcast your resume in a *shotgun* fashion (no particular target, just thrown out onto a cyber bulletin board) with hopes that someone will be looking for just your qualifications. However, because of the availability of the Internet, the response rate is dropping on these types of sites. The best sources are those sites where you can apply directly to a company or link to a company's Web site and apply there.

Internet postings can be effective when you post on (or respond to ads on) sites dedicated to recent graduates or to entry-level applicants. You are assured in these cases that the company is looking for someone with your kind of potential and may be less concerned with a long track record. Many companies welcome fresh knowledge as well as the lower salaries they pay entry-level employees. It is not uncommon for a company that is doing lay-offs also to be hiring new people for both of these reasons.

If you have experience, there are specialized sites and hard-copy publications where you can place your resume or position-wanted ad. Some are very discreet and protect you if you are searching for a new position while still employed. Be certain to look for the site's statement regarding its privacy policy.

Career Counselors or Recruiters

These professionals make their living by receiving a percentage of the starting salary for the employees they locate and bring to a company. Sometimes, the seeking company pays the fee to gain the convenience of not having to screen hundreds of resumes to find a fit. Other times, the placement person receives a fee from you—either a percentage of salary or a flat fee. Some just do resume preparation; others do employment testing, while still others place you on their Web sites or in their national databases; much like the multiple-listing services realtors use.

Two cautions: First, these people do not necessarily welcome entry-level applicants, and if they agree to take you on, they may put your search on the back burner. Second, some require an up-front fee with no guarantee of a placement. Be wary of these two scenarios. Read thoroughly before you sign anything to make sure you understand the fees involved, what you are agreeing to, and if there is any refund if the job does not work out.

Prospecting

The term *prospecting* is used because you are looking for "gold" anywhere you think you can possibly find it. It includes everything from targeting companies whose products you like and calling them *cold* (making unsolicited contacts for potential job openings) to telling everyone you meet that you are looking and what you are looking for. Job leads are everywhere! You may meet someone on the commuter train who works in the building of a company that interests you or in a city to which you are trying to locate. Standing in line at the car tag office or waiting for an oil change, you could begin a conversation with someone and find out the name of a contact or a networking group. People you know are the easiest, but not always the best, for finding leads in your field.

TRANSITION TIP
Jasyn Banks, Inside Sales

You have to see everyone as a potential job lead. Go places where there are people who are doing what you want to be doing. Introduce yourself to as many people as you can. Whenever you attend a professional function or even a club meeting, see how much you can learn about the people in the room. If you're hungry enough for the job you want, you'll overcome the fear of meeting people. Oh, and my advice to anyone for networking or for opportunities to get around the right people—learn to play golf. Executives and decision makers play golf; to get access to these people, do what they do.

Networking groups are formed for the purpose of exchanging leads and help. They can be taxing because every time you go, you feel like you have an objective of securing someone's assistance. The difficulty is that others in the room are doing the same thing. Get the host or hostess of the particular gathering to introduce you to the people you should meet—that is much quicker than casting about all night by yourself and much less frustrating. Some networking groups are on the Internet now, and you do not even have to go to meetings except for on-line chats.

Another source of leads from prospecting is your own curiosity. If you like a particular product, go the company's Web site, learn more about the product and how it is made, who the company partners with, how big the company is, and where the branch offices are. Investor Relations is another good section of the company (or their Web site) from which to obtain information. A letter or phone call from a knowledgeable person inquiring about joining a company because of a specific interest is better received than the general, unsolicited mailing. If you are interested in a technical position, call or e-mail someone in the engineering or production departments and ask for information or maybe even help.

In some companies, a salesperson is a good way in because salespeople are generally extroverts and like to talk to people. Many people enjoy talking about their jobs too. Questions such as, "What attracted you to this company?" or "What do you like best about what you do?" will often elicit lengthy answers. Trade show booths, especially when things are slow, are great places to meet people on the "inside" of the companies you would like to pursue. It is worth the money to find a large trade show in your field and make arrangements to attend. Solid job leads (and maybe actual offers) could be the reward; at the least you will meet many people who do what you aspire to do for a living, an important part of a career plan.

Preparation

Two types of preparation will best place you where you want to be: general and job specific.

1. General preparation involves building several alternate resumes that can be adjusted for a specific focus as needed, researching the industry and companies that interest you, asking your references for permission to list them, selecting and purchasing an interview wardrobe (one conservative, suit-like; one carefully tailored, business casual), choosing and establishing your professional look, having copies made as needed, creating a digital version of your resume, finding a computer with Internet access (or access

to one for an e-mail address), and getting a dependable phone answering system (not friend or family members).

2. Specific preparation involves a customized resume for a particular job interview, a list of job requirements matched with your qualifications and talents, a wealth of information about the company and its products and competitors, two or three leading questions you can ask the interviewer about the company or about her own experience with the company, affirmations and positive phrases to say to yourself on the way to the interview or a motivational tape to play, and a visualization of a successful interview.

If you need to develop the skills for introductions, answering difficult questions, taking tests, or the appropriate behavior in business and social gatherings, additional instruction or practice may be required. You should have enough understanding of the jobs in your field and a clear picture of how you fit into the position (and company) you are pursuing that you naturally exude that quiet confidence that wins the vote of the interviewer. As you begin your preparation, take a quick look at what you have. The resume is probably the first exercise you should consider as you begin to take a serious step toward that career.

Building a Resume

One instrumental tool in getting the job that starts you on your desired career path is the well-crafted resume. In this chapter, you will find several suggested formats. Each has successfully gotten job seekers to the interview stage, but you will need some guidelines to help you select the format best suited for your situation. A resume is laid out in sections. These sections elicit different levels of attention from the reader and must be strategically placed to achieve the most impact. If your resume is the commercial for the product (you), then it must be constructed with the goal of getting your reader to tune into what you have to offer. Each section of the resume must hold the potential employer's interest and pull him into the next section.

At the most basic level, you should have an attractive visual effect. Cheap paper and a type font that looks like an old dot-matrix printer does not impress anyone. If you do not do word processing, you will have to pay or ask someone to dress up the appearance for you. So many people today have access to desktop publishing and other word processing systems that employers expect a classy look. Your resume will be passed over and not even read if it looks hastily done or poorly presented. There is no need to get too fancy unless you are applying for a job in art or advertising. Neat and well-organized resumes do have an advantage.

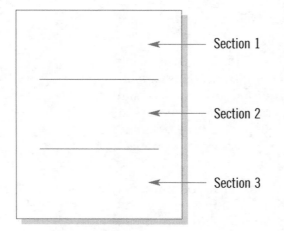

Section 1

Section 2

Section 3

The page itself should be well laid out, each section visually balanced; provide enough information to be meaningful, but do not overload the page with type. Also, as an employer scans the page, each section must hold her interest, both in relevant content and visual appeal. If you break the page down visually, into sections, each section should engage the reader.

Section 1

Section 1 contains **contact information** and your professional "introduction." Be certain that all contact information is current and correct. Also, be sure that whoever answers the phone you have listed or who records the phone message understands the need for appropriate conduct. A cutesy message may delight your friends, but an employer may not take you seriously.

Ann Allyson
406 Chadburn Ferry Road
Wierton, WV 57930
(406) 555-0095
annallyson@earthlink.net

If you provide an e-mail address in the heading be sure that it is professional sounding (no "surferguy@yahoo.com). Consider establishing an address to use just for your job search.

If the decision maker is over 40, he or she may require glasses to read small print. The resume in 12-point type that is easier to read without glasses could very well be picked up, with others skipped over. Of course, 14-point type would be overdone. Your contact information, especially, should be easy to read at a glance.

Also in Section 1 is the **professional capabilities** statement—what is great about you in 30 words or less. This is where you match who and what you are professionally with the specific job needs of a prospective employer. At one time, job seekers would include a "Job Objective" section. But job objectives often are too general to be helpful to a potential employer or too specific to keep doors open for the job seeker. You should know enough about the needs of a prospective job—at least about the job category—to be able to list your strengths that would qualify you for the job. These could be customized for various positions, thanks to the convenience of word processing.

Professional Capabilities: Problem solving and strong communication skills, including presentations, demonstrated in a customer-oriented environment. Familiar with database management software and fluent in Internet research.

This example might be a good statement of qualifications for a sales position. For a more technical position, a help desk, for example, you might arrange the information differently. Remember, in this section you should represent yourself as you want the employer in your chosen area to view you. If you have a unique or specialized skill or experience, or even professional certifications, placing relevant ones here would be helpful.

Professional Capabilities: Registered nurse with internship in critical care and four years' experience with a hospice organization. Can work independently in hospital or clinic setting. Familiar with computerized patient record management systems.

Section 2

By this point, the reader probably has some interest if the position needs fit and will read further for more detail. If there is no fit, then she is not likely to search your resume for something of value. She may retain or pass on your resume if she is familiar with other job needs of the company. Rarely does a reader look at a very general professional capabilities section and try to think of a place to use your skills. You must word that section to fit jobs you think are available. The same is true in the middle section of your resume, where you list all of the things you have done or know how to do.

For older, more experienced job seekers, a functional approach, describing what you have accomplished and how long you have been gaining skill in a particular line of work, might be best. List your accomplishments as line items.

Format A

Employment Highlights *[Some name this section "Employment Profile"]*

- Implemented client-server software system for 12-station local area network.

- Supported software programs as technical service representative for national accounts for major accounting software company.

- Demonstrated and conducted training on Excel in customer settings.

For less experienced people, or those embarking on a new career with mostly education to recommend them, a *managed page* approach is best. When people scan a resume, they generally lose concentration about two-thirds of the way down the page and are thinking about turning the page instead of focusing on what they are reading. In addition, those with little work history related to the job they are seeking seldom can impress a potential employer with their wealth of experience. So, the strategy is to direct the eye of the reader to those elements of your qualifications that fit the sought-after job.

This strategy includes putting achievements in school (recent achievements, not years before), honors in the military or civic and professional organizations, and course work during college, or grade point average high on the page. In addition, this strategy uses a "skills section" that shows all of the many talents and skills you have in a way that will impress the reader. Be certain not to overlook skills of a professional nature, though not necessarily in the specific field. For example, illustrating programs for the local theater group is graphics experience; it does not matter whether you were paid. Internships can also offer field-related skills, including projects completed in teams, and should be listed.

Format B

Education: Associate of Applied Science Degree

Graduation: June 2002 Major: Health Administration

Groves Community College

GPA: 3.8 out of 4.0

Accomplishments: Supported self 100 percent through school, member of National Honor Fraternity, Vice President of Toastmasters

Skills:

SOFTWARE	HARDWARE	PROFESSIONAL
Excel	Pentium III	Customer Service
MS Word	LCD (for presentations)	Speaking/Presentations
PowerPoint	Some MacIntosh	Technical writing (documentation)

A business-oriented resume plays up the managerial potential of certain skills or experience you may have. In this one, you give the skill, then where you acquired it.

Skills:

Project Management—managed relocation of telecommunication system to new facility.

Customer Support—maintained customer records and performed trouble call follow-ups in multimillion dollar business.

Budgeting—directed resources secured by fund-raising to programs in nonprofit organization.

Personnel—performed needs assessment, made recommendations, and secured services for training program in 100-employee company.

Technical—adept at business and market research on the Internet, Excel, MS Word, Adobe Acrobat; working knowledge of Visual Basic and client management system.

By this point, the reader is beginning to pay less attention to a line by line scrutiny of your resume. But, if he has seen something desirable, then there will be motivation to continue through your work history. Remember, this format is used when you have little or no actual work experience in the field for which you are applying. You are pulling desirable and employable features about yourself from other jobs, a prior career, or internships into the most visible portions of the resume, "putting your best foot forward" so to speak. Major school or volunteer projects can give you valuable skills and experience. Some companies are even beginning to look for community service experience in the well-rounded candidate.

Look at the following example and note the technical and nontechnical expertise required.

Rayana had just graduated from an associate's degree program in accounting from a community college. Her friend suggested she apply for a temporary job with the Internal Revenue Service for experience. She had never had a job in accounting, only her classes and labs. Just to quiet her friend, she read the description of the position.

Customer service representative—Internal Revenue Service

Expertise required: accounting, superior interpersonal and communication skills, problem solving in complex customer situations, ability to multitask, organization.

Because she had worked in customer returns at Sears since high school and had been given service awards twice, she realized that what was required for the IRS job was similar to her experience. Rayana put in her application, was called in for an interview, and was hired within two weeks.

Another format for this section of the resume is the classic "Work History" section. In this, you list your past jobs chronologically—from most recent to most distant. If you have worked only a few years, you might do well to use the preceding format and add a work history section afterward. You might have had a series of part-time jobs while in school, so your history might look erratic or undefined. If this is the case, you might want to sum up this time by saying, "Part-time jobs while supporting self through college included: fast food, teaching assistant, and retail clerk." Just as you try to put the strongest selling points highest on the page, try to put the least important information (such as dates of employment) on the right hand side of the page. This de-emphasizes them. (We read top to bottom and left to right.)

If you have gaps in your work history from layoffs, illness, or other reasons, the functional resume, Format A, is the best to sell your strengths before you have to explain why you were not employed for intervals of time. A general-format chronological work history follows:

Format C

Employment History:

April 2000–Present: Part-time jobs during college including Web page maintenance and database management.

March 1997–2000: Project Supervisor, Pacific Bell, Sacramento, California.

Directed installation of fiber-optic cable in two-county area. Brought two crews to deadline within budget.

June 1996–1997: Fiber-optic Cable Installer, Pacific Bell, Sacramento, California.

Worked up to crew chief in the first six months on job.

Prior to June 1996: Worked weekends and summers at sports park.

Section 3

This section can include whatever you deem desirable, whether it is professional organizations or achievements, awards, civic clubs, hobbies, or a willingness to travel or relocate. Every resume should have a "References" section, it seems, but most sources recommend that you simply say "References available upon request." Of course, you will have people in mind who have already agreed to say positive things about you. It is important to get the permission of those you submit as references. Do not press people into agreeing. If they turn you down, it is probably because they do not feel they know you well enough to answer questions from a potential employer.

This is by no means a definitive discussion of how to produce a winning resume. There are books and whole classes on the topic, but this discussion will get you started. (Note: www.myjobsearch.com and www.careerperfect.com have sample resumes for your reference.)

Remember that a resume is an ad for you as a product. You receive about 60 seconds of your potential customer's attention in the reading of your resume. Use strategy to put the good information about you in the most noticeable place. Allow each section to appear uncrowded and it will draw the eye of the reader.

You should show your resume to many people and get input. However, the resume has to sell *you*, so you have to decide what goes on there in the end. If the resume is "professionally" done (by a resume service), it is your responsibility to make sure it honestly represents you. And you should always proofread, even if a service has prepared it for you.

Keep in mind also what you have learned in this book. A resume is built to help you eventually command the job that will bring you joy. It is a document of the choices you have made on your career path and an introduction to the professional you wish to be.

A prospective employer generally scrutinizes a resume on four levels:

- *Level 1: Physical appearance*—notes at a glance type of paper, page layout, type fonts, clarity.
- *Level 2: Specifics scan*—looks for buzzwords, education cutoffs, and particular technical or customer skills.

(*Note:* These first two levels of scrutiny are generally completed in less than 30 seconds.)

- *Level 3: Initial approval*—likes qualifications and skills and may turn to second page or read work history or accomplishments area more closely.
- *Level 4: Final approval*—calls you in for an interview.

Interviewing

Many sources offer many approaches to succeeding in an interview: analysis of personality types, scrutiny of interviewer's clothes, practice with smooth answers to expected interview questions, and on and on. You are encouraged to check out the many Internet sources that offer hints on interviewing. (One definitive site is ww1.joboptions.com/careertools. This site even offers private question and answer sessions.) Also, talk to people who have recently interviewed successfully and secured a new job. Here, we will offer a few "nuts and bolts" to interviewing, along with some tricks.

Guideline 1

The person who interviews you may or may not be a professional interviewer.

The professional. This person understands the behavioral, legal, and financial implications of interviewing. She will not likely ask you any illegal questions, such as how old you are, if you are married, or whether you have disabilities. The professional interviewer will probably look at a variety of your qualifications including your personality type, your manner—how you conduct yourself—your overall approach to work, and your ability to work under pressure, in addition to the "technical" skills you have.

If a professional interviewer "likes" you because of an impression or "gut feel," it is likely because of his experience in the task of hiring. Many successful hires lead an interviewer to be able to recognize pretty quickly what a desirable candidate for his client or company is like. This person is less likely to have a personal reaction to you than a less experienced interviewer might; you may not even be able to tell if you have made a good impression due to his practiced reserve. Professionals (especially contract recruiters) know that their livelihood depends on successfully matching employees with companies. Mistakes of match or fit are costly to everyone involved and they know this.

The nonprofessional.   This might be a person who desperately needs someone to fill a painful gap in skill, knowledge, or experience, but may see the interview process as time consuming and potentially frustrating. Because of these conditions, she may make a quicker judgment of you based on fewer considerations. After a long resume-screening process, an interviewer may feel that all candidates called in are equally qualified—she is just looking for someone who fits in with the work group or someone she likes and feels comfortable with. The questions asked may seem random and undirected or sound like they came out of the same books you studied to prepare. When the exhausted interviewer (who may be uncomfortable meeting a lot of new people) finds one she likes, then in her mind the search may be over, regardless of who follows in the appointment schedule.

Guideline 2

Interview decisions are often made in the first minute of the interview (some sources say as little as 20 seconds). In education, this phenomenon is called the *halo effect:* a good initial impression will carry you through several possible mistakes. Conversely, though, this halo effect can tarnish the interview after a bad first impression. Even if your skills and qualifications are a good fit, you may not receive a job offer. This is why grooming, carriage, manner, and introduction are so critical.

Guideline 3

The classic interview "uniform," the dark suit, may or may not be the most appropriate. Many companies are using a "business casual" dress code. You should try to find out what clothing is expected because part of making a positive first impression is to look as much as possible like the people who already work there. If you are working with a recruiter or career counselor, follow that person's guidance. If not, try calling someone in the office of the company you are pursuing and ask politely what the expected dress for an interview might be.

"I have an interview there tomorrow, and I know companies have different dress codes. Can you tell me what might be the most appropriate to wear? I would really like to work there and want to make the best impression I can."

Another way to handle this is to visit the company (always a good idea so you can be sure you know how to get there) and ask if you can go to the breakroom for a snack or soft drink. On the way there, observe the employees to see how they dress and wear their hair. Though you will probably be expected to appear more conservative than some you might see, you will at least have some idea of the general style.

Says one placement professional, however, "I believe that most employers still say that interviewing is a game of sorts and the applicant needs to play by the rules. I also think that it depends on the position being interviewed for— if the position is a professional one (requiring a degree for example), then a suit is the best choice. This is versus a warehouse loading position where business casual in the interview is okay. Also note that how you dress for the interview does not necessarily correlate to how you dress on the job or how the interviewer is dressed. (Goes back to the game . . . you are expected to put your best foot forward)" (Boyer, 2001).

Women candidates might want to go to the suit department of a department store or specialty store and get advice.

Guideline 4

Your interview may not be in person. The phone interview is becoming more and more common as the logistics of interviewing candidates all over the country become more difficult. Phone interviews are particularly difficult for those who are used to making a good impression by watching the reaction of the other person throughout the conversation. Not being able to see the reaction of the person conducting the interview can leave you feeling anxious and tentative. Some larger companies have video-conferencing facilities, but that experience is not always a great deal better, due to the slight delay in the transmission.

Do as much as you can to encourage an in-person interview, even offering to meet someone at the airport on a layover. However, some people just do not want to take time for every candidate and might interview you from the car or airplane. Looking on the positive side, the phone does offer an exchange where you can ask questions and clarify points. Also, you can glean some reactions from the voice. Thankfully, sometimes a phone interview is only a *rubber stamp*, where the manager just wants to chat with the person his staff has already chosen. Either way, a relaxed, confident, and even manner is at least as important as the words you offer.

Look in a mirror while you talk and make sure you smile. A smiling person sounds different on the phone. Although you have the option of dressing casually because you are on the phone, if you dress as if you were going to the interview, it can help to put you in that frame of mind. It is very easy to get too comfortable on a phone. Also, you may want to stand up—it helps to project your voice. Do not eat, drink, or smoke while on a phone interview. Avoid the sounds of TV, radio, or kids in the background.

To stay focused have a notepad by the phone to write down notes. These should include:

- the main idea of the question just asked (keeps you from straying off the point)
- notes on the company or position (details you can review after the call)
- any names mentioned
- questions about the company
- the procedure for the next level of decision

Guideline 5

The interview may or may not be for a real position. Sometimes, companies talk to potential candidates to see what is "out there" in the way of skills or availability. This happens rarely to the entry-level person, but if it does, it is an opportunity to establish your value, to make the company understand that you are an asset that someone should find a place for. This kind of interview also may occur when a contact has gotten you in to a company to see someone who can make hiring decisions (or at least recommendations), commonly called the "foot in the door."

For this type of interview, do a great deal of preparation on the company and its products, directions, and values (often available in the financial statement or on the Internet)—this will make you appear to be keenly interested in the company's welfare. Additionally, if you can show what a match you are for the company, then the lack of a clearly defined position may not be such a hindrance to your aspiration.

Additional Guidelines

1. Manner. Your professionalism, reliability, poise, and intelligence may be gleaned from your manner and may be a large part of your evaluation. The elements that go into manner include: punctuality, tone of voice, diction, grammar, discretion and judgment (knowing what not to talk about), walk, handshake, facial expression, and social graces.

2. Punctuality. Always arrive early enough to locate a parking space and the office; do not check in with the receptionist until a few minutes before your appointment time.

3. Tone of voice. Nervous people speak in strained and flat tones. Relaxation of the throat muscles through yawns or voice warm-ups can help. Singing on the way to the interview (in the car, not in the building) is an excellent voice relaxer. Volume should be conversational, but watch for signs of the interviewer being overwhelmed or having difficulty understanding.

4. Diction and grammar. No one expects perfection in this area, but the ability to speak clearly, so that people from all parts of the country can understand you, is an important part of your qualifications. Poor grammar is often taken as a sign of a weak education or a lack of attention to polishing your manner. Strong regional accents and the incorrect use of verb forms are the most notable of these considerations. Adolescent phrases, such as "like" and "awesome," may make the interviewer see you as immature.

5. Discretion and judgment. Being too personal or discussing tasteless subjects can make a terrible impression, even when the conversation has turned casual and may even be taking place in a bar. Talking negatively about past jobs or other interviews is also considered inappropriate. If you have any doubt as to the suitability of any topic, stay away from it. You are being interviewed for a job, no matter how relaxed the situation is, and are expected to speak with integrity and candor. Lying and faking knowledge also fall in the category of things to avoid. Finally, if alcohol is offered over an interview lunch or dinner, just say no. You cannot afford to be impaired, even a little.

6. Walk. Striding forward confidently, especially when the interviewer is holding open a door or walking with you around the building, denotes assuredness with your ability to do the job. The interviewer should not have to wait for you to gather up things in order to walk in—be ready. It is possible to walk confidently, even when you do not feel that way; pick up your speed a little and you will move better.

7. Handshake. Practice, practice, practice. In Western culture, we often size up a person by the handshake. If you are from a culture that avoids this kind of contact or that believes a softer handshake is a sign of respect, remember that the expectation is a firm grasp of the whole hand. Eye contact is expected with the handshake as well. This is the moment you connect with the interviewer, if only for a second. An excellent rapport may grow out of a good handshake. Damp hands from nervousness may be tolerated in someone young or inexperienced, but try to dry your hands just prior to the greeting.

8. Facial expression.   Relaxed muscles around the eyes and cheeks suggest a calm demeanor and a genuine interest. Note how your face feels when a song that evokes a pleasant memory comes on the radio; that is a good approximation.

9. Dress.   If you do wear a suit, and you are a man, have the shirt starched and use a silk tie (synthetics do not tie as well). Though the classic charcoal or navy works in many cases, try to use a variation that works well for you. Image consultants can tell you the colors that best compliment you to give you that very "together" look. Also, make-up counters at many department stores will do a color consultation for free. When you wear colors that are right for you, you are more likely to elicit a positive response to your appearance; if you do not coordinate colors and shades, the interviewer may notice the clothes, but not remember you as "looking good."

Be certain that what you wear fits. Something too tight or obviously too large makes you look like you have bad judgment not only about your appearance, but also about how to behave appropriately in business situations. If your budget is tight, remember to check out consignment shops. The more upscale ones may have clothing that is still very much up to date and in good condition.

For both genders, minimal jewelry and cologne would be the guideline, and do not forget neatly trimmed fingernails. Women, keep earrings to quarter size or smaller; men, an earring is still considered somewhat unprofessional, at least for the interview.

10. Questions.   Lists of sample interview questions are available many places for you to look over to prepare. Obviously coached and memorized answers will not make a good impression; however, you should certainly have already thought out some reasonable responses to standard questions, such as "Tell me about yourself" and "Why are you interested in a job with our company?" Amazingly, some candidates cannot adequately verbalize an answer to "How did you choose your particular field?" Trying to bluff your way through questions you do not know the answers to only makes you look more foolish than not knowing the answer and admitting it.

TRANSITION TIP   *B.D., Special Projects Supervisor*

Don't be afraid if you are a "tough case." I was older than most of the candidates as well as having a history of a felony conviction and alcoholism in earlier years. My prior employment background was in the arts, and I was applying for jobs in my new degree area, engineering. I also had been told that I had the kind of personality that just naturally rubbed some people the wrong way. But a professor agreed to coach me on the interpersonal stuff, and another of my profs called someone he knew at a large company that had hired many graduates of my college over the years with very good results. What really helped, though, was understanding very clearly what I had to offer—what skills and talent transferred from my prior arts career experience, and what my personality type was particularly suited for. I've found my niche here in a very short time and am doing well, with a couple of promotions already. My advice? Know what you bring to the job, get cool with who you are, and be able to explain what is really good about you. Finally, realize that a lot of people out there can, and are willing to, help you.

11. Social graces. This area is often overlooked by candidates preparing for an interview. Some companies may hold a reception for applicants to meet employees or may take an applicant out to dinner. This time is very much part of the interview because the hiring company wants to be sure an employee knows how to behave in polite company, especially in the company of a customer. If the interview moves to food, be sure you demonstrate table manners that reflect professional courtesy.

There is no specific do or don't regarding what to eat, but if you have the freedom to order, get something fairly small (so you don't have to spend all your time eating to get through the amount of food) and not too messy; you are there to talk. Bowtie pasta, for example, is easier to eat gracefully than linguini. If the company is large, there is a possibility that you might be taken to a really nice restaurant. A little research on foods and wines as part of your general interview preparation is not a bad idea. You really ought to know what calamari is before someone orders it for you. (Grocery stores are excellent for learning the names of things, as are cookbooks.)

What to say and what not to say at a business social gathering are important also. Never speak disrespectfully of anyone, even political figures. Remain positive in all that you say, and if you are in a group, monitor the volume of your voice. When you are nervous, you may tend to talk more loudly or more softly than usual. Avoid personal topics, like health and appearance, and if someone takes issue with a point you make, concede: "You have a point there. I'll have to think about that." Make sure you find out who the important people are in the room and introduce yourself.

Salary Expectations

One common complaint from employers is that candidates have unrealistic expectations about salary: they either have no idea about the "going rate" for their own industry or they have an inflated (and unsubstantiated) view of their own worth. A candidate who has done too little homework about the industry or about the type of position shows a distinct lack of initiative and seriousness about the process. An excellent source of salary expectations and hiring and salary trends is the National Association of Colleges and Employers (NACE) Web site, www.naceweb.org. Some highlights are included in Table 20.1.

Data for liberal arts and social sciences were not listed in this particular report (NACE, February 6, 2001). The site noted an increase in sales positions over information technology positions for the first time in several years.

| TABLE 20.1 | Average starting salaries for some professional positions. |

	AVERAGE STARTING SALARY	PERCENT + OR −
Accounting	$38,739	3.8%+
Business Administration	$36,314	1.3%+
Economics/Finance	$40,297	5.7%+
MIS	$44,879	4.7%+
Computer Engineering (includes both software and hardware)	$53,443	14.3%+
Civil Engineering	$39,852	9.2%+
Electrical Engineering	$50,850	6.6%+
Mechanical Engineering	$48,340	5.8%+
Computer Science	$51,581	5.9%+
Information Science	$44,251	1 %−

(Note: Communications companies hires received $47,583, which is 10.8% higher than last year.)

Data may be difficult to find for your particular field, but publications for industry or professional organizations will include some general figures, though you may find a great deal of discrepancy in the highest and lowest starting offers. Remember, averages are just that, averages; they take in the top and the bottom and include the prestigious schools as well as the small state colleges. Salary offers vary by region, size of company, capital constraints, and policy, and many other factors. Exceptions are found on both the high and low end. Just like a car, you are worth what someone is willing to pay to bring you on—no more, no less.

Occasionally, an employer will make a "lowball" offer (an offer lower than you would expect to receive). This could be for any of several reasons:

- strong feelings about probationary conservatism—to keep the risk low until your suitability is proven
- the company might want to see if you are willing to sacrifice and "invest" yourself in the company
- maybe you do not have exactly the skills they want, but they would like to bring you on with hopes that you will increase your value on your own initiative

Whether the reason is a budget crunch or simply seeing just how cheaply they can get their needs filled, you will have to make the decision whether the offer is good for you. Some considerations along this line include:

- future potential—for example, growth in a large company or significant additions to resume
- culture and conditions—the particular ambiance of the workplace or geographic location
- role in goal support—the degree to which the credentials gained from the duties or by association with a "name" company will contribute to your goal activity
- benefits trade-off—educational reimbursement, health plan, flexible hours, professional freedom, bonus potential, or company stock
- risk—the company is a startup in new technology that could flourish or flounder, company rumored to be up for sale or going public, highly competitive and volatile market, history of high turnover rate, or potential for family disruption due to transfer

Many of the considerations you have about your career in general will enter into the decisions you make about the right match between you and a particular job—money is just one consideration. If you are just coming out of college with student loans or if you are recovering from consumer debt or a job termination, you may not currently have the luxury of taking on an exciting, but perhaps risky, job. Relax. You will likely work for a minimum of 40 years. This gives you plenty of time to explore several job options.

TRANSITION SKILLS SUMMARY

Determine the job fit

Search all sources

Build a resume

Use interviewing skills

Understand salary expectations

GOAL SETTING

My self-nurturing goals to preserve my personal and relational health during a job search are:

_____

_____

_____

My self-advocacy goals to contribute to my career management in my job search efforts are:

_____

_____

_____

COACH'S CORNER

"Reading" an interviewer helps you determine your strategy during the interview. A lot of what the interviewer communicates may not be words. Preparation is essential, but eventually, it is just you and the interviewer. There are some ways to assess what is going on to determine how you are doing.

1. Determine the mission of the interviewer. If it is to screen 50 applicants, then the purpose is to get rid of the obviously unsuitable as quickly as possible for the next "real" round of selection. If you can find out in advance what the situation is, all the better, but if not, here are some signs that there is not much interest:

    a. When the interviewer sits down, he immediately (or almost immediately) looks down and writes or reads notes or questions. This could mean that the interviewer is inexperienced and needs the prompts on the paper for a guide, but it may suggest disinterest as well. A flat or monotone voice will signal lack of interest as will the interviewer's not making any attempt to show enthusiasm or to make you feel welcome.

    b. If the interviewer seems to try to "sell" the company and position to you, it may mean that you have made a good impression and would seem to be a good fit. It may also mean, however, that due to some element of the job (possibly undesirable location, travel, or salary), the interviewer knows it may be difficult to secure commitments from strong candidates who have many choices.

    c. An interested interviewer will lean slightly forward and may make eye contact intently, appearing to scrutinize you more closely. However, hands or feet fidgeting may show boredom or impatience.

2. If you establish rapport, the questions will seem more natural and relaxed. Be careful, however: that tone may be merely to see if you will let your guard down and say something inappropriate. The same applies if they leave the room. The interviewer may watch you from outside the room or have the receptionist look to see what you do during the time you are alone. You should pick up or take out company literature and have a question formulated for the interviewer about it when he returns.

(continued)

a. Some hints for establishing rapport: "I know that you have constraints on your time today, but I believe I have more than just a resume to offer. I am teachable and believe my background is just a launch point. I really look forward to expanding into being an asset to the company."

b. Note the room in which you are interviewing. Is it the person's office? If so, what is around? A family picture on the wall or desk might suggest a family orientation. Awards or artifacts can be conversation pieces. The more quickly you can move the conversation to the interviewer and his experience with the company, the more quickly you will have a "real" interview instead of a canned one.

3. If you sense that you have been dismissed in the interviewer's mind, you have a chance to "punt" anyway. You can stop the interview and say, "Look, I'm very new at this interviewing thing, but I have researched this company and its products and would really like to work here. What information can I give you that would show you what a good fit I would be?" It's a long shot, but sometimes that is just the thing to jog the interviewer out of a general boredom with so many candidates. Energy and interest are two very appealing qualities, and few interviewers would overlook either.

GENE MINOR, Interpersonal Communication Specialist and Executive Development Coach; e-mail: lgminor@mindspring.com.

CHAPTER 21

Lifelong Career Management

T he following quotes reflect the experiences of a number of people who made significant changes in career direction after they had worked a year or so. In each case, they were hired for an entry-level position that their skill or knowledge qualified them for, and they used that position as a stepping-off point to explore other task areas and to develop new skills and experience. Experience is a great leveler: the clever and capable people bubble to the top fairly quickly, and the less capable eventually settle into their places as well. People who start out in the workforce with MBAs or engineering degrees may enter with a higher starting salary than someone with a bachelor's degree in business or technology, but the earning potential often evens out fairly soon, based on the talent and career management skill of the individual.

"I didn't know what I wanted to do for the long term, just that I needed to build as much on my resume as I could as quickly as I could—computer skills, productivity records, etc. My first job was long and hard hours, and I didn't like it very much, but the experience looked great on paper when I was ready to change."

"My first job was in a movie rental store. Imagine, me right out of college, a hot-shot with a finance degree working in a video store. But I turned around three of the locations and made them profitable. With that record, I moved into a position

Taken from: *Transition Management: A Practical Approach to Personal and Professional Development*, Fourth edition by Sandra L. McKee and Brenda L. Walters

at a bank in the loan department. That experience introduced me to a client who was CEO of a high-tech startup, and she invited me to work there—no job description really, just carved out my own place. Now I'm doing business development and handling purchases and mergers—at 30."

"I got out of school and immediately went international. No husband, no geographic ties, and the excitement and money were all in the international arena. My systems degree opened the door, and now I direct overseas purchasing."

"Though my degree was in accounting, I worked an internship in a small company that let me try different things out. My interest grew in the area of marketing, and I focused my skill building there. I had a great mentor, so I really picked up the job quickly. That experience landed me in a major market research firm by my second year out of school—and last year I bought a house."

"My original focus was design. When I graduated, though, I was more interested in the business end and sought out a company that sold their designs through their own exclusive outlet stores. I was able to use my art background to get in, but I've since eased myself more into the marketing and strategic end of the business."

One interesting career management story is Michael's. He performed on Broadway for many years, got a degree from Harvard University, then decided he needed more "marketable" skills and sought a bachelor's degree in information systems from a technical institute. He is now the Chief Information Officer at the company where he works. Some people do a stint in the military for a career starter; some have a family first, then move into education and a profession later. For some, graduate school becomes a means to an end; for others, a sales position with a company or in a field that they want presents a threshold through which to pass into upper management.

Career Success

Arby's restaurants, in a survey of customers, reports that most people had their first real feeling of adulthood when they got their first full-time job. Perhaps, but *career success ultimately comes when you are being paid to do things you like and are good at, and when you are paid a wage that allows you to meet your needs.*

These statements are obviously subjective, contingent on a lot of individually defined words: "things you like and are good at," a "wage that meets your needs." How you define each of these concepts is truly an individual response. This chapter's objective is to explain how to reach that point, and perhaps more importantly for someone starting out, how you decide what that point is. As one career explorer phrased the idea, "I want to be able to work where I want, not just where they'll let me."

Understanding the keys to career management will give you:

- professional freedom
- autonomy with regard to your career future
- opportunities to contribute to the community
- time to involve yourself in meaningful relationships

In this book, you have up until now looked at how to make changes, how to solve problems, and how to maintain and enhance relationships. In the area of your career, the principles are the same, even though they may be applied somewhat differently. Whether you feel like you simply have not found the right place career-wise or are just looking at the beginning of your job path, the plain truth is: *You spend most of your waking hours pursuing work. If your job does not contribute to your life in a meaningful way, then you are missing a great source of personal fulfillment.* The following examples illustrate the point.

Jemal makes $26 per hour at the car manufacturing plant. He has been bored with the job for some time, but because he earns a reasonable wage and has great benefits, he feels he would be foolish to leave. Melaney is an insurance claims representative. Her job is to process client claim forms. Though she feels that she is paid well and is liked by the people she works with, she is not using her accounting degree and her job has no real value to her.

Both of these people are unhappy with their current career paths. Neither seems to know what to do about this struggle. Being unhappy, or maybe even just not being terribly fulfilled, often fails to motivate someone to make changes. Occasionally, it takes being laid off or fired to cause a close examination of the reason for a successful career choice.

Is the Job Fulfilling?

A lack of fulfillment or a failure in the form of the loss of a job are only two of the work or career problems you may face. Stress and a sense of struggle, of just not being in the right place, all of these are symptoms of a poor job and employee match. Work-related stresses invariably spill over into your personal life and can affect families and even harm personal health. So, problems with work life do not just stay at work.

Where are you now? As you have seen in prior chapters, *understanding your current situation is the beginning of a new direction.* Perhaps you have just decided to move to a new job, to a college education, to a different and more lucrative or satisfying career path. Wherever you are at this moment, you can use career management to guide you toward the most reward in your work. *Career management is a careful process of discovery and design—discovery of what you really want in a career, and design of the job that will bring you the most satisfaction.* The beginning point for designing a meaningful career path is to explore the attitudes you have developed over time about working. In Activity 21.1, you will be asked to begin a careful examination of what work and a career mean to you.

21.1 ACTIVITY

Answer the questions about your attitudes toward work. Where possible, give an example to explain your answer.

1. What impression do you have of your parents' work? Do they enjoy it? Do they think it is important? Is it just a way to earn money?

_____

_____

_____

2. What experiences have you had with work? Do you work now? Have you worked in the past? Was it a positive experience? What is your strongest impression about it overall?

_____

_____

_____

In a career, we often find the same cause-and-effect connections that we do in our personal relationships. For the most part, we receive what we expect. If we expect work to be a meaningful contribution to an overall satisfying life, then we make choices and direct our effort to that end. If our view of work is that it is a drudgery that has as its sole purpose to provide income and no more, then that is likely what we will settle for. The really seductive situation, though, is the one where we either expect or are receiving a substantial income, though we might not find the working conditions or job tasks ideal. Maybe the work is great, but the location requires a long commute or places you in a town or part of the country you do not care for.

Dwayne was experiencing stress at work. He was absent more than other workers, and he seemed to have a lot of conflict with his coworkers as well as his boss. As a medical technician, he did testing and analysis tasks in a lab. Though competent at what he did, he showed no enthusiasm for his duties, and his behavior with friends and family was becoming more and more negative. One night he confessed to a coworker, "I want to work with patients more and be treated like a real professional." Eventually, it came out that Dwayne wanted to be a nurse, but with a disabled father to support, he didn't feel he could stop earning an income long enough to complete a nursing program.

Feeling trapped, Dwayne had become more and more frustrated with his job. He had become convinced that he had no choices about his current situation.

What about you? Maybe you have chosen a direction in your professional life and are now gathering credentials or skills that will prepare you to pursue that direction. Maybe, instead, you are embarking on a career with no clear direction as yet or understanding of what a satisfying career might be. Viewing your work as a set of choices that will lead you closer to happiness can give you a sense of freedom and joy.

1. What is Dwayne missing in his work every day?

2. Is his situation likely to get any better without some specific action on Dwayne's part?

3. How might his life be different if he were to redirect his career?

Does the Ideal Job Exist?

There may be a work area that will suit you but doesn't even exist yet. The world of work is changing all the time, so try to keep your thoughts open as you begin to choose your career path. Instead of a job name you think you should pursue, you might try to define a set of conditions you would ideally work within. Here is an example.

Not "I would like to be a lawyer"—instead, "I would like a job where I get to analyze problems and research the answers to those problems. I would also like to be respected for my ability to do my job well. I would like to be able to work with people (or alone). I would like to share ideas with other people in the same type of work."

This description could apply to many jobs in many different industries: real estate title searches, research assistant, marketing analyst, or troubleshooter. Because many of us do not know the names of jobs that we might enjoy, a great deal of self-assessment will help. (See the appendix for a list of self-assessment tools.) An ideal job for one person could be most unpleasant or stressful for another. The key is understanding enough about yourself and your professional needs to seek positions that allow you to capitalize on your strengths and preferences.

Chou went to college because his parents said he should and because he did not really have anything better planned. But as graduation neared, he still had no career direction. He was receiving a degree in business, but preferred to spend most of his time on his skateboard. When his parents expressed concern about this, he answered, "But Tony Hawk makes his living on a board and he's an old guy." Chou knew that only a few boarders are good enough to make a living at that sport, and he had never even entered a competition. Thus, his chances were pretty slim. He could not see himself in front of a computer all day or working construction full-time as he had one summer, yet he knew he had to move on to some type of job.

Lucy was a 15-year sales veteran with a major telecommunication company. She consistently got good bonuses for her sales and was highly respected at all levels in her company. The company downsized and began offering early retirement buyouts for people who wanted to leave the company voluntarily. Presented with the option of doing something different with her life at the company's expense, she took the opportunity to examine what she really wanted. Lucy is now nearing graduation as a physical therapist. She already knows, however, there are no openings at the hospital in her small town.

Both of these people have to do some serious self-assessment as well as career research—not just job research because that may become limited to just a survey of job titles and duties. Career research requires an investigation into what people actually do all day to carry out their jobs in different career areas. For example, a customer service person generally comes to the job enjoying contact with people, having good communication skills, and possessing the ability to learn about a company's products and procedures. Customer service representatives can be anything from retail clerks to software troubleshooters or client liaisons in many different and diverse fields. Both Chou and Lucy need to discover a career design framework to chart their career destination.

A Career Design Framework

Having a place to go for eight hours (or more) a day where you do things that make you feel valued is truly satisfying. *Meaningful work makes individuals feel motivated and enthusiastic every day.* Sometimes it takes a while to arrive at your career direction. After you figure out where you are going, though, the steps to get there are easier to discern.

A U.S. soldier was stationed overseas in a country that had quite a few American cars among its imports. One of the area residents had purchased an American-made van and sought out the serviceman for advice on operating it. Among other devices, buttons, and levers, the serviceman pointed out the cruise control, saying, "This manages the speed of the car and lets you relax while you drive." The resident thanked the serviceman and drove happily away. An hour later, heading down a long stretch of road, the driver set the cruise control and climbed into the back seat to have tea. He was discovered late that day with his vehicle spun out in the middle of a sandy plain. He was unhurt but covered with tea.

Stepping into the back seat while you put your professional life on cruise control is liable to cause more problems than just spilled tea. Applying a framework to your career design process will help you focus your efforts. To remember the steps in the process of developing your career plan, remember the word "ARRIVE."

- **A**ssess your skills, talents, traits, and interests
- **R**evive your curiosity
- **R**each for a goal
- **I**nvest in your journey
- **V**erify along the way
- **E**njoy your success

When you open up your thinking, you dramatically improve your potential for arriving at a satisfying career future. Just by expecting satisfaction from your career path, you are increasing your chances for achieving that satisfaction.

The first consideration in pursuing a career that will bring you fulfillment is to determine what work activities you like. Dr. Fred Ott of Georgia State University describes the process this way: Your primary goal in considering a career direction is joy. This idea, interestingly enough, is fairly new to our culture. For generations we have been told, "Get a good, steady job and stick with it until retirement." Nothing was ever said about enjoying that job.

Today, however, we are seeing so much stress-related illness that we are beginning to look to the workplace as a likely contributor. When your health is affected by emotional factors, then negative work environments can be a very real threat. Because you have begun the process of looking at your career path in terms of your own satisfaction, you will likely find problems that you have to deal with. Many of you may have already started this and are now in a new job, or in a college or a training program to make changes.

Assess Skills, Talents, Traits, and Interests

Throughout this book so far, you have been examining the elements that make up the package that is you. In addition to this examination process, you have been adding life-management skills. During your educational process and in the jobs you have had up to now, you also have established a repertoire of specific skills for your industry. If you have attended a career or technical college or training program, defining your job-related skills may be easier than if your education was in a broader university because of the focused curriculum at career-oriented schools. However, cataloging what you bring to the needs of the world of business is necessary for mapping out your journey.

Skills

Assessing your skills should include listing everything you know how to do: equipment you can operate, hardware, software, and interpersonal skills, such as customer service, sales, or training. Skills are sets of knowledge you acquire through experience or training that can be demonstrated in some observable or measurable way.

You must be very careful and objective in this aspect of your assessment. Note the comments by an agency whose job it is to assess and place contract workers in a specific field.

"People come to us right out of school, and we ask them to rate their skill levels in the various software packages used in this field. Most rate their knowledge as a 9, but upon testing, we find they rate a 4 or 5 at best. What happens is that they become very knowledgeable in one or two areas of the software, but have no exposure at all to other capabilities that our clients require" (Sherra Bell, Industry Resources Recruiter).

At job search time, you will be expected to substantiate your claim of a skill either by demonstration or by examples of jobs or training you have had. For this part of the process, though, you are taking an initial look at what you have to offer.

Talent

Assessing your talents may require some thinking outside your assumptions of what an industry might need for a particular job. Talents are abilities you are born with and may have enhanced through training, but not necessarily. Performance in many areas can be enhanced by skill training, but this section addresses those areas that an individual has a natural capacity for. Math aptitude, verbal ability, language acquisition, the talent of being able to read people and situations, creativity, music, visual–spatial awareness, fine motor skills, organization, simultaneous multitasking (not experiencing stress from a highly unstructured and busy environment—such as advertising), and written expression.

Many companies and specialists test for these talents and may uncover some you are not aware of simply because you have not been in a position to use them, such as a language acquisition ability. Even without elaborate testing, you already know some things just come easy to you. Those areas are probably where you have talent. As intelligent beings, we can learn to do just about anything. Our talent areas give us an edge.

Traits

Traits are those aspects of our character or operating style that we need to examine carefully. If they are not in line with the expectations of the workplace, immediate action toward correcting discrepancies is in order. Traits can describe our personal or professional self. Punctuality, dependability, self-discipline, persistence, affability, moodiness, energy level, distractibility, ethical orientation, and values; all of these are traits that you have to consider in your assessment. If you are punctual, dependable, and persistent, and have many examples of your past behavior to attest to these traits, then they should be part of your self-description. If, however, your energy level is low or you are moody, you need to take these traits into account when you consider work environments and activity or stress levels.

Performance traits are behaviors and, as such, lend themselves to changes in the pattern. If your value system dictates or allows certain behaviors (e.g., smoking) that potential employers would not find desirable, you might want to examine that value system. If you have not been punctual or dependable in the past, try to determine the reason and take corrective action. Personality traits can be observed in testing as well as in behaviors (e.g., tolerance for ambiguity, Type A behavior, introversion, extroversion, need for inclusion, locus of control). These are part of our personality or the way we view the world. Knowing your predispositions, such as a low tolerance for ambiguity (a complex or rapidly changing environment would be stressful) or extroversion (you prefer to interact with people rather than work alone), can help you look at jobs that suit your operating style.

Many assessments of personality traits are available to help you develop a vocabulary to describe the type of person you are: a discovery virtually impossible for an interviewer to make in a short interview when trying to determine your suitability for a job. Your chances of finding a satisfying and interesting job improve dramatically when you know what type person you are and know how to uncover the conditions at various workplaces. The closer a match you are with the characteristics of the jobs in your career area, the less stress you will experience and the more "at home" you will feel.

Interests

Curiously, though, our talents and skills are not always our interests, especially in multitalented people. A young woman who tested extremely high in math ability preferred to direct her career to her voice talent. A man who naturally can ride a horse well may never be interested in that and may use his body awareness for tennis. This is why we need to look beyond our skills and talents to our interests. Consultants can help people match the activities they seem to prefer to do with jobs that require those activities. You may be able to write computer programs and have a good math aptitude, but you enjoy more the part of your job in which you assess the needs of users and design systems to meet those needs. Therefore, if you are a programmer and only 20 percent of your responsibilities involve assessing user needs, you may actually end up spending 60 percent of your time with users because that is what you enjoy. Then, you will be stressed when you have to do the bulk of your job, those programming tasks you do not like, in less time.

Thus, knowing what your interests and motivations are may be at least as important in your eventual career success as your skills. You will be willing to invest more time and energy into those high-interest activities, and will, according to research, experience less stress on the job. What is a stressful set of work conditions for one person may be the place where another person thrives. While one enjoys sitting at a terminal writing manuals and reports all day long, another would consider that a maddening drudgery. Some feel much more energized when they interact with people, whereas others might find that much people exposure to be taxing (Kolbe, 1990).

When you actively and honestly assess your skills, talents, traits, and interests, you come closer to a realistic and workable description of the right career fit for you.

Revive Your Curiosity

Learning is a part of succeeding in any new activity. You must learn new skills and information to be able to progress in your life or your job. To do this, you might look at the style of the real experts on learning: children. Children live to learn and savor every new idea and experience because of their natural curiosity.

One way children express curiosity is through "Why?" questions. They want to know how a fire truck works, why the sky has clouds, and where the moon goes in the daytime. By being curious, children learn about their world. You have the same opportunity. When you see people who appear to be doing the type of job you think you would like, ask them how they like their work. Or, if you see an article on the field you are interested in, read about what others have to say. A product you use or a service you have contracted for recently could be starting points for researching new, potential job categories you had not thought of before.

> Curiosity is asking questions, wondering about issues, exploring ideas. It stretches the imagination. It makes "What if . . . ?" become real.

Reviving your curiosity may take some effort, but the returns are tremendous. Your curiosity will lead you to discover helpful information by asking questions and noticing things that might help you progress on your career path. Become nosy about public meetings and trade shows; attend seminars on things that interest you. Amazingly, sometimes a career path becomes lit with neon just because your curiosity led you into a particular room.

The best advice for someone who wants to move forward in life is this: "Be in the room." Of course, this sounds a bit cryptic, but the following situation will explain.

> "I had been in operations for an insurance company for a year, a decent job, just not very exciting for me. My hobby on the side was studying and trying to build an all-electric car. Out of curiosity, while on a vacation in New England, I took a morning to attend a conference held by a clean air organization. At one of the seminars, I heard about a company that was building electric buses. I talked to several companies to learn more about this interesting area. One I talked to was looking for someone for their operations department. I made a quick career change."

Maybe this sounds like "dumb luck," but the opportunity would have gone unnoticed if the person's curiosity had not led her to the conference. In addition, if she had attended in a passive way, she might not have learned some interesting information about her hobby. But, by asking questions, she became aware of the potential of what was being discussed. Otherwise, nothing of career benefit would have occurred.

Curiosity can make a party or even waiting time in a car repair shop a valuable career contributor. Listening to a conversation about market influences on a particular industry or asking how a particular company got started can enrich your career life on many levels. You are in the middle of a world of information and opportunity each day. A key to this process, though, is getting out and into new "rooms." Dennis Waitley, a noted motivational speaker, advises that the way to get into the career you want *is to be around people who do the kind of work you are interested in.* He recommends professional organizations as well as seminars conducted by leaders in the industry. Associating with these professionals can create opportunities and expand your knowledge. By knowing what factors will bring you closer to your goal, you can tune in to new events, people, and situations that will be helpful to you.

Chou read skateboarding magazines and went to shops, where he asked a lot of questions about distributors, designers, manufacturers, and consumer preferences. He developed a list of ideas to explore about companies that manufactured boards and about places boards were sold. He also looked at other products that were sold in the same places as skateboards and the types of people who competed professionally, as well as the ones that rode casually. That led him to extreme sports parks where he talked to shop owners and park managers.

Lucy's challenge was to think about her goal in different ways. She talked to physical therapists about their work and the equipment they used. That led her in two different directions: to therapy equipment distributors and to temporary agencies that managed contract workers. She discovered that many salespeople for equipment did not have a therapy or even health care background. She also discovered that resource agencies often handle all types of contract skilled professionals and many in her area had no specialists in the health care fields.

Many transitions in our lives began with wondering: "I wonder what it would be like to . . . ." Endless curiosity leads to the discovery of endless thresholds to new tiers of career fulfillment.

Focusing your effort toward specific career goals is a two-step process:

1. determining the focus
2. learning what is required to reach the ultimate job goal

Determine Your Career Focus

A good focus definition will make your changes work for you. A key point to remember is: *The job focus definition should be simple and attainable.* In this chapter, you will narrow your vision down to focus on a specific industry or set of conditions. In addition, you will discern paths to those industry or condition goals.

Some people drown themselves in endpoint statements that are too detailed or limited or are intimidating in their size and complexity. An endpoint focus statement for a very intense law student read, "I will pass the bar exam in Texas and be admitted as a junior partner in ABC firm by August 2004 at the salary of $68,000 per year to include a company car and benefits." On the other hand, a housewife who wished to return to the workforce wrote as her defining statement, "I want to increase my accounting skills in order to secure a position where I can feel respected and can experience growth."

Chou began looking at his definition and focus: "I want to have a job that gives me time to skateboard; I'm not that interested in a 'people' position; I like a casual dress atmosphere and probably would rather be in a small company, without corporate hassle. I don't really care where I live."

Lucy wanted "to be in a health-care related position where I can use my degree and make a difference in people's lives in a personal way. I like being able to direct my own activities each day rather than having tasks assigned to me. My salary should be at least $40,000 per year to maintain a standard of living I am comfortable with, but benefits are important also. I would prefer to stay in this area."

ACTIVITY 21.2

Develop an endpoint definition statement for yourself—where you would like to end up professionally. It is okay to have more than one, but try to keep your statement simple and direct.

I would like to focus my energy in the direction of:

_____

_____

Later on, I would like to move into:

_____

_____

Learn What Is Required to Reach Your Goals

Now that your curiosity has been stimulated and your focus is becoming clearer, you are beginning to find out what is required to reach your goals.

Maybe schooling, training, or new experiences are needed. This is part two of reaching for a career definition: identifying the competencies required to reach your endpoint, then developing the process for acquiring those competencies. In many ways, you will leverage what you know at any stage in your goal pursuit to learn more or acquire additional skills that will help you achieve your end result.

Once you learn the competencies required, or maybe even the experiences expected, to reach your ultimate dream career situation, then gaining those competencies and experiences leads to your near-term goals. You may find that the career dream you desire requires that you have experience living in a foreign country. Though there are many ways to accomplish this—military, school abroad, job in an international company—you have a clear goal to reach. Thus, you will begin to invest time in acquiring the necessary competence.

One complaint from students and from those making a career change is that they cannot get experience in jobs to discover what they really would enjoy and what is involved in different types of jobs. An excellent aid to this discovery process is community service work. Many duties and responsibilities in volunteer and charitable work parallel those of industry.

For your own contribution to the community, Habitat for Humanity, United Way, Red Cross, an historical society, and public radio and television stations can always use volunteers. Whether your motivation for community service is for professional advantage or personal altruism, the net effect is that you gain visibility and acquaintances in many different fields.

Check out the boards of directors of the local arts councils or other service organizations. Being involved with a pet charity of someone important gives you the chance to be around others of importance, while doing a valuable service for someone else. Also, some large companies have particular nonprofit organizations they support with money and hands-on activities. You can meet people from a company you think you might enjoy and learn something about the company in casual conversation.

You will be able to practice, and become expert at, skills you have acquired, and you can learn new ones. From a personal perspective, you derive an enhanced sense of your own worth when you give to others. Working with people who are in need helps keep your perspective on the whole of live more grounded. You also meet some pretty terrific people who will enrich your spirit.

Invest in Your Chosen Area

Philip and Adrienne wanted to be in business for themselves, but they had heard that over half of new businesses fail. They were curious to find out the reasons for this high failure rate. They went to seminars, read articles in magazines, and talked to small business owners. What they learned is that most people who go into business know their product or service well, but know nothing about managing and marketing a business.

Time

Curiosity leads Philip and Adrienne to a guide for meeting their goal. One thing they must do to achieve their dream is to learn more about business management and marketing. So, their goal now has sub-goals that they can do one at a time. If they are serious about what they want to do, they will spend some time each day adding to their business knowledge. If your goal is important to you, you will devote time each day to activities that will lead to your achieving it. If this is not the case, you may lack conviction. This may be the time to analyze your goal to make sure it interests you enough to pursue it.

The summer after Chou graduated, his parents gave him the option of traveling for a month prior to starting life on his own. In preparation, he spent some time every day either on the Internet, looking through magazines, or sending e-mails to make appointments to meet with people at skateboard manufacturing companies, shops, and skate parks. He asked about what positions they might have open and what qualifications were needed. Then he planned a trip through several states to meet with people in the industry.

Motivational speakers will tell you that the only bad idea is one that you do not act on or that you dismiss because you think you can't make it happen. *Finding opportunity is helpful, but acting on opportunity is what moves you closer to where you want to be.*

ACTIVITY   21.3

From the information you have gathered, pick one of the elements needed for you to reach your career goal. Then, list one or more activities related to this element that you can spend some time on each day.

Element 1:

Activity: _____

How long will this activity take? _____

Time schedule for activity: _____

Element 2:

Activity: _____

How long will this activity take? _____

Time schedule for activity: _____

Conviction

Attaining life goals requires commitment and energy. You have to constantly give yourself pep talks to keep your level of enthusiasm high. Nothing important is accomplished without enthusiasm. Others may or may not understand your goal or your wish for the goal to be fulfilled, so, they may not be as supportive as you would like. This is unimportant. *You can be your own supporter. It is your goal, your joy, and you are entitled to feel good about it.*

You can do this by activating your goal in your mind. Use present tense statements such as, "My chosen career path is a source of joy," "I devote effort toward my goal," "My goal is vital and positive." By talking about your goal in terms of your "here and now" thinking, you make that goal part of your present reality. You invest thought and enthusiasm into the process as well as your time gathering qualifications along the way. Without a real emotional investment on your part, you probably will not see your way through all of the barriers it will take to reach your dream.

So many people stop goal activity because they talk themselves into believing that the goal is, after all, not attainable. Many goals are attainable over time that are not remotely in your realm right now. New jobs and new industries emerge daily; the conditions, salary, and position you ultimately aspire to just may not exist at the present. That does not preclude your finding it a year or 10 years from now. Your challenge is to keep the self-talk positive whether the day is good or bad, or whether your friends are supportive or not. Your goal has value and merit. Remind yourself of that often.

One thing you should do for yourself is build confidence in your goal activities. You do this by engineering successes along the way. On the way to your final goal of a fulfilling career position are many small goals that need to be accomplished. As you define these goal steps, it helps to make each one small enough so that you can complete it successfully in a limited amount of time. Few people achieve great things by huge leaps; more often, they win little victories as they go. These little victories reinforce a clear sense of purpose and give you the opportunity to affirm your progress on a regular basis.

Chou really wanted a job in the skateboard industry, but his friends who boarded worked at pizza delivery places or video stores and teased him about going for a "real job." But Chou wanted his own place and a high enough income to be able to travel to different sports parks around the country. "My goal of working a full-time job in the extreme sports industry will give me the personal life I want and a job I enjoy." Another affirmation Chou wrote for himself was, "With my degree and my knowledge of the sport I am well suited to a career position." On his mirror he taped in large letters "BOARD AND BUCKS."

Lucy received a lot of approval for her decision to pursue a health care provider position, but she ran into a barrier with the lack of full-time positions in her area. She resisted discouragement by reminding herself, "I have a lot to offer with my professional background and new specialized skills. Using a creative approach I will design or discover a position that will pay me for both." Still enthusiastic, she went to a half-day exhibit for personnel and contract worker agencies. One of the companies was promoting a new division in health care services that would be locating in the area. Earlier that week, she had attended a meeting of physical therapists where the conversation had centered on the lack of variety in the work and the unavailability of therapists for home-bound patients.

ACTIVITY 21.4

Describe how reaching your career goal will lead you to a satisfying life. Don't forget to remind yourself regularly about your potential. Many of the most successful people do it every day.

Reaching my goal will:

_____

_____

_____

Action

Talking to yourself in a positive way helps to keep you motivated in the face of all sorts of barriers to your goal-directed activity. Once you move your goal ideas to the status of goal actions, you are well on your way to success. *Daily action reinforces your quest by directing your energies regularly toward your desired end result.* In addition to this daily activity, you will become more alert to situations that might expose you to opportunities.

During his summer travels, Chou attended three extreme sports events, visited the home office of two in-line skate and skateboard companies, and did

Internet research on the size of the industry. At one of the events, he talked with the owner of a sports park and found that he was looking for an assistant manager to coordinate all of the separate activities and programs. The owner appreciated Chou's ability to understand the terminology and the types of activities a sports park offered.

He was also impressed with Chou's research on the industry as a whole and with Chou's good grades in his business courses. One of the "perks" (benefits) of the job was that Chou could skateboard any time he was not working, and he especially enjoyed being able to meet all of the "stars" of the sport when they came to do exhibitions or compete. He accepted the job on the spot. He was able to move ahead with his goal activities.

For you to do the same thing is quite easy. Here are the guidelines:

1. Define a short-term, intermediate focus that is relatively easy to accomplish.
2. Acknowledge your successes as they occur.
3. Affirm your progress often.

Accumulating small successes will give you the confidence to move forward and face the challenge of the larger steps. Successful action leads to more attempts and more successes. With many successes to your credit, temporary barriers to your goal activity will seem insignificant.

Verify Along the Way

Pursuing an ultimate career goal should be like mountain climbing: stop periodically to enjoy the vista because everything looks different from each level the higher you go. At the base, you see the beauty of the lower rock formations and the clouds further up the mountain. When you are in the clouds, you see only what is immediately around you, but you still know pretty much where you are in relation to where you are going if your compass and equipment are correct. Finally, from above the clouds, you see the sky and perhaps a distant peak. Two-thirds of the way up, you may decide that it would be much more satisfying to snowboard all the way down the mountain or to hang glide over to another peak altogether: choices you might not have even considered at the base.

The Endpoint

When you set your direction for your life, an occasional stop along the way, either by choice or by circumstances, allows you to survey the territory, to take stock of where you have arrived. Sometimes, because you can see something different at one level than you saw at an earlier one, you might want to redirect your climb toward this new destination. If your dream is happiness, be wary of defining that in a purely situational way; that is, as a specific set of circumstances. Each new threshold you pass through places you in a new position and a new prospect. When your view changes, so might your definition of what will make you happy.

The single-minded pursuit of a goal—a practice advocated by many motivational and positive thinking books—will likely do what those books promise: get you to the goal. But what happens if somewhere along the way an avenue or opportunity opened up because of a new skill acquisition or an unexpected contact? If that might redirect you from your original endpoint, in a strict sense of pursuit, you should ignore it. However, there is no reason for a focus so narrow that it ignores options or limits overall potential for dream fulfillment.

Verifying at regular intervals that you still want the original endpoint or direction allows for breadth of scope and creativity on your part as well as flux in the workings of the universe.

The Impact on Others

Another area of our lives that we should check every now and then is the effect of your goals on those dear to you. In your confident charge toward your career path of fulfillment, you must be cautious that you maintain balance. The people you care about are affected by your decisions and choices as well. Personal goals that are harmful to others bring negative long-term results. You must have a clear vision of your goal, but you must also have a heart.

Terence, a restaurant owner in a large city, reached his dream of opening a second restaurant. However, the children rarely saw their father unless they went to his restaurant. In this case, Terence's goal activity was succeeding, but at the risk of damage to his family.

Jennifer worked for two contract companies as a graphic designer in order to build her portfolio so she could get a position at a large ad company. She was able to manage because she worked at home most of the time. She and her oldest friend, Maria, for the year since they had started working, used to meet every Thursday night for sushi and mutual support. Though Jennifer knew Maria was going through an ugly divorce, she stopped going on Thursdays and ignored Maria's repeated pages while she pressed to meet a deadline.

Admittedly, it is easy to get lost in the pursuit of a particular definition of success,

1. Is Jennifer entitled to her goal-directed activity?

2. What price is her friend Maria paying for Jennifer's degree of focus?

3. What might be your recommendation for a way to maintain both career-goal focus and balance with those close to Jennifer?

especially if things are going well. But, *personal relationships sustain us far more profoundly than professional accomplishments ever can.* It is a sad case, indeed, when a person begins to see work as the sole source of joy or achievement.

Achievement does require sacrifice, but sacrificing those you love for the sake of a goal may lead to an empty victory. Those who say it's lonely at the top may well have alienated friends and family along the way. This is just not necessary. Some of the most successful and busiest people in the world fiercely protect their family time and priorities.

You will have to make your own decisions about how you want to allocate your time. But, if along the way you stop long enough to include those closest to you in your goal setting and in the steps you are planning, you will find a solid support base. When they understand what you are trying to obtain and where they fit into the picture, they will be your biggest fans. Also, by including them in the process, you will prevent their feeling threatened or left out of your life.

Others' goals and needs have value just as yours do. You are not the only one going through transitions to reach higher levels of satisfaction in life. Verify where they are with the decisions you are making. To maintain connections with other people who also have goals and dreams, you will be required to give and take in all areas of your life. The ability to do this will make your arrival in *Success City* a celebration for everyone.

TRANSITION SKILLS SUMMARY

Assess skills, talents, traits, interests
Revive curiosity
Refine your career focus
Invest time, conviction, action
Verify the goal and its impact on others

GOAL SETTING

My goals for my ongoing emotional and relational development are:

_____

_____

My goals for my ongoing career management are:

_____

_____

_____

C O A C H 'S   C O R N E R

Many people these days want to know what the route to entrepreneurial success is. Of course, there is no formula, but there are a few common elements to those who make it.

If you are in a corporate environment, you need to find your way into P&L (Profit and Loss) responsibility, such as marketing, operations, or general manager jobs. Stay away from human resources, public relations, and administration. You need to have a track record of results—for an entrepreneur, results are all that matter. Be prepared to think outside the box and document successes doing that. While still employed, you will need to network with entrepreneurial types to stay fresh and on top of potential opportunities.

Once you prepare to go out into the entrepreneurial arena, there are two routes: create your own start-up or join one in the early stages.

Option 1: Your own venture. Ascertain the reality of the market. A great product does not necessarily invent a market. Is someone willing to pay to meet a need? Write a business plan (before you leave your regular corporate job) to figure out the necessary resources—what will it take to finance the business? The assumptions of the plan are more important than the figures themselves. How long is the sales cycle, for instance? If it takes one year to close a sale, then you need funding for one and a half years. Realize it always takes more time and more money than you expect. Circulate your plan and network with other entrepreneurs for feedback and advice. SCORE's retired executive volunteers will help you, and there may be similar organizations in your area. Consult books on startups and research details of the industry and potential customer target groups. If a 30 percent close rate is expected, that means you close 1 of every 30 calls, and one salesperson cannot handle it profitably. You also have to have a clear understanding of all cost and revenue drivers. Financing can come from friends and family, or an "angel" funding (a wealthy individual who looks to invest in early-stage entrepreneurial corporations). Another source of financing is loans from the Small Business Administration, but you will need collateral or assets to secure these debts. Venture capital is a less likely option; less than 10 percent of all businesses are funded by venture capital. Women generate many times more startup proposals than men, but less than 4 percent of all venture capital money goes to women. Finally, one very risky approach is to use credit card sources. (This has actually been done successfully with a $100,000 debt.)

(continued)

Option 2: Joining an entrepreneurial company that is already in business. Locate a likely company through events that venture capitalists and technology companies go to; call attorneys and accountants and find out what is going on. Read business papers to find out what's hot. How do you get in? You will have to demonstrate that you can produce results: generate more revenue, make more customers happy, or reduce costs. You might also get an edge if you are willing to work on a trial basis with no pay (a month) or will take a low salary in exchange for stock options. But you need to figure in the risk. The majority of new businesses fail, and people who invest in or are involved in them know this and expect it as part of the game or process. But greatness never occurs without risk. It's best, though, for your own peace of mind, or at least to arrive at a close approximation of the actual risk, to do your own due diligence, to investigate the same as a potential investor would.

Look at the market potential, the size of the customer base, product need, and buying power. Figure out what the sale price would be by studying sales of similar companies. There is, ultimately, a possibility that you are not suited to an entrepreneurial situation. Are you risk-averse? Do you need a lot of structure? Does rapid and unpredictable change bother you? Do you have little or no cash reserves or alternate income sources? If any of these conditions are outside of your comfort level, you would be miserable, and you just wouldn't be a good fit.

It can be a very rewarding experience whether you end up cashing in big or not. You have to consider the overall value of the experience, however. Are you in it for the final sale or for the excitement and creativity of the whole entrepreneurial situation—the team—people you respect and are inspired by, the win–lose element, the variety, the high energy level, the learning experience? There is also the chance to contribute, to have input due to the size of the company, to stretch and take on all sorts of different responsibilities. It's more than the small chance at hitting the jackpot that draws people to this kind of situation. I think the spirit, energy, and potential are at least as much of an attraction and reward.

KAREN ROBINSON, President and CEO, consultant and advisor for early stage entrepreneurial enterprises; e-mail: krobinson@npcml.com.